PRAISE FOR INNER DIVINITY

"*Inner Divinity* is a beautiful weaving of different methods that create a holistic model of healing for body, mind, and spirit. Mara Bishop is a brilliant writer and healer who empowers us with simple practices to heal all aspects of our lives."

—Sandra Ingerman, MA, author of *Soul Retrieval* and *Medicine for the Earth*

"Mara Bishop offers an organized left-brained approach to the right-brained world of intuition. She combines powerful stories of her work in counseling clients and humorous family anecdotes from her role as a mother with healthy doses of practical wisdom and spiritual magic to create this useful guide to the ordinary and non-ordinary realms."

—Larry Burk, M.D., Former Director of Education, Duke Center for Integrative Medicine

"Mara Bishop's primary contribution in *Inner Divinity* is as an architect of the sacred in our lives. Bishop has crafted something elegant, simple, and profoundly wise: a way to organize powerful spiritual precepts one building block at a time. She does so in a compassionate and steady way, combining structure with options for each of us, to help us stay the course and become all that we are meant to be."

—Cecile A. Carson, M.D., clinical associate professor of medicine and psychiatry, board member, Society for Shamanic Practitioners

"*Inner Divinity* is a treasure chest of inspirational teachings for just how to 'craft your life with sacred intelligence.' As a resource it is well-organized, clear and to the point. As an instrument for personal motivation this book sings with Mara's voice of compassionate wisdom. We can feel the strength and comfort of her presence throughout!"

> —Nan Moss and David Corbin, Faculty, Foundation for Shamanic Studies, authors of *Wisdom from the Sky* and *CloudDancing*

"Mara Bishop has written a book that not only demystifies the ins and outs of shamanism and intuition, but makes them available to everyone by including clear and easy exercises."

> —Karen Webster, intuitive consultant, teacher, and author

INNER
DIVINITY

INNER DIVINITY

Crafting Your Life with Sacred Intelligence

MARA BISHOP

M.S., TH.M., C.S.C.

iUniverse, Inc.
New York Lincoln Shanghai

Inner Divinity
Crafting Your Life with Sacred Intelligence

Copyright © 2007 by Mara Bishop

iUniverse books may be ordered through booksellers or by contacting:

iUniverse
2021 Pine Lake Road, Suite 100
Lincoln, NE 68512
www.iuniverse.com
1-800-Authors (1-800-288-4677)

First Edition

ISBN-13: 978-0-595-40743-9 (pbk)
ISBN-13: 978-0-595-85108-9 (ebk)
ISBN-10: 0-595-40743-9 (pbk)
ISBN-10: 0-595-85108-8 (ebk)

Printed in the United States of America

For My Parents

Companion CD now available.

See the *Resources* section for ordering information.

GUIDED MEDITATIONS
selected from the book

INNER
DIVINITY

Crafting Your Life with
Sacred Intelligence

MARA BISHOP

MEDITATIONS

1. Grounding
2. Psychic Boundaries
3. Nature
4. Inner Guide
5. Animal Spirit
6. Dialogue with Your Body
7. Love

CONTENTS

# ACKNOWLEDGMENTS

In writing *Inner Divinity*, I was supported by many people in different ways. Professionally, I am grateful for wonderful teachers, especially Michael Harner, Sandra Ingerman, and Karen Webster. My work would not be possible without their willingness to share their expertise and their inspiration. I particularly thank Sandra for her unfailing encouragement of my writing and healing work and for allowing me to draw from much of her work in this book.

From within my family I especially thank my parents for their biological contribution to my existence and their constant love and support. Without either one this book would not be possible. Many extra thanks to my mom for countless hours of editorial and advisory help. Thank you to my husband for his unconditional love, and his support for me and my unconventional endeavors. Thanks to my daughter for making me laugh and enjoying cuddles as much as I do. Thank you to my many ancestors who created a path for me, especially to Grammy for pioneering and supporting our shamanic work.

Good friends and colleagues helped me in the process of creating this book. I especially thank Teresa Leigh for her confidence and enthusiasm for who I am and what I do and Rona Marren for her courage and sound advice. I thank Diana Henderson for her loving wisdom and kind counsel, Dr. Larry Burk for his unique perspective and helpful suggestions, Linda Wescott and Iris Silverman for their editorial services, Jill Over for her gentleness and big heart, and Tory Pryor for her professional advice and generosity of time.

I honor and thank the beautiful, patient, and kind spirit guides and teachers who've been willing to work with me.

 INTRODUCTION

WHAT IS INNER DIVINITY?

"The divine is not something high above us. It is in heaven, it is in earth, it is inside us." Morihei Ueshiba

Inner divinity is your natural state of being. It is the spirit you were born with and underlies who you are today. We come from the spirit world. We are born into physical bodies, but do not lose the spiritual life force that existed before our birth. You are divine from your core. Your inner divinity is your unique source of peace, power, and happiness. Many of us have forgotten that we hold that source within us always. This wisdom is the key to your healing and your joy. By remembering your inner divinity, you bring harmony to every aspect of your life.

WHY THIS BOOK?

"We ourselves feel that what we are doing is just a drop in the ocean. But the ocean would be less because of that missing drop." Mother Teresa

I wrote this book to share my journey toward understanding inner divinity. I grew up Catholic, a regular albeit sensitive kid who enjoyed art and watching the wildlife around the pond at my house. I had friends, but often felt different, as if I didn't quite fit in. I probably couldn't have explained it like this at the time, but it felt as if there was more to life that I was missing. I caught glimpses of magical moments, usually with my family, when everything felt "right," as if I was connected to something larger and anything was possible.

I went on to college and majored in art and communications. I still sensed I was missing something ephemeral just outside my perception. A few years after I graduated I began having more frequent intuitive experiences, like precognitive dreams. They were usually about ordinary things, like my father slipping comically on a walk in the woods or a tabloid headline I'd see the next day, but they started my exploration of consciousness. Then I had an interesting experience that helped me understand the concept of inner divinity.

During a time of emotional crisis, I went for a walk around a pond near my home. As I walked, I searched for an external sign to guide me through a difficult situation. I looked to the trees and I looked to the sky, imploring them, and God, to give me an answer to my questions. Suddenly, a voice boomed inside my head, "It's in you!" I was startled, but I got the message. I already had all the information I needed. The insight and wisdom I craved was inside of me. I wish I could say that I incorporated the realization into my life fully at that time, but I didn't. Truly believing and understanding my divine nature is an ongoing process.

Several years after that experience at the pond, I began my formal education in consciousness, intuition, and spiritual healing. I apprenticed with a gifted intuitive. I trained with the faculty at the Foundation for Shamanic Studies and received graduate degrees in Energy Medicine and Theology. And perhaps most importantly, I learned from my own spirit teachers. Increasingly, I started to see the world through "shaman's eyes." When we filter the world through shaman's eyes we sense our interconnectedness, see the intangible aspects of everything around us, and feel the assistance available to us.

Throughout my life I've benefited from the support of the spiritual world, and also from my family. My parents and grandparents were my models for living, always generous and loving. It is my good fortune to work closely with my mother in shamanic and intuitive practice, and to have worked with my grandmother as long as she was able. On the other end of the generational spectrum, one of my great joys is motherhood. My daughter has provided many opportunities for me to practice what I preach. She has taught me how deeply interconnected we are, having the power to affect each other for better or worse. She's taught me to watch my thoughts and to lighten up! The lessons I've learned from within my family apply directly to my work with clients.

I've been in private practice seeing clients since 1995. I work with a variety of methods, including intuitive counseling, shamanic healing, and energetic healing, in an integrated approach to spiritual healing, personal growth, and emotional well-being.

I teach workshops and give presentations on shamanism and intuitive development, among other topics. Throughout my experiences in life, learning, teaching, and seeing clients, there has been a common thread: go inside to learn the truth.

Advice, healing, and support are provided when you connect to the seed of the divine within you as you live and breathe. You have a vast potential for creating and experiencing the world in partnership with the universe. Being in union with the spirit of the universe enables you to reach your true potential and find balance with the world around you. There is a bud of perfection inside you that is waiting to blossom. It grows every time you are kind to yourself or someone else. It grows because you have a spark of light in you that cannot help but shine. There are ways to foster that light and help it grow brighter, maybe even help others see their own light. This inner divinity is your birthright. It cannot be taken away from you. Whether you let that light flicker softly deep inside or whether you stoke it into a powerful inner fire is your choice.

HOW TO USE THIS BOOK

"There is a desire deep within the soul which drives man from the seen to the unseen, to philosophy and to the divine." Kahlil Gibran

Inner Divinity is divided into seven sections that build on one another. Each section examines an area of life where you will benefit by engaging your sacred intelligence: in your relationship with yourself, other people, your environment, your intuition, your spiritual support, your health, and your future. I share much of the information I've conveyed to clients over the years. Although each person is unique, with a distinct set of circumstances, gifts and challenges, some central messages come through repeatedly.

Each section includes exercises for using the concepts practically in your life. Throughout the exercise sections in this book, I'll instruct you to "meditate" to get information or gain awareness. Think of meditation in its simplest sense here—becoming still and quiet. Simply relax your mind and body, breathe deeply, and listen. Open yourself to receive guidance, knowing it may come to you in different forms. You may see images, hear sounds, feel things in your body, or have a sense of knowing. The information may be subtle, just a fleeting impression, or strong. Simply pay attention and accept what you receive. I suggest that you get a notebook and write down as much as you can about your experiences in doing the exercises. You can also record your dreams, intuitive insights, and any thoughts and impressions that you want to remember. It can be helpful to go back after some time has passed and review what you've experienced. Many of these exercises can be done as a shamanic journey. See the *Resources* section at the end of the book for information about finding instruction in shamanic journeying. Or, if you have another method of tuning in for advice and guidance, feel free to use it.

Section 1 addresses your relationship with yourself. The nature of your internal interactions is the foundation for all other relationships. Your inner communication sets the tone for your external communication. It is important to create space for silence and reflection. Connecting with an inner voice can guide you in a supportive and loving way. When you learn to treat yourself with respect and kindness, you create healing energy that is reflected back to you in your life. Becoming aware of personal biases and beliefs allows you to experience the world with fresh eyes. *Section 1* lays the groundwork for connecting to your unique source of wisdom and power.

As you learn to sense the spark of the divine within you, you begin to see divine light in others. *Section 2* builds on these new concepts of relating to yourself by demonstrating healthier ways of relating to those around you. Creating strong nurturing relationships supports your vision of a life filled with meaning, cooperation, and passion. I'll address the nature of successful interpersonal communication and the profound effects of forgiveness. *Section 2* helps you understand how personal energetics impact your relationships, and how your awareness of these subtle interactions can affect your satisfaction in relating to others.

As you see the divine shining in everything, the world and its inhabitants take on new vitality. *Section 3* guides you through creating harmony in your environment. From learning to manage the onslaught of information from the media, to creating sacred space, to engaging the elements of nature, this section helps you develop a partnership with the world around you. By paying attention to the way you and your environment affect one another you learn to work cooperatively, creating a fertile ground from which your ideal life can grow.

Connecting with your intuitive sense links you directly to your divine energy. *Section 4* delves into the nature of intuition and how you can put it to use in your life. This sacred intelligence is innate in all of us. It can be developed with intention and practice. I explain methods of accessing your intuition and advise you on developing it safely and ethically. When you listen to your intuitive voice, you tap a source of spiritual and practical guidance that aids you in crafting a fulfilling and joyful life.

What is God? In *Section 5* you'll address that question for yourself and consider different sources for spiritual support, starting with the core of your own divinity and branching outward to the community, the spirits of nature, creativity, and being in service. I give tools for assessing your spiritual support network, for developing a sacred foundation and for strengthening your existing means of spiritual sustenance. Through the ages, prayer, meditation, and shamanic practices have linked us to the divine. You'll find ideas and support in *Section 5* for evolving your own spiritual practice.

Section 6 explores spiritual and energetic healing modalities. Although you are ultimately in charge of your own healing, there are many ancient and modern resources to help you on your path to health. The concept of a universal spirit of healing has existed through the ages and that philosophy is applied today through methods such as shamanic healing, Reiki, distance healing, and herbal medicine. You learn to engage your physical and energetic bodies in dialogue to understand what you need to create ideal health.

The future frightens and entices us. *Section 7* discusses how you can participate in the creation of the future. From following your inner calling, to honing the power of your intention, we explore ways to call a positive future into being by staying connected to the divine in the present moment and using ancient tools of prayer and visioning.

This book provides many options for remembering and reconnecting to your divine identity. That identity is unique to you, as is the combination of methods you will find most effective. Some of these methods will feel more comfortable than others. I encourage you to try them all, and then go back to the ones that feel especially helpful and repeat them. Find some subset of practices that works for you. Perhaps add some methods I haven't mentioned, or create some new ones. The choice is yours.

Evolving in your life is an individual process; there is no map that charts the path for everyone. Enjoy your individual path and be kind to yourself along the way. I do not presume to have a formula for happiness that will work for everyone. I'm offering a sampling of ideas, exercises, insights, and experiences. I hope they will provide some fuel for your own search for a happy and inspiring life. Only you know your deepest dreams and passions, only you can engage your spiritual companions, and only you are blessed with an opportunity to know yourself in this life from the *inside*. Trust your instincts before you accept what anyone tells you. I may say things you don't believe. That's okay. On the next page you may read something that facilitates a great change in your life. Stay open, be gentle with yourself, and do your inner work.

A word about terminology: I use words such as "divine," "God," "goddess," "universal life force," and "spirit" somewhat interchangeably throughout this book. Many of the words we use to describe spiritual energy have powerful connotations. Some of us are comfortable with the word "God" and others are not. The same holds true for "angel," "power animal," or "Spirit." Please substitute the words that feel most suitable to you. We are all living reminders of the existence of God. We are sacred souls, as well as physical beings. Understanding this interplay of spirit and flesh has perplexed the human race for a long time. Over time, we have developed limited definitions of God. Please don't let semantics get in the way of your open consideration of the ideas and exercises in *Inner Divinity*.

We live in partnership with the spirit world. Without the help of the beings in that world, our potential for creating balanced, healthy lives is greatly decreased. It is also important to define the term "harmony" as I use it in this book. We create harmony in our lives by living with integrity, by opening to our own sources of inner wisdom, by expressing gratitude, by engaging the spirits for the higher good of all. To have a harmonious or balanced life does not mean living a "perfect" life, one without challenge, disappointment, grief, or anger. It means having developed the inner resources and the spiritual partnerships to allow life to happen and to participate in it fully and gracefully.

Much of what I write about may feel familiar to you at the conscious level, or at a deeper level of knowing. I've distilled what I've learned from many gifted teachers and healers, from my spiritual guides, and from the writings of others, both ancient and modern. These ideas and practices in total are what have worked for me, personally and professionally. I'm not always successful in following my own advice, but I've witnessed the positive effect these methods have had on my clients, my students, and me. I do the best I can. And that is all *you* can ask of yourself.

INNER DIVINITY AND WORLD RELIGIONS

"Ye are gods; and all of you are children of the most High." Psalms 82:6

The concept of inner divinity is explained in ancient spiritual practices and religions. Early Christianity supported the idea that the "kingdom of heaven is within you," the joys of experiencing divine union are available to you now. Instead of creating a hierarchy that distanced humankind from God, Jesus embraced the divine that resided within himself and within everyone around him.

The Quakers rejected the hierarchical structure of Christian churches in the seventeenth century, believing instead that God's light and power is inherent in all individuals. They assert that with the gift of that light comes the responsibility to create a ministry from within. Quakers emphasize the importance of silence, from which they experience guidance from and communion with God.

In Buddhism, there is no concept of an external God who is separate and superior to human beings. Divinity or enlightenment is a state accessible to all people. The teachings of Buddha are focused on helping people attain a state of enlightenment or "Buddhahood" for themselves. As such, Buddhists don't perceive a disconnection from their own divine natures. They are simply working to express the elements of themselves that are most like the Buddha: compassion, the ability to be inwardly still, and detachment from the traps of the ego. A Buddha is a person who comprehends that he embodies the true essence of life.

Hindu practices, such as yoga, teach that divinity lies within each human being. The word "yoga" is Sanskrit for union. The spiritual practice of yoga involves uniting with the divine power that exists behind the body, mind, and ego to attain knowledge of the inner self. The awareness of one's inner divinity is enhanced through managing the breath, chanting, meditation, and entering certain physical postures that align the physical body and the energy body.

The goal of Islamic mysticism, or Sufism, is also union with the divine, considered to be the true reality. Sufis seek an *experience* of oneness with God on a profound bodily and spiritual level. Sufis attain this state of union with the divine through various practices, including art, dance, and music. Rhythmic chanting, the pounding footsteps of dancers, and monotonous drumming all help practitioners enter into an altered state of consciousness where union can be felt most deeply.

Shamanic cultures also use monotonous sound to enter into a state of union with Spirit. Sonic driving is the technique of rapid percussion, typically using drums or rattles. Through this method, the shaman is able to journey to other worlds to connect with spirit helpers. Shamanic cultures are animistic, believing that all living things, including the elements of nature, possess spirit or divinity. Humans accept their place in the world alongside these spirit beings. Spirits are honored through ritual and ceremony. There is a strong belief that everything in the universe is interconnected, from the spirits to human beings to the smallest frog. All life is honored for the divinity it embodies.

In looking back through time and into the philosophies of many world religions, we see the threads of the concept of inner divinity. Throughout this book, I hope to help you find the threads of a deeper, practical understanding of *your* unique divine nature. It is then your job to weave those threads into the rich, living tapestry of a fulfilling life.

PEACE, POWER, AND HAPPINESS

"Most folks are about as happy as they make up their minds to be." Abraham Lincoln

A part of God's sacred nature exists in all of us. Everything is interrelated. The best way to begin to live fulfilling lives is to operate from the premise that we're sacred beings living within an interconnected web of life. Then we must put that concept to work operationally. I'm a practical person, so I can talk about embodying the divine for only so long before I ask myself "What does that mean?" "What do I need to do in my life to live connected to my divine nature?" In the coming pages, I will give you practical advice about how to "plug in" to your divine energy and put it to use in your life.

By using your sacred intelligence, or intuitive sense, as your guide, you can begin to create a life that is more fulfilling because it is aligned with your true nature. By engaging the world and the beings you encounter consciously and respectfully, you cultivate inner peace in your relationships with yourself, your family, and your environment. When your actions and deeds reflect that inner peace, you are changing not only your consciousness, but also the world around you.

A helpful analogy for thinking about the interrelatedness of everything is the hologram. Michael Talbot's book *The Holographic Universe* uses the hologram as a vehicle to understand the complex universal organism of which we're a part. He expounds on quantum physics, which asserts that the universe is structured like a hologram, with each part "accessible" from any other part. What does it mean to be able to access anything in the larger universe from the point in time and space that you occupy right at this moment? By shifting your viewpoint, as you do when you look into the depths of a hologram, you can connect to anything, affect and be affected by anything. You can access the vast wilderness of nature from a tiny blade of grass in your backyard. By paying attention to that tiny plant, you can tap into nature on a much larger scale. By focusing individually on sending love out to the universe, wherever you are, your heart can merge with the heart of the universe. If we're not limited to previously accepted ideas of space, time, matter, and energy, the wonders of the universe become more accessible and the nature of reality becomes more intriguing.

Our daily lives are infused with the sacred. We've come to separate our spiritual selves from our physical, mental, and emotional selves. This separation is an illusion; yet that illusion can dramatically influence the way you live. You are whole. You are complete, with an abundance of inner resources at your disposal. You don't need more money, a more prestigious job, a more understanding spouse, or a better body to be happy. You have all you need to be happy at this moment. The key to your happiness is internal, not external. Let your intuition and innate wisdom be your guide down life's stream. Enjoy the sights and the sounds, the rapids and the calm spots, and know you are safe, you are not alone, and you are loved.

You have the tools you need to live life connected to your source of peace, power, and happiness. By developing and understanding your relationship to your inner resources, you often find clues to reaching a state of peace. Peace comes from acceptance and from faith. Peace comes from finding what makes you happy and doing it. Peace comes from being able to slow the chatter of your mind. Peace comes from living in the moment with lightness and humor. Peace comes to each of us in different ways. Your sacred self is a unique resource. By connecting to your inner divinity, you can uncover what helps you reach a state of peace.

One purpose of this book is to remind you of the power you already hold. Power comes from many sources: personal spiritual practice, acting with integrity, moving past fearful states of mind and into loving ones. You increase your power when you have the courage to do what you know is right, when you give of yourself, and when you take care of yourself. Your inner power is the fuel that drives your life. When you have the courage and the strength to face adversity and push through, you tap your inner power. When you recognize that you affect others with your words and actions, you grow in responsibility and compassion. The ethical use of your own power is vital to your ultimate spiritual health.

From a state of peace and personal power, many people find happiness. We serve others best from a state of happiness. Joy radiates and ripples, washing everything around it with its golden energy. Likewise, misery spreads, casting a long shadow. To strive for a state of happiness is not self-serving in a negative sense, but serves the self appropriately. It is your job to secure your happiness as best you can.

There is no true happiness in objects or status. Pleasure and happiness are two different things. Many of us seek pleasure in sensory experiences; however, happiness goes deeper than the fleeting enjoyment of a slab of chocolate cake or a great round of golf. Happiness is finding a true sense of peace within. Everything in your life doesn't have to be perfect for you to be happy. Rather, you experience happiness when you align with your true self, whatever your life circumstance may be. By working actively with your sage inner self, you can create a life that brings you joy.

I encourage you to follow your passion and your intuition. Instead of letting the spark of your inner divinity smolder, fan it with all your energy. Coax it into a vibrant and glorious blaze. Recognizing your sacredness, knowing that you come *from* God and are *of* God, is part of an ever-unfolding path. Creating harmony and balance is a continuous, demanding, and exciting dance. Your sacred core is the source of your peace, power, and happiness. From that source you can create your ideal life. *Inner Divinity* is about opening doorways that allow you to see and experience your divine nature and to behold the beauty, power, and joy that are rightfully yours.

The stories and conversations portrayed herein are factual to the best of my knowledge and recollection. I apologize in advance for any errors on my part. Please note that the names of clients and friends have been changed.

SECTION 1: YOUR SELF

Creating a Healthy Relationship with Yourself

You are your primary caregiver. Once you become an adult (and even earlier for some people) you become responsible for your own safety, state of mind, and level of contentment. The way you treat yourself is important, not just physically—we all know we should eat a healthy diet and exercise—but emotionally. Are you kind to yourself? Do you speak to yourself in encouraging and thoughtful ways? Or are you your own worst critic; a cruel judge of your body, your abilities, and your potential? By becoming aware of the way you care for yourself, you begin to see the filter through which you experience the world.

You are primarily a spiritual being. Your fundamental nature is intangible, yet you live in a tangible world in your physical body. When you forget this fundamental aspect of your existence, it creates stress and confusion. One lesson of being human is reconciling your spiritual core with your material vessel. Your body is more than packaging for your soul. In the search for peace or enlightenment, some people become confused and seek to deny their physical natures. Our goal is unity, not separation. We need to learn to live effectively in both the physical and spiritual dimensions. Recognizing that your divine nature and your body are distinct yet interrelated calms some of the discord that surfaces when those two aspects seem at odds. One aspect does not need to be denied in order to accept the other. The way to peace and happiness is to reconcile your many facets, your entire being in all its complexity.

Just as you cannot lose your physical self, you cannot lose your divine self. Your inner divinity connects you, always and forever, to the sacred source of all that is. The illusion of separation is what causes suffering. I see many people who worry that they are not as spiritually connected as they should be. They try to reconnect, when really all they need to do is remember. One of my clients, Joan, had a dream that was troublesome for her. She saw a cloudy sky; light was pouring down from above through a break in the clouds. As she watched, the clouds closed together and the light was gone. She worried that she was going to become lost, separated from the source of her spirituality. It simply isn't possible. We can *forget* our connection, but we can never lose it.

You have the power to manifest your dreams. You have the support to transform yourself and your life as you choose. Your divine nature is a spark of creative power and peaceful knowing within you. It is your greatest asset in finding happiness in the world. It will speak with you if you are willing to listen and it will guide you where you need to go. Your inner divinity is a direct link to the power of the universe. By consciously creating a safe and supportive space inside yourself, you become aligned with the transformative power of the sacred. This alignment can have miraculous effects in your life.

INTERNAL DIALOGUE

"When a warrior learns to stop the internal dialogue, everything becomes possible; the most far-fetched schemes become attainable." Carlos Castaneda

Internal dialogue is the constant stream of communication you have with yourself. You talk silently to yourself all the time through your thoughts. This conversation may be about you, other people, what is happening in the moment, the events of the past, or your concerns for the future. This "self-talk" may not always take the form of words or sentences, but you are constantly processing thoughts and perceptions.

This internal dialogue is often described as "monkey mind" or chatter, something to be turned off if possible in order to achieve a state of peace. Being able to still your inner communication is beneficial. However, it is also important to understand *how* you communicate with yourself. The constant flow of information and emotions you process affects you and how you perceive your life. Your perceptions are your reality. Your expectations and biases influence how you interact with the world. In other words, the way you *view* life shapes what you consider real. Understanding the dialogue that forms those perceptions is important for two reasons. First, identifying what kinds of thought patterns you replay mentally helps you see yourself more clearly. Second, developing an awareness of that dialogue is the first step in altering it to better suit your needs. If you don't even realize you are communicating with yourself most of the time, you don't question or analyze the content of that communication. You accept it as true. Often these internal dialogues are fear-based. Other people's opinions are incorporated as your own. You may make assumptions about yourself and others that are inaccurate. By becoming aware of the conversation, you begin to understand how it has affected you throughout your life.

Start by simply paying attention to your inner dialogue. As you go through the day, notice the tone of your communication. Does your inner voice whisper the true wishes of your heart, or does it echo your worst fears? Does this voice encourage you to take care of yourself, or to act impulsively or self-destructively? Become aware of how these "talks" you have with yourself make you feel. Does the voice sound like your own, or does it repeat someone else's words?

Imagine having a constant companion who is kind and supportive, loving and patient; someone who praises you and gives you the benefit of the doubt. Take a minute and let yourself feel it. What is it like? Now imagine that companion berating and belittling you, criticizing you and telling you that you aren't good enough. What is that like? Envision the things you accomplish, and the sense of peace you have, with the first companion. Now imagine how hard life feels with the second.

Your "self-talk" largely determines the tone of your life: it fosters a nurturing environment for you to thrive and grow, or it plants seeds of doubt and fear. Even difficult truths can be heard more clearly when the voice is kind. If your inner dialogue isn't supporting you, change it. You are your own constant companion through life and you control how you communicate with yourself internally.

Other people can influence your internal dialogue. I've often joked with my mom that there is a little Dad inside my head. I find myself asking the same kinds of questions he would, approaching a situation the same way, speaking to myself silently the same way I believe he would speak to me out loud. For example, my father doesn't replace things frivolously. Recently, I went to buy new sneakers because the soles of my old ones were coming apart. I found myself in an internal debate about replacing or fixing the shoes. "I can fix these," I almost convinced myself. The Dad voice always returns me to a logical way of thinking. If I am about to make a decision without doing the research or thinking out all the ramifications of that choice, I hear the voice pushing me to have solid data before taking action. I didn't mean to add his voice to my internal dialogue, but his influence on me was strong and I internalized my perception of his reactions to life. A good friend of mine realized she was frequently concerned with what "they" would think. One day, I asked her who "they" were, and she realized she had internalized her mother's fears about other people's opinions of her. She didn't have anyone in mind, but she'd taken her mother's thinking on as her own.

Frequently these inner voices are those of a parent. As adults we have the freedom to choose which voices we accept and which we reject. Once you've become aware of the different conversations you have with yourself, you can purposefully weed out those that don't serve your best interests. Communication that is not nourishing, truthful, and supportive can be gently dismissed. Over time, as you listen to it less, its volume will decrease and so will the effects those conversations have on you. Conversely, as you become a more mindful listener, the voice of your inner divinity, the true voice of your soul, will sound louder and clearer.

Don't underestimate the power of your thoughts. You shape your reality from the inside out. I'll talk more about how to do this in *Section 7: Your Future*. Your internal dialogue is the entryway to creating a life that sustains you. Much of the power you generate with your thoughts is derived from the emotions at the root of those thoughts. When you think and feel from a place of love, especially for yourself, you move forward with faith and courage. You are able to take risks to attain your goals because you know you are fundamentally safe and loved. When fear is the root of your thoughts, there is conflict. You are constantly fighting the fear inside your mind. That conflict seeps into the other relationships in your life and how you perceive the world around you. If you believe you are in danger as you walk down the street and tell yourself that repeatedly with your "self-talk," you will find ample evidence to support your theory. The people you pass will look suspicious. You will be especially attuned to news items about crime or violence. If you've allowed fear into your energetic space, it affects how you, in turn, appear to the world—apprehensive, suspicious, and aloof.

One day a friend of mine planned a walk in the state park. Her boyfriend told her she shouldn't go because there were probably "molesters" there. He believed the park was a dangerous place for a woman alone. Perhaps someone planted that seed in his mind when he was young, or possibly he saw a news story about an incident in a park, but she didn't allow his fear to become part of her internal dialogue. She replied by asking him how many times he'd heard of incidents in a state park versus incidents in people's own homes. "Oh," he said, "I never thought of it that way." Often it takes someone else's challenge to our assumptions and beliefs to make us aware of the inner dialogue we engage in unconsciously.

Remember that you can take control of your thinking. Becoming aware of your inner dialogue is the first step in realizing how it affects you. It is the backdrop for how you see life. If it isn't serving you, recreate it. Your mind can be trained to function differently. Physiological changes can take place, supporting your effort to create a more harmonious inner reality. Neuroscientists have documented that brain cells can adapt to new ways of thinking, essentially changing the way our brains work. By gradually replacing our negative thinking with positive thinking, our nerve cells and neurotransmitters rewire themselves and inner transformation begins. We can actually train our minds to be happy.[1]

Start by clearing negative communication from your thoughts. When you catch yourself being judgmental or harsh, stop and change the message. Imagine what you can accomplish with an inspiring voice playing in your mind. Do everything you can to listen to that voice. Your inner divinity is the ultimate source of truth, love, and happiness. You have the power to create a healthy internal environment, an environment where you can thrive and find peace.

PERSONAL ENERGETICS

"Everything that irritates us about others can lead us to an understanding of ourselves." Carl Jung

Inner divinity is a soul-quality residing deep within you and connecting you to the source of all things. There is also a more tangible energy body that overlays and interacts with your physical body. This energy field, and the life force that flows through it, animate you and directly affect your state of physical, emotional, and psychological health. Many ancient spiritual traditions have recognized that living things have a light body in addition to a physical one. In the Vedic tradition of the Indian subcontinent, this force is called *prana*. In China it is *ch'i*. In the Pacific region it is *mana*. The Jewish mystical theosophy of Kabbalah refers to it as astral light.[2] I'll talk more about how different cultural traditions describe this life force and how modern science is validating its existence and studying its relation to health in *Section 6: Your Health*. I'll give a brief overview of the human energy system here so we have a common language on which to base later discussions.

We each have an energetic personality, a way of interacting in the world and relating to others that is as distinct as our voice. You are born with your energetic personality; however, it also evolves and changes as you do. In many ways our energetic personalities mirror what we believe our character traits or outward personalities are. For example, shy people often hold their energy close to their bodies and suspicious people can be closed energetically to those around them. Extroverts send their energy outward quickly to connect with others, and aggressive people may emit overpowering energy. But your energetic personality is subtler than your physical actions. You may try to act a particular way even if it goes against your nature. For example, you may wish to appear more easy-going or spontaneous than you are naturally, trying to accept last minute changes in plans with a smile, but typically your energy is a more truthful representation of your true nature. For the more sensitive people around you, your "acting" may be undermined by what is sensed about you on the energetic level.

Your spiritual source flows through a system of channels and energetic vortices called the chakras. Levels of the human energy field, or auric field, expand outward from the body in increasingly subtle layers. Each layer of the auric field has a different function, as does each chakra. The seven major chakras are located approximately in a vertical plane along the spine. Each layer of the field is associated with one of the chakras. The first, or root chakra, located at the base of the spine, is linked to the first auric level, and so on through the seventh chakra, located above the crown of the head. The first chakra is associated with physical functioning and sensation, and autonomic functioning of the body. The second, or sacral chakra, is located below the belly button in the lower abdominal region and is associated with emotions. The third, or solar plexus chakra, is located in the middle of the body near the lower rib cage and is associated with linear thinking and mental activity. The fourth, or heart chakra, is located in the chest region (along the spine as all the major chakras are), and is associated with love and compassion. The fifth, or throat chakra, is in the throat area and corresponds to communication. The sixth chakra, or third eye, is located above and between the eyebrows and is connected with celestial love and recognition of the divine within all life. The seventh, or crown chakra, located at the top of the head, is connected to the higher mind and comprehension of your true spiritual nature.

THE CHAKRAS

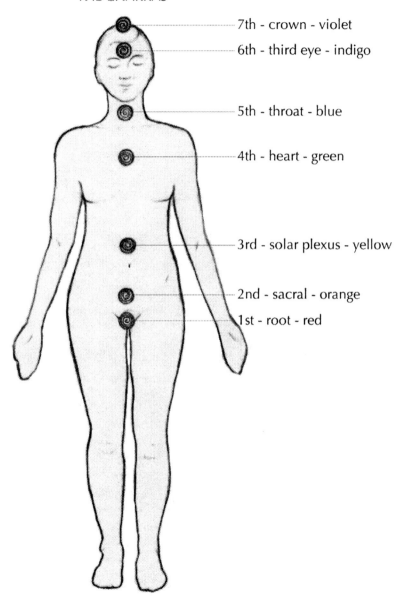

7th - crown - violet

6th - third eye - indigo

5th - throat - blue

4th - heart - green

3rd - solar plexus - yellow

2nd - sacral - orange

1st - root - red

Chakra	Color	Physical Areas	Emotional Issues
1st root	red	Adrenal gland, bones, immune system, legs, feet	Grounding, survival, safety, stability, tribal relationships, social law, family order
2nd sacral	orange	Sexual organs, large intestines, bladder, pelvis, appendix, hips	Sexuality, sensual pleasure, interpersonal relationships, creativity, money, power
3rd solar plexus	yellow	Pancreas, muscles, digestive system, kidneys, liver, spleen	Will, personal identity, fear, joy, trust, self esteem, integrity
4th heart	green	Thymus gland, heart, circulatory system, lungs, breasts, arms	Love, hatred, compassion, healing, anger, faith, grief, resentment
5th throat	blue	Thyroid, parathyroid, neck, shoulders, mouth, teeth, trachea	Communication, translating ideas, self-expresssion, truth, decision-making, criticism
6th third eye	indigo	Pineal gland, eyes, brain, ears, nose	Intuition, vision, intellect, emotional intelligence, open-mindedness
7th crown	violet	Pituitary gland, central nervous system, cerebral cortex, skin	Divine union, spirituality, connection to the higher self, values, humanitarianism, faith, big picture thinking

The level of energy flowing through each chakra at a given point in time relates to your ability to process the consciousness and issues associated with that chakra. A closed chakra indicates a difficulty in functioning in the areas associated with that chakra. Conversely, when energy flows freely through the chakra, it indicates a state of balance or health in those areas. Ideally, the chakras process your personal energy at the levels you can handle, with increasing openness as you grow and evolve. When energy flows through each chakra smoothly, and throughout the system evenly, you are healthy. When energy stagnates you experience disease or imbalance. [3]

Each of our chakras is open at different levels at a given time. This energetic snap-shot may be consistent for an individual over time, or it may change. The energy associated with the chakras that are open are typically the ones other people sense about us first. Expressions like "She's all heart" or "I go with my gut" refer to the kind of personal energy which is engaged most intensely at that time. Personal energy can be highly evolved in specific areas and less developed in others. For example, I've known people who have smoothly functioning thought processes and are very intellectual (open third chakra), but who are guarded when it comes to love (closed heart chakra). There are many books that teach the fundamentals of the energy system and the chakras. I will describe some healing methods to sense and balance your chakras in *Section 6: Your Health*. For now, start thinking about where you have had illness in your body, especially chronic problems. Observe which areas in your body feel weak and which feel strong. Think about the emotional issues you've had in your life. Where are your challenges in relating to yourself and others and what comes easily to you? If it feels right, start to make correlations between these things and the chakras that are associated with those areas. For example, if sickness usually hits you in the throat first, think about how you communicate. Have you been holding back your opinions, or are you having trouble expressing yourself?

Start paying attention to your energetic personality as it relates to your heath and how you show up in the world. Your divine nature is the seat of your energy personality. When you accept your energetic make up as you accept your body and your personality, life will feel more understandable and peaceful. When you stop trying to change to fit someone else's ideal, you begin to build your personal power. As your sense of peace and power grow, your life begins to flow, harmony ensues and happiness is not far behind.

THE SACRED SPACE OF SOLITUDE

"I love people. I love my family, my children … but inside myself is a place where I live all alone and that's where you renew your springs that never dry up." Pearl S. Buck

To find out who you really are, spend time alone. Solitude is invaluable as you seek to understand your inner divinity and your true nature. Interacting with other people is an important part of your existence and growth process. It's also fun and rewarding; however, when you spend all your time with other people you cannot fully understand your relationship with yourself. It is in the hours spent in your own company that you learn your taste in food and movies, your natural sleeping patterns, the tone of your internal communication. For some, those personal preferences are fairly fixed and remain constant even when they are around other people. For others, personal preferences can be easily influenced and change according to whom they are with. From within the sacred space of solitude your natural rhythms, preferences, and imagination express their instinctual tendency to create harmony.

Some people crave time alone, while others do whatever they can to avoid it. Early on in my marriage my husband and I would joke that I needed some "alone time." My husband was respectful of my need to hole up or explore on my own. Being alone allows me to clean out energetically. I can be engaged exclusively with my own thoughts and feelings, without the immediate concern for others' needs or moods. When I'm not conforming to someone else's schedule, I find I go to bed earlier or eat different foods at different times than I would with someone else around. When we're with other people we interact not only on a physical level, but also on an energetic level. Emotions send strong signals. Have you ever spent an evening with a person who is angry? They don't have to express it overtly, but you can tell. When you're with that person you are soaking up the emotion of anger. You may begin to feel angry or sad, or you may react in other ways to their energy. Likewise, you are affected by a happy person's energy. It is difficult to understand yourself, and what you need to find balance, when you have to distinguish which emotions, opinions, and preferences are your own or those of your companions. People who are intuitively sensitive or empathetic often have difficulty in this area. Others are somewhat more oblivious to the energetic and emotional dynamic of those around them and may be less affected, at least at the conscious level. Find out who you are by spending some portion of time alone each day.

This is a challenge for some people. If you come in contact with many people in your personal or professional life, it is especially important to make time for solitude. Alone time is hard to come by with small children in the house, but even a few moments stolen in a hot shower or during naptime can help parents stay balanced. You don't need a weekend retreat in the mountains, just a few hours or even a few minutes to breathe in only your own energy. Figure out what your own "recommended daily allowance" of solitude is and, like a multivitamin, try to take it each day.

If you are averse to spending time alone, ask yourself why. Be honest. Do you simply want someone to share experiences with, or do you feel somehow inadequate or uneasy on your own? When faced with solitary time, are you uncomfortable making choices by yourself? Do you go along with the group or eat what your partner likes because it's easier than speaking up for yourself? If so, take a look at why. When you are alone, do you bombard your senses with the constant sound of TV or radio? Television is as fully charged with emotion as any person sitting in the room with you, or any crowd you might mingle with. Noise drowns out your inner voice.

It is in the moments of solitude that you connect most fully with your inner divinity. Quiet time alone filters out extraneous sensory input, letting the discernment of your shaman's eyes clarify your vision. Inner peace is a state that involves interaction with the world, but it originates in and emanates from your relationship to yourself. You will find your inner voices speaking up when you've given them the respect of your attention. In the silent moments you spend listening to your heart and soul, you will find the unique guidance you need to live the life for which you were made.

ATTITUDES

"Human beings, by changing the inner attitudes of their minds, can change the outer aspects of their lives." William James

Faith vs. Fear

Fear is a paralyzing force. It can also be an instigator of irresponsible action. It has been said that there are only two primary emotions—fear and love—and that all the other emotions are variations on these two source emotions. Love is a sense of unity. Fear is a feeling of separation or disconnection from the world around you. The body responds to fear with neurological and endocrinological changes. The autonomic nervous system is responsible for enacting a stress response. In extreme situations, this response prepares the body to take immediate self-protective action. Typical reactions include an increased heart rate, increased blood supply to the muscles and the brain, the release of glucose into the bloodstream, the dilation of the pupils, increased breathing rate, and an increase in sweat gland activity.[4] Fear feels uncomfortable. When immediate protective action is not warranted, neither is the extreme physiological response induced by fear. Some basic fear instincts are necessary for survival; however, in most cases fear is not a helpful or healthy emotion. Fear causes us to react to a perceived threat from a place of imbalance. Fear finds our weaknesses and our insecurities and exploits them. It pulls us from our center.

Fear is, in most cases, a result of not living in the moment. There are certainly times when fear is an appropriate real-time response; for example, if you are about to be hit by a truck, or if you just stepped on a rattlesnake. But usually we're responding fearfully to a future possibility. It doesn't help your emotional, physical, or energetic bodies to behave as if you are constantly under threat, worrying that bad things will happen at any moment. Your body feels the *potential* suffering as if it were happening *now*. That is the power of your imagination. You can feel the effects of fear without a threat ever being present.

Subsidiary emotions of fear are pettiness, jealousy, selfishness, arrogance, bigotry, duplicity, and cruelty, among others. When fear-based emotions surface for you, start by asking yourself what you are afraid of. Once you've answered that, you can address the root cause and not let fear-based emotions run your life. Being fearful does not prepare you to handle negative events in your life. Some people expect the worst, thinking they will be emotionally prepared for it and somehow hurt less. It doesn't work that way. By focusing on the negative possibilities, you are suffering in advance for something that may not even happen. A better approach is to have confidence that you can handle anything in your life with grace in the moment. Allow life to happen and experience it in real time. Better yet, work to feed the vision of the life you want.

When you have faith or optimism, life presents itself differently. You accept that challenges arise, but feel a sense of underlying safety and support helping you through those times. When you have faith in something outside yourself, a higher power, you recognize that you are not always in control and can accept uncertainty and change without becoming fearful. In some ways, faith lifts the burden many of us carry of feeling that we're solely responsible for everything in our lives. During stressful or upsetting times in my life, faith has kept me from despairing and helped me to stay centered. If you have faith in the universe and act accordingly, you will accept the twists and turns of life with grace and gratitude.

Fear clouds your judgment. Simply being optimistic is helpful in creating a happy life. Having faith is not a naive belief that everything is going to be perfect, it is knowing you are equipped to handle whatever circumstances arise. If you are not equipped, you will ask for help; if there is no help, you will survive, or you won't. But life will somehow go on. Events will come to pass, ones you perceive as positive, as well as negative. If you can stop labeling everything that happens as one or the other, you will go a long way toward experiencing life fresh in the moment. Your perceptions will be clear. You will act for the highest good that you can in each situation.

Love and Compassion

When we think of compassion, we generally think of acts of kindness or generosity toward others. However, if you treat yourself lovingly, you not only create
a healthy environment for your own growth and happiness, but then naturally
extend that love and kindness to others. The Tibetan word for compassion, *tse-
wa*, refers generally to a state of nonviolence and a wish for all beings to be free of
suffering. The Dalai Lama advises that if we wish first for ourselves to be free of
suffering, that feeling will expand outward if we tend to it, consciously spreading
our intentions for others to be free of suffering as well.[5]

Many people feel disconnected from themselves. It is not surprising we have forgotten the sacred spark we carry within us at all times. In order to be fully present with
others, to offer love and empathy, you need to begin to love yourself. Practice compassion toward yourself. Forgive yourself. Be kind, indulgent, and gentle to yourself.
This is not selfishness; it is self-care. Practicing compassion and kindness in your
relationship with yourself helps you treat others that way too. By creating an energetic atmosphere of love and respect for yourself, you can create that atmosphere in
your family and in your community. Think for a moment about how you would
treat a newborn child. You would beam love down on your baby with every gaze.
You would encourage her in adventures as she learned about her world. You would
try to teach her how to share and have respect for others. You would hold her when
she cried and rock her gently to sleep. You would tell her how beautiful she is inside
and out. Begin treating yourself as your own newborn child, a precious being under
your care. It is what you are. Feel the power in that responsibility, the power to affect
someone's life for the positive. That life is your own.

I know many people who are compassionate and kind to others without extending the same courtesy to themselves. Some of us are much harder on ourselves
than we are on the people in our lives. I see clients who feel they are unworthy,
unlovable, or defective in some way. It saddens me to see wonderful people who
don't appreciate their uniqueness and their beauty. When I say simply, "You are
wonderful. You are just fine the way you are and can stop beating yourself up,"
often their emotions well up and tears start to flow. It is such a relief to hear those
words. We don't get enough unconditional love from external sources, so please
start giving yourself some.

One of my clients, Allison, is a lovely human being, but often thinks she is unworthy. She and her father are very different people, and she internalized the feeling
that he was disappointed in her because of those differences. This became part

of her internal dialogue. Instead of loving and appreciating herself, she continually finds fault. Her dad was a linear thinker, rational, non-emotional, critical, and sharp. Allison is radically different. She has a beautiful, flowing, and creative energy. She is deeply affected by her emotions. She's lived her whole life essentially rejecting her true self. She accepted her father's way of being as the ideal, and compared herself accordingly. She judges everything she does and comes up short. Life reflects the idea that she isn't competent or acceptable back at her.

Allison purchased a new house. Eventually she discovered a crack in the foundation of her house. On a deep level she felt she must have made a mistake. She had done nothing wrong. When she bought the house she'd had it inspected. She did everything a thorough and rational person would have done, but she judged herself harshly for not finding that crack. The crack was an interesting metaphor. She needed to patch the crack of the foundation of her life with a mortar of love. It sounds corny, but that was the key issue I saw for her. She needed to love and accept who she was at her foundation. She needed to be kind to herself and she would stop feeling confused and depressed.

Start paying close attention to how you are feeding yourself with your thoughts. The energy of your mind and your heart is your most immediate environment. It supplies you and those around you. Is the emotional environment you are creating in each moment a nurturing and loving one? Intentionally send yourself an extra dose of loving thoughts from time to time. You can focus love on your body, or on allowing yourself to be who you are instead of working to be someone else. For those of us who are driven, the kind message may be to relax a little and know that you are capable, and everything will be taken care of as it should. Stop comparing yourself to other people. Start loving yourself the way you are.

Confidence inspires faith. When people are comfortable in their own skin it feels good to be around them. You cannot find peace outside of yourself. You can work from the inside out, knowing that all the resources you need to find that peace are within you waiting to be discovered. Michelangelo described his approach to sculpting as simply letting the figure out of the material that encased it. The figure he was working on was already fully formed, trapped inside the block, and simply needed to be uncovered from the excess stone.[6] Release yourself from your self-created prison of worries, doubts, and fears. Emerge as your true self, a perfectly formed living sculpture.

Gratitude and Appreciation

Living in a state of appreciation is transformative. It's not about being a Pollyanna, putting a sugar coating on everything, or denying what truly needs fixing. It's about recognizing the positive in each situation, or the divine order of things, even when it seems difficult. Simply shifting from a complaining attitude to a grateful one shifts the energy surrounding you, changing the way you feel.

I've spent some difficult nights lately, where sleep was scarce and emotional tensions were high due to an illness in the family. As I lay in bed, I shifted my energy from the tension of the day and gave thanks for the people who were with me, the safety and comfort of my bed, and the knowledge of my husband and daughter safe nearby. I focused on those things, rather than my three–day–old headache, aching back and worried mind, and things snapped into perspective. I didn't deny the discomfort and exhaustion I felt, but by shifting to a state of gratitude I actually felt much better about the situation. I knew I was where I needed to be, doing what I needed to do.

An appreciative attitude often makes painful circumstances more bearable, and brings light and movement into dark and stagnant mental states. Martha Washington said, "I am still determined to be cheerful and happy, in whatever situation I may be; for I have also learned from experience that the greater part of our happiness or misery depends upon our dispositions, and not upon our circumstances."[7] Your attitude has a remarkable effect on the way you experience life.

Japanese researcher Masaru Emoto documented the cellular nature of water. Initially, Emoto used a machine called a Magnetic Resonance Analyzer, to measure and record the crystal structure of water. He noticed that each crystal was unique, some more beautiful and perfectly formed than others. After perfecting his technique, he photographed water from sources around the world and began to experiment with how sound and language affects water. He proposed that if scientific studies confirmed plant life was affected by the way people spoke (encouraging words produced healthy plants, and discouraging words sick ones) that the same might be applicable to water. He found that water's crystalline molecular structure changed dramatically when exposed to particular words. The words "love" and "appreciation" created the most beautiful and harmonious configuration of water molecules. Our bodies contain up to 70 percent water.[8] Surround yourself with love and appreciation and you will find your molecules coming into harmony and balance. Don't deny yourself your feelings, but allow your inner divinity to guide you to the most healthful ways of being in any situation. Does your heart feel good when you are complaining and agitated? Does it feel better when you calm down, let things fall into perspective, and simply do the best you can? Experiment with this in the moment and see what happens.

As you are striving for the next acquisition or accomplishment, don't lose sight of what you have. It is fine to have ambitions, to want to improve yourself—tone your body, get more education, learn how to skydive—but you don't need those things to be complete right now. They are extra. As you are striving, always remember to come back to a place of wholeness. Reassure yourself that you are acceptable in the state you are in. Be the best you can be in every moment of every day. Our capabilities vary from person to person and from day to day. There are days when I'm energetic and enthusiastically accomplish a lot, and other days when I'm tired and moody. It does you no good to compare yourself to others, or to the "you" of a week, month, or year ago. You are constantly changing and evolving. As you strive for a better job, remember to stay in appreciation of the job you have now. As you strive for a better living space, remember to appreciate the safety and warmth that your current living space provides. My bathrooms are old and falling apart and I spend a fair amount of time fantasizing about their renovation, and even feeling embarrassed by their decrepit state. But when I stand in the shower and my stress melts away, I'm so thankful for indoor plumbing and steaming hot water.

Gratitude opens the door to seeing life in a whole new way. Typically, it is easy to be thankful for things that feel good, e.g., gifts, a sunny day, opportunities, and compliments. It is harder to be grateful for things that feel difficult, like the loss of a loved one, an annoying co-worker, or a bad haircut. It is from these difficult circumstances that you often learn the most. Challenging times prod you to reach into your deepest self and be your best. The most trying people in your life can teach you the most, because they push your buttons. They spotlight the areas on which you need to pay attention. When things are going your way it is easy to become less conscious of yourself. When things go badly you're forced to look inside. It's easy to be a good sport when you win, but what does losing teach you? How often does losing a job allow you the opportunity to find something better? Sometimes it simply gives you the confidence that you can survive. It's not always easy to see the positive when you're in the middle of a crisis. Although it is not always easy, I try to have faith that life is unfolding as it should, and to be thankful I am here to experience it. When you're appreciative of life, regardless of the details, you can partner with divine energy and slip more easily into the universal flow. The lessons from adversity are rich; the lessons from harmony are sweet. Enjoy them both as best you can and know that each contributes equally to who you are.

RESPECTING YOUR NATURAL CYCLES

"The goal of life is living in agreement with nature." Zeno

Everything that exists in material form has a cyclical nature, a life cycle: birth/ death, growth/degeneration, activity/dormancy. These cycles revolve endlessly on macro and micro levels: from the creation and destruction of solar systems, to the rise and fall of civilizations, to the birth and death of a tiny insect. As human beings we are invariably affected by the rhythms of nature around us, and most dramatically by the modulating cadence of our own bodies. Numerous built-in clocks, known as the circadian rhythms, influence your body. Circadian rhythms help regulate when your body naturally wants to change its state. For example, they cause you to get sleepy when it is dark and stay alert when it is light. On a basic biological level, these rhythms have a tremendous impact on the way we experience the world. When we try to keep our lifestyle in balance with those natural cycles, we feel more comfortable. If you have ever experienced jet lag, you know that jumping ahead (or behind) in the normal cycle of night and day can affect you dramatically. Your body gets confused. When your natural rhythms are disturbed, your usual indicators for when to sleep or eat go haywire. Respecting your internal biological cycles positions you to function at your best.

Simple adjustments can help you accomplish your responsibilities with less stress. For example, pay attention to when your energy levels are highest and when you crave a nap. Plan for the energetic peaks and valleys of your day, scheduling important meetings in the morning if you are an early riser, or later in the day if you need a while to gear up. In addition to circadian rhythms, the newly discovered, shorter duration, ultradian rhythm indicates that keeping your nose to the grindstone for long periods of time without breaks is not the most effective way to work. Every ninety minutes your body naturally slips into a state more conducive to daydreaming than to work.[9] Instead of fighting this natural period, try taking brief breaks to refuel and avoid burning out. Fighting these natural cycles puts undue stress on your systems.

We also have personal psychological cycles, and are clearly affected by the phases of the natural world. Personally, I feel my life spirals in evolving patterns, phases repeated, some added, some left behind. There have been times when my work energy level is extremely high and I get more accomplished. At one point, I was employed full-time at a university, working on a master's degree, seeing clients, teaching classes, pregnant, and preparing myself and our home for our new baby. An enormous amount happened, but I surely do not have that level of industry and stamina all the time. If I held myself to that standard, I'd be disappointed with my energy level during the other equally valuable cycles I go through. Slower rest cycles nourish me so I can survive my bursts of energy.

There are times when I sit down to write, even when I don't feel like it. I know it is what I should be doing in that precise moment. I also know when it is time for me to stop. There are times when my nagging voice tells me I should be writing, but my true inner voice tells me I should be doing something else, napping for instance. I love the days when I'm given permission to nap! I happen to be in a cycle right now where much of the time I don't really want to do anything. I enjoy life and things get done, but my natural inclination is to move slowly and be indulgent with myself and my time. A South American tribe has a word for the motivation that propels the spurts of productivity we experience. If they don't have "gana" it is not the right time to work.[10] The community respects the ebb and flow of the individuals' cyclical levels of energy.

It's important to discern what your natural cycles are telling you. Sometimes they speak through your body. Perhaps you need more sleep in the fall and winter? Sometimes they speak though your intuition; perhaps you get the urge to clean out your closets or start a new project. Paying attention to what your body and spirit truly want from one day to the next is challenging. Electricity allows us to forget that it's dark and we should be asleep. A consistently long workweek prevents many of us from adapting our cycles with the seasons. A tulip bulb needs to have a dormant phase before it can bloom. The tulip needs to feel the embrace of the cold January earth in order for it to burst forth in April with colorful blooms. The tulip doesn't question that it must stay still and rest, preparing for the time to grow and develop quickly. We often live in a fast-paced environment and have many demands on our time. We have come to believe that we should be moving, producing, creating, doing something all the time; that to justify our existence we must be *busy*! Until we get the flu, or sprain an ankle, or receive some other message from our bodies or the universe that forces us to stop and rest. Just as the tulip refuels in winter, we must give ourselves time for rest in order to be as productive as possible.

Some businesses are recognizing the benefits of allowing employees to rest when their bodies need it most. Companies like Deloitte Consulting, architectural firm Gould Evans Goodman Associates, and Lowney & Associates, an engineering consultancy, are among the companies creating comfortable spaces for their workers to enjoy a brief nap to refuel. David Birch, chief executive officer of Cognetics Inc., an economic research firm in Cambridge, Massachusetts, explains, "Creativity is important in what we do. If I don't nap, I burn out by 1 or 2 o'clock. Napping doubles the length of my day from a creative point of view." According to William Anthony, a Boston University professor and author of the book *The Art of Napping at Work*, "The rationale is a productivity one—workers are sleepy, and when they're sleepy on the job they're not productive." [11] Our health, happiness, and productivity are affected by the degree to which we honor the cycles of rest and activity that we instinctively need.

I've found myself acquiring things lately, objects from family members, yard sales, wherever, things I like, but don't necessarily love or need. I stopped for a minute today and remembered a time a few years ago when I was giving away many things; things I liked, but just didn't need. Why the difference now? I'm in a different cycle. We all have phases of contraction and expansion: periods of acquiring and letting go, outwardly creative times and inwardly contemplative times, energetic cycles and sleepy cycles. We are not machines. Even the cells of our skin, the largest organ of the body, are entirely replaced every four to six months. [12] Red blood cells are replaced every 120 days, and the cells in the digestive tract last for only four days. [13] Our bodies are recreating themselves constantly. If you cling stubbornly to life as you know it, you block the doorway of transformation, preventing your own development from happening naturally. You keep yourself from evolving as you need to, and make yourself miserable in the process. We are a part of nature and the natural world is changing all the time. Our environment is in a spiraling state of flux. The moon waxes and wanes, as do the tides. Trees grow leaves in the spring and then drop them in the fall.

It is not practical for most of us to adopt an agrarian schedule, sleep when it's dark, hibernate in the winter, or tell the boss "Sorry, I have no 'gana.' I won't be in today." However, you will feel more comfortable if you pay attention to the ways your body phases affect you. Observing the rhythms of the natural world around you also helps restore a sense of balance and connectedness. Nature is the embodiment of the creative power of the universe, divine energy. We share in that spiritual nature as much as the plants or the rivers. Often we forget our connectedness, not only to the natural world which supports our bodies, but to the spiritual world which supports our souls. Paying attention to the fluctuations in your own natural rhythms and inclinations is a way to honor your divine nature, your creative core. Paying attention to the oscillations of your environment reminds you that we are one: one vast being on this planet, in this universe. To disconnect from our natural cycles and environment is to invite disharmony and disease into our lives.

19

KEEPING YOUR BALANCE

"God turns you from one feeling to another and teaches by means of opposites, so that you will have two wings to fly, not one." Mevlana Rumi

Grounding your energy is analogous to grounding an electrical wire: it is a way of safely discharging excess energy that has accumulated in your body. Grounding is essential to keeping your balance as you delve into spiritual explorations and open up to intuitive information. It is particularly important for people who are sensitive. Energy is around you all the time: your energy, other people's energy, and the energy of places you live or visit. Each of us perceives energy differently and is affected by it to varying degrees. When you work intensely with energy, as you do when you are opening your body and heart to new ways of being in the world, it is crucial to keep your balance. When your circuits are feeling overloaded you cannot function from a peaceful place. You may feel edgy or emotional for no discernable reason. Your thoughts may become obsessive, or your body may react with a headache or stomachache. Do not let yourself get overloaded. Discharge excess energy. When energy builds up it can hurt you, it can be sent out negatively to someone else, or it can contribute to the general soup of negative energy around in the world.

There are many ways to ground; different techniques work for different people. Grounding can mean literally touching the ground. Simply placing your hands on the earth, or walking barefoot, helps discharge some of that extra energy. When you ask the earth to help you ground, be careful about what intention you're holding. Instead of sending negative energy into the earth, ask for the earth's help in neutralizing what you cannot handle. The earth is not an energetic garbage dump, and we need to work conscientiously with her. Ask for permission to draw on the earth's power to balance the energy that is too much for you to handle. Do it respectfully and you will feel a tremendous difference. I recommend this kind of grounding frequently to clients and use it myself. It is simple and effective. Gardening is one of the most peaceful activities for me. It gets my hands in the earth and my energetic system responds by feeling more connected and harmonious.

Trees are remarkable partners in grounding. Their energy is solid and receptive. When clients are feeling particularly off balance or panicky, I frequently suggest that they go and put their arms around a tree or sit at the base of a tree. There is an exercise at the end of this section that walks you through a complete grounding meditation with a tree companion. Simply step outside and connect with a tree. Ask permission of the tree before you start. You can simply be with it and feel the strength that emanates from it, or you can ask if you can actually merge your energy with the tree. Mingling your energy with a tree, visualizing your roots deep in the earth and your leaves and branches swaying in the breeze is one of the best therapies I know.

Breathing deeply can help bring you from an unbalanced state into harmony. Gentle, repetitive breathing, while sitting in a chair with your feet flat on the floor, can bring you back into a comfortable awareness of your body. Doing physical activities can ground you. When you are emotional, are you ever drawn to clean out your closets, eat a big meal, or take a walk? Many people who run for exercise describe that jogging at the end of the day helps them to release the tension that has built up. Physical tension also translates into energetic tension. This kind of physical exertion is particularly effective if there are issues of anger and frustration involved in the overload. Stress management techniques help us to release excess energy our bodies have generated during periods of difficulty, strain, or excitement. Our bodies have natural, physiological responses to stressors, such as increased muscle tension, rapid heartbeat, or sweaty palms. Sometimes called the "flight or fight" response, these reactions are signs that the body is ready to take action quickly. When stress is short term, the body relaxes and the reactions abate, bringing the body back to stasis, or balance. However, when we experience long-term stress, from either internal or external triggers, the body stays activated and tense. Chronic tension results in an over-production of energy which can ultimately cause serious harm to the body, including hypertension, headaches, ulcers, and TMJ. It's important to learn how to discharge stress from our physical bodies, as well as our energetic bodies, as the two systems are inextricably linked.

Stress can result from positive events too; a new job or a newborn baby can be wonderful welcome events, but are also tremendously stressful. On a recent trip to my acupuncturist I explained the long list of activities from the week before. I was headachy and exhausted, but told her all was well and the events were happy ones, making light of a very taxing time. She said that our bodies often can't tell the difference between a wedding and a funeral. Your body reacts in a similar way physically to happy or sad events.

Grounding can also bring you back "down to earth" when you're having trouble focusing or are confused. Eating hearty foods like pasta or nuts can help you reconnect with your physical systems when you've been focused on the intellectual, spiritual, or fantasy worlds. Some energy healing practitioners and teachers will offer snacks to their clients after a session or training. Especially when you have a group of people doing spiritual work, it's easy to become disconnected from the physical realm. Engaging your physical body through eating, walking, stretching, and breathing consciously will help you regain your sense of balance.

Balance is when energy is flowing freely throughout your body. Your system is healthy when you are incorporating energy from above and from below, and the path for that energy to travel is clear and unimpeded. A connection to your higher self, or to divine spiritual energy, is most closely related to the functioning of your upper chakras. Your ability to draw and use the flow of earth energy is related more to the lower chakras. The goal is to have your entire energetic system working in balance. There are many healing modalities that are primarily concerned with this flow of energy. Acupuncture, for example, utilizes the meridians, or energy pathways, to create a smooth flow of *ch'i* throughout the body. Practitioners use thin needles and other tools to speed up or slow down the movement as needed. Acupuncture is based on the understanding that all systems of the body are interconnected and affect one another. More healing systems are outlined in *Section 6: Your Health.*

Reconnect with the earth and you will feel more peaceful. Reconnect with your body, and you will learn quickly that you contain all the elements of the earth within you. You are made of water and air and minerals. The interconnectedness of the systems of your body and the systems of the environment hold the key to finding balance both in your personal life and for the planet.

LIVING IN THE MOMENT

"Now is the only time. How we relate to it creates the future. What we do accumulates; the future is the result of what we do right now." Pema Chödrön

Each of us has a temporal focal point that shapes the creation of our lives. When you view your life through the lens of the past, your present and future are colored by your past experiences. The beliefs you adopted as a child continue to affect your choices and the way you experience your life today. Many adults are still operating with a child's view of the world, one formulated from their limited range of experiences and understanding. As adults, it is time for us to reassess the expectations and assumptions about the nature of reality we created as children. We update many things as we grow older, but our outlook on life often remains stunted and fixed in the past. Some people are future oriented, believing their happiness and contentment lie in some future state. They often believe that between the present and the future, certain things need to happen to bring about their desired state, perhaps buying a house, losing ten pounds, or finding a boyfriend.

Neither of these modes of being, past or future fixated, are viable ways of being to create the life you want. When you look only to the future, your present is experienced as a constant state of lack. When your consciousness believes you are lacking what you need, you recreate that state of lack each day, thereby making the future state of happiness more difficult to attain. When you live only from the past, you operate under limiting beliefs. By engaging so much mental energy with your past patterns, you often doom yourself to relive them.

The concept of being present in the moment is an ancient one. Buddhists believe reality exists only in this moment. Keep your attention focused on present time, as it contains the seeds of all things. Through meditation, chanting, and other mindfulness techniques, Buddhists focus on the present moment. The techniques can be quite simple and easy to use. Breathing exercises and sitting meditations help practitioners bring body, mind, and breath into oneness. Emphasis is placed not only on developing a discipline used during short periods of time, but in incorporating basic mindfulness practice into daily activities. For example, Thich Nhat Hanh, Zen Master, poet, social activist, and author, has said when we are washing dishes, we should act as if we are washing the baby Buddha, or Jesus.[14] This level of attention to each moment and the tasks at hand become second nature, giving a new awareness and appreciation for "now."

For many of us, the past holds a mix of painful and happy memories. Typically, it is the painful ones that stick to our psyches like burrs to our cuffs. It is from fear of reliving those painful moments that we actually empower them energetically. We spend our mental energy trying to *avoid* something rather than *create* something. Energetically, the thing we're trying so desperately to avoid will often play out in some way. Conversely, if we focus intently on creating an ideal state, that too will be more likely to manifest. In each moment there is the opportunity to create a new reality.

When you surrender to your circumstances, life can be much less of a struggle. I'm not suggesting you become complacent, but accepting. At each moment you're in a given situation: hot/cold, tired/energetic, joyful/depressed. Seek balance between accepting each moment (opening yourself to what it has to teach you and appreciating it for its uniqueness) and doing what you can to create each subsequent moment more to your liking. You can acknowledge that your current job has afforded you certain benefits (a roof over your head, training, good contacts, etc.) while also recognizing it is not a healthy place for you to be working. Complaining about the negative aspects of your job does nothing to change your future. Taking the practical steps to find another job, creating vibrant and tangible visions of your next job, and praying or asking for help from the universe will all put you in good stead to change your future. This is an active way to create the life you want, while enjoying the life you have.

Healing work helps release the hold the past has on us mentally, emotionally, and spiritually. There are several techniques I use to help bring a client's energy out of the past and into the present. The shamanic technique of soul retrieval is especially helpful. (See a more detailed description of this technique in *Section 6: Your Health*.) Soul retrieval reunites people with spiritual parts of themselves which disconnected during times of crisis. It helps people to heal the energetic and psychological damage caused by traumatic events of the past, without having to relive the trauma itself.

We tend to fossilize around painful incidents from the past. We find it much easier to remember an insult than a compliment, a painful event than a pleasant one. We carry around resentment toward people we feel have wronged us, not realizing that instead of punishing the culprit we're punishing ourselves and depriving ourselves of living fully in our lives. We cannot be fully present and functioning at our highest capacity when so much of our energy is spent reliving the past and clinging to its pain. It makes it harder for us to focus, to be clear, and to respond appropriately to people and events in our present life.

Don't judge yourself for your emotions in the present or the mistakes of your past. You need to forgive yourself before you're truly able to forgive others. Start by releasing yourself of guilt for what you've done, or neglected to do, in the past. The only benefit of guilt is to guide you in your future actions. If you acted a particular way and felt remorse afterward, you can use the memory of that experience to change your behavior if you're faced with a similar situation again. Learn from your mistakes, don't live in them. Accept the past for what it is and move on. The future will arrive without any help from you, so live in the moment.

BEING LIGHT

"A merry heart doeth good like a medicine ... " Proverbs 17:22

"Being light" is a valuable skill. It allows you to step back and take a broader view. To see yourself and the happenings of your life, without becoming too attached or serious, allows you to flow through life gracefully. I've learned to laugh at myself when I act foolishly, putting the telephone in the fridge or forgetting an ordinary word, like "hardware." But sometimes laughing at myself is a challenge. When I realize I've been judgmental or self-centered it's not so funny. However, I can usually lighten up enough to appreciate the humor of my eccentricities and foibles. If you do something embarrassing, and you laugh at yourself, the moment passes. If you have great success, thank the universe, chuckle at your good fortune and keep your success in perspective (e.g. no swelled heads). When times are rough and you laugh at something, anything—yourself, a good joke—the edge comes off. After suffering from ankylosing spondylitis (an excruciating condition involving severe swelling of the joints and spine), Norman Cousins discovered that experiencing positive emotions, especially laughter, through movies and books helped ease his symptoms.[15]

There are clinical studies documenting the benefits of laughing on our health. Laughter calms the body's stress response and increases immune activity. Salivary immunoglobulin A or IgA is believed to protect against some viruses. In studies, subjects viewed a humorous video. Afterward, their salivary immunoglobulin A (IgA) levels were tested, showing an increase in salivary immunoglobulin A (IgA). Furthermore, people who say they "turn to humor as a way of coping with difficult life situations" had the highest initial concentrations of salivary IgA, suggesting that a consistently cheerful approach to life enhances one's immune capacity.[16]

When you laugh at yourself you lift an energetic load. You literally "lighten up." It is easy to become immersed in your thoughts and circumstances to the point where you lose perspective and everything becomes heavy. Humor and laughter clear away toxic emotions and free you to move out of intellectual or emotional ruts, the grooves that lead to compulsive and limiting thinking. We can all be ridiculous. We see it in others all too clearly. But acknowledging our own quirks and faults, and recognizing they are funny sometimes, can be more difficult. Often the personality traits that cause us the most duress have the highest humor quotient. My daughter, at age three, told my husband and me to "be easy" when we acted impatiently. During a moment of frustration for me, she said "Mom, take it easy, temple, temple!" She meant "temper, temper," a misquote from *The Lion King* movie, I believe. She made me laugh and I was able to pause and disengage from my frustration. Little ones can be a great source for reality checks.

Once you learn to step back from yourself you begin to see your life more clearly. Some of the most difficult circumstances are borne more easily when you say "Oh well, it's just life. Let's do what we need to do and have as much fun as we can along the way." Ultimately, much of life is out of our control, so instead of letting circumstances get you "heavy," where nothing flows and you feel miserable, be "light" and you'll get back into a harmonious flow.

We are so afraid that people will see us at our worst, doing something that exposes our ignorance, or our incompetence, or whatever we doubt about ourselves. We easily become overly concerned with hiding those weaknesses from the world, instead of acting truthfully about who we are and admitting we are not perfect. Take a chance, be goofy, have fun and fun will be attracted to you. Be light and the light will grow around you.

Children can teach us so much when it comes to living in a light state. The simple and joyful act of play is one of the fastest ways to get out of a dark mood. Play without a goal. As adults our energies are typically focused on accomplishing something: a job, housework, errands, etc. Children play just to have fun. Carve out some time in your life to do something purely for fun. Draw without a care for the end result, just for the enjoyment of making colors and shapes. Put on your favorite music and dance or sing for yourself. Be honest about what is genuinely fun for you. Personally, I'm not a big game or sports lover. These are generally considered fun things, but to me they aren't. Finding play time is one of my challenges. I know it's good for me, and the spirits have prescribed play to me for a long time. In fact, when I first felt a connection to a spirit guide, I asked how I could find him again. The response was "Play!" Playing more will translate into a greater sense of peace. It unwinds your energy and relaxes your spirit.

Lightness also helps release your attachment to outcomes. We often have specific desires for how situations will turn out. Sometimes we get rigid and see only one possible positive outcome. In reality, there may be many positive possibilities for a given situation. The best may be one you hadn't considered, or allowed yourself to hope for. Keeping an attitude of humor, playfulness, and detachment helps you realize there are larger forces at work in your life. You cannot control every detail. Requesting spiritual assistance, and praying for what is needed, is typically healthier than becoming calcified around the desire for a particular outcome.

Perfectionists often have trouble with being light. When you obsess on every detail of your life, where's the humor? Personally, I wrestle with an overactive brain and the driving force to "do." I typically get a lot done during the day and create and recreate "to do" lists at lightning speed. I frequently hold myself to impossible standards. Some part of me feels I should be able to do everything well, do it with patience and kindness, and look good in the process. Then when something in my life isn't exactly how I want it to be I can obsess about it. Sometimes it takes someone else, a friend or my husband, to encourage me to lighten up and stop being so hard on myself. Then I can snap out of it and see the funny image of myself running around in a frenzy, cleaning, writing, taking care of my daughter, zoom, zoom, zoom, making sure I've accomplished everything possible!

When you feel life acts upon you and everything is serious, especially yourself, you give up your power. You tend to feel victimized by life and powerless to change it. When you can see the humor in life, when you can play through life, you take your power back. Laughing at yourself, with kindness of course, breaks the cycle of perfectionism and control. You've gained personal power because you've learned to channel your energy from draining ways of being to energizing ones. This release gives you the flexibility and the acceptance needed to feel peaceful. Clearly we're happier when we're laughing than when we're angry or frustrated. Bedtime at my house can be a source of frustration for me. My daughter has a tendency to drag out each step of the process. It can be infuriating or adorable depending on my mood. When I've said, "Come and brush your teeth" for the fifteenth time, it's infuriating. One night when she was three she said to me "You are the best Mommy I never had." That soothed my irritation quite a bit. Once at Christmas time, instead of following my orders, she stood there naked and irresistible and burst out with a robust rendition of "Deck the Halls with Boughs of Mommy!" How could I stay mad? When she does something funny, she snaps me out of my mood and I can enjoy the whole process with a little perspective, enjoying this precious and fleeting time in our lives. An Apache myth describes how the Creator gave human beings many abilities—to speak, walk, see, hear, and so forth—but was not satisfied until they were able to laugh. The Creator said "Now you are fit to live."[17]

PERSONAL POWER AND ETHICS

"… Everything can be taken from a man but one thing; the last of the human freedoms—to choose one's attitude in any given set of circumstances, to choose one's own way." Viktor Frankl

Your personal power is your energetic integrity. There are ways of being that contribute to your reserve of personal power: acting honestly, treating yourself and others with respect and kindness, remembering to stop and connect to the spirit world. There are ways of being that detract from your personal power: cruelty, deceit, attempting to control others. Socrates describes this concept of personal power simply as that part of us which is benefited by doing what is right and harmed by doing what is wrong. The way you use your personal power affects you profoundly. It is at the heart of your energetic relationship with the world around you. It influences everything: the way you see yourself and experience your day to day life; your relationship with others; your connection to your sources of spiritual wisdom, and your physical health. When you are aware of your personal power and use it wisely and conscientiously, you increase it and experience your connection to your divine self more fully. When you abuse your personal power you tend to lose it and become detached from your inner divinity.

Fortunately, you can often change the results of the use or misuse of your personal power. First, ask yourself a few questions. To whom or what do you give away your power? Take a brutally honest look at your tendencies. No one else needs to know what you discover, but being honest with yourself is critical, so look hard. Have you sold out, or would you sell out, for money? Have you allowed, or would you allow, someone else to abuse you emotionally or physically in order to feel loved? Have you manipulated, or would you manipulate, someone to have control over them? Have you lied, or would you lie, to get what you want? This is a short list. There are many more ways that people give away their personal power. Make a mental list of what circumstances make you vulnerable and work to act differently when they come up again. Don't fret over what's happened in the past, just reverse the trend. Start making deposits into your spiritual bank account instead of withdrawals.

Truth, Acceptance, and the Shadow Side

You are in service to yourself when you are truthful. When we communicate with ourselves, honesty is important, and often a struggle. Get clear about your motivations, your fears, and your wishes. When "talking" to yourself, let go of any false ways of being you have adopted, such as overly self-deprecating modesty or passive-aggressive behavior. You don't need to be polite to yourself, you need to be straight with yourself. Acknowledge your emotions and opinions and accept them for what they are. If you have made mistakes in your life, own up to them. Admit you are not perfect and then appreciate yourself for who you are as a whole. Accept credit and blame where they are due and move on. It is difficult to understand what is true when you are hiding from yourself. Shine a light into all the recesses where you have hidden the parts of yourself you do not want to see.

We all have a shadow side, traits or tendencies that we're ashamed of, or wish to suppress. It's important to acknowledge all aspects of your being, the light as well as the shadow. Both sides have much to teach you. It is often most difficult to be truthful with yourself when you are looking at shadow side issues. It is not helpful to fight or indulge them. Simply be truthful with yourself *about* yourself. Then give thanks for all your parts and let them be. When you accept the totality of who you are, you increase your personal power. When you reject parts of yourself or are fixated on certain aspects, you decrease your power.

My client Mark provides a good example of wrestling with the shadow side. We uncovered through dialogue and journeying that he was overly engaged with his shadow side. He was well aware of the havoc that indulging those dark aspects had wreaked in his life (affairs, drug abuse, irresponsibility), but hadn't understood that for his whole life his focus was on those aspects of himself that he considered "negative." He'd been criticized as a child and made to feel unworthy, so he rebelled. In his early years, he focused on the fight against the parent who rejected him. Later on, he incorporated that parent's words into his own internal dialogue and focused on fighting himself. He fought his nature at every turn, feeling he was going to be overcome by his shadow side again. As an adult he didn't want to repeat his mistakes. But since he was only engaging his shadow side, and thought he could overcome it by fighting it, he was simply feeding it more energy. Through journeying I helped him recognize he needed to infuse his thoughts with lightness. He needed to appreciate himself and refocus his energy on his wonderful qualities, his creativity, and spontaneity. By bringing light and love in, he was more easily able to find balance in his life. Combat wasn't going to ease the shadow side effects, but only make them fight harder to keep control. His personal power increased as he ceased fighting and accepted his whole, divine being.

I recently realized I'd been judging someone unfairly. I'd stopped discussing a certain part of my life with someone close to me. I thought he was closed and judgmental of me and my interests. A more accurate description of what happened was that I was defensive and overly sensitive. I felt uncomfortable in a few conversations, mostly from my own projected fears and insecurities, so I shut down. Then I blamed him for the lack of communication. Ouch. Not very pretty. I really thought I was right in my opinion until he asked me to defend it and give examples. When I have a case to make I typically have my evidence dated and in color-coded file folders. Not literally, but I do have an elephant's memory when I get angry. I couldn't come up with much to defend this point. It was the tip off for me that I'd made a mistake. I hurt a relationship I cared about deeply. I learned about some aspects of my shadow side: I can be defensive, closed, and judgmental. I apologized and promised myself to be less defensive and judgmental in the future.

Transmute the darkness from your life, as you accept your shadow side. We all have fears, judgments, and issues that trip us up over and over again. They keep us from feeling connected with our true spirits. Bring all those things to light and deal with them—with yourself first. Remember it is equally important to recognize your light, "positive" qualities as it is the "negative" or shadow aspects. The act of being truthful has tremendous power. It takes courage, and a certain level of humility, to admit the truth about your deepest self. By having the fortitude to face yourself in this manner, a new world of honesty and integrity opens for you in your dealings with others. When you're open, you clear the blocks to communication with your divine self and with the guidance available to you through that higher level of your being. Mahatma Gandhi said, "Happiness is when what you think, what you say, and what you do are in harmony." This is living with integrity.

The Razor's Edge

Shamanic practices, and many other traditions, address the concept of personal integrity. They speak about the importance of acting impeccably: to tell the truth, to be compassionate, to be kind. When you walk your path embodying those qualities, you generate personal power and you can sleep at night knowing that you've done the best you can.

For many shamanic cultures, there are particular ways of behaving that are acceptable to the individual and the group. Performing rituals to honor ancestors, killing animals only for use and not sport, and showing gratitude to the spirit world are ways that people in many indigenous cultures behave according to their concept of harmonious living. The Ten Commandments set forth a Judeo-Christian code. Religious and secular groups have explicit or implicit codes for interacting with the rest of the world. Come up with your own set of standards to uphold. You can use existing spiritual systems as a guide, but explore what you believe are the most important qualities to adopt in your life. Then do your best to follow them, knowing full well that there will be moments when you don't.

Shamans talk about walking the razor's edge. The analogy explains that being fully on your spiritual path is like walking on the thin edge of a razor. You can't help but fall off. The trick is to get back on and keep trying to walk along its narrow edge. This is not about perfectionism. You're not perfect and neither am I. Nor are the greatest spiritual teachers of our time or times past. Do your best and leave it at that. Don't judge yourself when you don't live up to the standards you have set. You're capable of different ways of being at different times. Personally, if I'm tired and cranky it's a challenge for me to stay in a place of peace. I accept that about myself. I've worked over the years to transmute the frustration and anger I feel when in that emotional state, so the mood lasts for increasingly shorter periods of time. I've practiced keeping that energy to myself instead of spreading the misery around. Do I always succeed? No. Just ask my husband. But when I fall short, instead of judging, I look at how I want to act differently next time.

There are many aspects to the personal code I try to follow. I try to tell the truth and be kind. I try to be grateful for the amazing good fortune in my life. I try to be patient and respect the environment. I try to keep things in perspective, I try not to be self-engrossed, and I try not to lose my temper frivolously. Those are important parts of my code. I fail frequently with some parts and am fairly good at others. I recently had a trivially annoying day trying to buy a piece of computer equipment. I'd been shopping around, bought something only to have it arrive broken, thought I'd found another one and when I got to the store discovered it wasn't the right thing. This whole process was of very little importance in the scheme of things, but I really wanted this gadget and was fuming after my final attempt to obtain it failed. I stomped. I swore. Fortunately, I didn't yell at the salesperson. Then I got over it. I didn't judge myself for being angry, myopic, and somewhat ridiculous. I let it go. I accepted my emotions, tried to manage them responsibly, and then let them wisp away. Without perspective or awareness of the dynamics of emotional energy, this kind of thing can snowball.

This is a trivial example of falling off the razor's edge and climbing back on, but the larger things in our lives can be treated the same way. I've found myself being judgmental, unforgiving, greedy, and oblivious. I've likely committed as many "sins" as anyone, but I haul myself up again, trying to walk a straighter path the next time. Be true to yourself, remember the way you want to be in the world, acknowledge your weaknesses, and have the strength to get back on your path.

CLOSING

"When the whole is understood as an inseparable mixture of organized parts, then we may understand ourselves as part of this great wondrous whole, and within ourselves be complete once again." Anodea Judith

Accept who you are and seek out your true nature, your true preferences, your true opinions, and your true yearnings. One of the noble truths of Buddhism is that humans experience *dukka*, a sense of dissatisfaction, or that something is lacking. We suffer with this uneasiness because we're disconnected from our true natures. Until we reconnect to our sacred selves, we will not be content.[18] Look within and call forth your authentic essence. Remember who you truly are and you will find peace.

You have no choice but to live with yourself. Given the permanent bond you have with the being inhabiting your skin, doesn't it make sense to develop a kind, enjoyable, and evolving relationship? How you speak to, think about, and care for yourself establishes your first link to the rest of the world. If you can't love yourself fully, it is a challenge to love others without strings and expectations. If you can't forgive yourself for your mistakes, it is difficult to forgive others for theirs. If you can't accept your own weaknesses and personality quirks, it is likely you will find them irritating in others. Model your best behavior to yourself first. Try loving, encouraging, and forgiving yourself first, and you will become a loving, encouraging, and forgiving person to others.

When you respect yourself and your personal boundaries, others will respect them too. When you're having fun being yourself, others are drawn into playfulness. Enjoy the unique and fantastically imperfect creature that you are. When you recognize that you blossomed in this world from a divine seed, you can't help but feel awe, gratitude, and joy at being exactly who you are.

EXERCISES FOR SECTION 1: YOUR SELF

Refer to the *How To Use This Book* section in the *Introduction* if you have questions. Relax your body and clear your mind before you begin, be open to the information you receive, and write down your experiences when you are finished.

* Meditate on this question, "What do I need to change about how I care for myself?"

* Meditate on this question, "What do I need right now to remember my inner divinity?"

Internal Dialogue

* Monitor your internal dialogue.

  ○ Identify the voices of other people that have been incorporated into your internal dialogue.

  ○ Modify your self-talk as necessary to create a nurturing environment inside your mind.

Personal Energetics

* Pay attention to your inner body and how it reacts in different situations.

* Meditate on each of the chakras. Sitting quietly and with your spine straight, focus your attention on the root chakra for a few moments. Visualize the color red and simply pay attention to that area of your body. Work your way up the spine, paying attention to each chakra and color in order, until you reach the crown chakra. Refer back to the chakra chart for the colors associated with each chakra.

The Sacred Space of Solitude

* Create some time each day for solitude and silence.

* Pay attention to your reactions to being alone or in silence.

Attitudes: Faith vs. Fear

* Meditate on this question, "What are my deepest fears?"

  ○ With each answer, go deeper and ask again until you feel you reach the core fear.

  ○ Meditate and ask for a ritual to release the fear.

  ○ Design an affirmation/vision replacing that fear with faith.

Attitudes: Love and Compassion

* Practice sending yourself love and kindness each day.

* Do something nice for yourself each day for a week—then keep doing it!

Attitudes: Gratitude and Appreciation

* Make a list of what you are grateful for and give thanks.

* Meditate on this question, "What are some positive aspects of myself which I need to appreciate more?"

Respecting Your Natural Cycles

* Keep a journal of your natural cycles.

   O Note how you feel energetically and emotionally each day.

   O After a period of time, look back and see if there are discernable patterns.

* Pay attention to your natural sleeping patterns.

   O Notice if they change over the weeks, months, and throughout the year.

   O Try going to bed at different times and see if it affects the number of hours you need to feel rested.

   O Try waking up without an alarm clock (programming your body to rise when you need to, by setting that intention the night before).

* Pay attention to the phases of the moon for several months. Keep a journal about how you feel and how the phases of the moon may affect your moods, energy, productivity, etc.

Keeping Your Balance

* Walk barefoot, get your hands in the dirt, or embrace a tree.

* Grounding Meditation
  (*This meditation is included on the* Inner Divinity *companion CD. See the* Resources *section for more information.*)

  Sit upright with your feet planted firmly on the floor. Close your eyes. Breathe deeply. Imagine yourself sitting in a beautiful forest. You are at the base of a very old and large tree and a brook is babbling nearby. The sounds of the forest surround you. Feel the tree trunk strong against your back. Picture its vast root system beneath the earth. Picture its spreading branches reaching up toward the sky, soaking up the sun. With each breath, feel yourself more closely connected to this tree. Smell the earth and the forest all around you. Hear the birds and other living things in the forest and feel yourself become one with the tree. Merge with that strong, solid, grounded tree energy. Now as you breathe in imagine you're breathing through the roots of the tree, through your roots, drawing up the calm, balanced energy from deep in the earth.

As your breath fills your lungs, imagine that it is reaching to the tops of your branches, nourishing each and every cell with exactly the energy it needs. With each breath, relax more and more deeply, soaking in the energy of the tree, the earth, and the forest. Any troubling emotions, either yours or those you picked up from others, are neutralized and gently melt away. With each breath, breathe through your roots, drawing up that deep calm earth energy and letting that nourishing air reach out to the tips of your branches. Take several moments simply to enjoy this state of balance and harmony with nature, and with your own body, mind, and spirit, paying attention to those roots reaching deep within the heart of the earth.

Take several more deep breaths. Come back into your body now, sitting at the base of the tree. You are once again separate and feel the tree strong against your back. Thank the tree for helping you ground and regain your balance. Relax, soaking up the sound of the brook and the birds and the insects. Breathe in the fresh sweet air of the forest. Feeling at peace with yourself and nature, take a few more deep breaths and when you're ready, open your eyes.

Living in the Moment

* Make a list of your current beliefs.
   O What works? What doesn't? Let go of outdated or unhealthy beliefs.
* Practice staying present in each moment.
   O Wear something or post something near your work station or kitchen sink which will help you remember to keep your energy focused on the present moment.
* Practice Thich Nhat Hanh's meditation. Sit quietly and repeat the following affirmation silently or out loud:
   Breathing in, I calm my body.
   Breathing out I smile.
   Dwelling in the present moment,
   I know this is a wonderful moment.

✳   Meditate on this question, "What have I not forgiven myself for?" Then
    let it go.

Being Light

✳   Laugh at yourself!

✳   Make a play date with yourself, a friend, or a child.

✳   Choose an issue that is important to you and release your attachment to
    the outcome. Ask for help from the spirits, and your higher self. See the
    issue as a symbol or word and hand it up through the clouds to a pair
    of strong kind hands. Allow those hands to hold the issue and see that
    things resolve as they should.

Personal Power and Ethics

✳   Meditate on this question, "Where am I not being truthful with
    myself?"

✳   Meditate on this question, "Where am I investing my power?"

    ○   Consider how you are using your power. Is it a productive and healthy
        use, or is it draining you in some way?

✳   Meditate on this question, "When in my life have I misused my power?"

    ○   Ask for a ritual you can do to heal the effects of that misuse.

✳   Make a list of what areas are most important in your life and focus on
    putting your power into those areas.

SECTION 2: YOUR RELATIONSHIPS
Living Harmoniously with Those Around You

We live in relationship to other beings. Our personal relationships shape our expectations for, and interpretations of, our life's experiences. Our connections to other humans are sometimes rewarding and sometimes painful; these interpersonal encounters are often our best teachers. The way we relate to others is shaped by the way we relate to ourselves. Once you perceive the divine within, you recognize it more easily in others, which fosters an attitude of love and respect toward the people you encounter. In this section, I'll describe some basic ways you can use your inner divinity to interact consciously with the people in your life. Your relationships will benefit simply from your being who you truly are. We'll also discuss interpersonal energetics. Every being on this planet has a spiritual identity, a frequency that is perceived by others. Much of the confusion we feel in relationships is in interpreting or misinterpreting the energy of others.

Sometimes the oldest adages hold the most wisdom. Love thy neighbor as thyself. Do unto others as you would have others do unto you. If we can detach from our egos enough to understand another person's point of view, we can treat them as they wish to be treated. I want to be treated kindly and fairly. I want the people who are close to me to say and do things to make me feel loved and appreciated. I want my wishes to be honored and my feelings to be respected. Everyone has a different list, but we often misunderstand each other's needs and wind up pitting ourselves against each other. We become so concerned with our issues of dominance or insecurity, or the wrongs we feel have been done to us, that we are unable to understand each other enough to live harmoniously.

One of the beautiful effects of recognizing your inner light is that you develop the power to relate to others more humanely and compassionately. As you see yourself more truthfully and treat yourself more kindly, those ways of being naturally translate into your relationships with those around you. Everyone has experienced hurt or trauma. We have all wounded others and been wounded ourselves. At a fundamental level, we're collectively sharing the experience of living. Within that collective experience, there are multitudes of ways in which we express ourselves and a vast array of life events that affect us. We're all trying to get through life with a minimum of pain and a maximum of satisfaction. We can help each other achieve those goals when we understand how much we share in simply being human.

COMMUNICATION

"Communication leads to community, that is, to understanding, intimacy and mutual valuing." Rollo May

Just as we communicate with ourselves constantly through our inner dialogue, we also communicate to the beings around us. We're sending out messages all the time, some intentional and some unintentional. We convey our opinions and emotional states through verbal language, body language, and the language of our energy. As with learning to observe and adjust your inner dialogue, becoming cognizant of your communication style is a first step in interacting responsibly in your relationships.

The Power of Words

Verbal communication is the most tangible way you convey your thoughts and feelings to those around you. Start by simply observing yourself for a while. You may be amazed at the things you say and don't really mean. Have you ever said something like this? "I hate that guy!" or "I'm going to kill her!" Did you really mean it? Words have amazing power. Remember a time in your life when someone said something hurtful to you. It may have been a seemingly innocuous statement, or a joke not intended to hurt at all. We all have experienced the devastating effects of cruel or thoughtless words. You have internalized them, formulated opinions of yourself based on them, and let them influence you for long periods of time. Now think of how often you may have affected someone else with your insensitive words. When I do this, it's sobering. I think of the times I said something spiteful out of anger. I think of the times I told loved ones they weren't capable of living up to what I really wanted from them. As I've grown older I've become more aware of the power of my words. I choose them more carefully, and with forethought for how they may affect the receiver. I still must work hard to choose fitting words, but when I do it seems that conflicts resolve more quickly and relationships deepen.

In our relationships we can plant seeds of hope and reconciliation in the minds of those we love. Is the language you use encouraging or disparaging? When you speak to your child, do you convey your faith in her ability to choose well, or do you fill her with fear of failure? Do you support your partner with words of praise or do you complain about his shortcomings? Do you inspire your employees to be their best or limit them with criticism? Of course, we must be truthful in our communication. Good intentions do not excuse us from being honest, but the kind delivery of our thoughts is important.

I once had a friend try to comfort my complaints about my figure by saying I had "childbearing hips." I think she was trying to be kind, but her choice of an unfortunate phrase haunted me. Another time I shared a new painting with an acquaintance who had showed interest in seeing my work. Her comment was "Oh, that's busy, isn't it?" It was not the response I was hoping for. Neither of these people meant to hurt my feelings and they didn't need to give me false praise, but if they had chosen their words more carefully, they could have inspired me to feel good about myself and my work.

Once my daughter was trying to speak conscientiously. She was admiring her grandmother's softness and asked her "What's a nice way to say fat?" Even as a young child she wished to express truth, but in a way that wouldn't offend, and in fact would compliment her beloved grandmother.

Your speech is the most direct way you engage the people in your lives, both personally and professionally. As you strive to speak consciously and with awareness of the effect your words have on the receiver, you create accord with those around you. As you experience the effects of that accord, you will begin to see the level of satisfaction in your relationships grow.

Listening

Listening is as important as speaking. When people talk to you, do you ever catch yourself watching their mouths move while you think about something else entirely? Instead of paying attention to what they are communicating, are you formulating your response before they even finish? I've found myself doing both these things. When you're paying more attention to your inner dialogue than to the person speaking to you, you're not really listening. You may be hearing the words, but not necessarily understanding what the speaker is really trying to convey. We can often get away with this shallow level of interaction when we're shopping or making simple arrangements. It's not ideal and it doesn't respect the people we're engaging. We're so used to multitasking that deep meaningful communication is unusual and fast verbal "transactions" are more common. I recently found myself talking into two phones at once! I was having conversations, speaking and trying to listen to two people simultaneously. It was a challenge to say the least, and I'm sure I wasn't an effective communicator on either end. In my own defense, the pilot light on our furnace had gone out and it was cold; I was trying to make arrangements to get it turned back on. However, in many ways my life is set up to encourage the quick convenient use of technology. In this case, it turned out well and one furnace repairman came out while the other was saved a trip. But it made me think. I was talking to one person and couldn't really listen to them because I had another conversation going on in the other ear. How often do you do other things as you converse and how does that deteriorate the level of your listening? So much is conveyed through a person's eyes, tone, and body language. If you open up with all your senses to receive what is being shared, you can connect at a much deeper level than when you're distracted.

We often listen selectively. Like many people, I have a hard time hearing criticism. I can be sensitive and defensive. When someone I respect has something negative to say, no matter how mild or well-put, it looms in my mind. Their comment may have been surrounded by praise, but what I remember is the criticism. The inverse can be true as well. We can be remarkably good at hearing what we wish to hear. Hearing is the first step, obviously, but the next step in listening is processing what you've heard in a balanced and thorough way.

When you listen intently you can understand not only what is being said, but what is required of you in response. In some interactions, the person sharing with you wants help or advice; sometimes they just want to be heard and to share their feelings. One of my clients recently came to me with some concerns about her relationship. Her partner was getting frustrated with her because she complained about the same issues over and over. My client simply wanted to share her feelings, but her partner assumed she wanted advice about how to fix her problems. Since the partner had already given her opinion on how to fix them, she was getting frustrated with hearing them repeatedly. My client's issues aside, she simply wanted to be heard. In fact, she didn't feel supported by her partner's attempts to solve her problems. They had two different ways of listening and responding. They had good intentions, but they weren't expressing their own needs or listening to their partner effectively. My client needed to make it clear that she just wanted a shoulder; she didn't expect, nor did she want, a plan of action. Her partner needed to listen more intuitively and in the present moment instead of rerunning tapes of their previous conversations. She was tuning out once the conversation started, because in her eyes they'd had it already and she knew what to expect and how she would respond.

My husband and I did this recently. Late one night when we were both tired (never a good time for intense dialogue), I shared with him my excitement about a new idea. From my exuberance and my history, he thought I was ninety percent sure I was going to pursue it. I wasn't really that sure, but was excited and wanted to share it. He moved from the sharing phase into the practicalities and challenges of making it happen. I hadn't thought those through, so from his perspective I hadn't done my homework. I felt attacked for not having a good plan, when I hadn't even gotten to the planning stage. The conversation went badly. Neither of us really understood why the other was upset. I needed to be clearer in what I wanted from that conversation. We both needed to listen more sensitively to what the other was saying, without responding defensively. We agreed the next day not to have important conversations when it's late and we're tired.

Be precise in explaining your needs, and listen attentively to perceive what the other person needs from you, and your conversations will be more satisfying and more productive. Words are the most overt way that we communicate, but our body language and the language of our personal energy are also powerful indicators of our true feelings.

Body Language

Sometimes we respond based on how people appear, rather than what they actually say. When people don't look you in the eye, what judgments do you instinctively make about them? Are they shifty or just shy? Hard to tell sometimes, but you know you're affected. The way they engage you in subtle, physical ways shapes your opinion of them. Of course, remember that people perceive *you* at all times, too. When you're in line to buy groceries, you can choose to be friendly to the check out people, or you can look away and ignore them. With each interaction, you have a wonderful opportunity to add lightness to the world. With each interaction, you can choose to effuse a warm and welcoming energy. You don't have to be fake or put on a perky act, just be aware of what energy you want to share with the world.

We can manage this to some degree as we become aware of it, but sometimes it is beyond our control. Some of us naturally look happier and more approachable than others. For example, I tend to look serious and even scowling when I'm lost in thought or just going about my business. I know from experience that people have judged me based on my expression rather than any real interaction with me. I noticed it for the first time in college. Repeatedly, people would come up to me at parties asking what was the matter. I was just sitting in a chair or relaxing, but they thought I was upset. One girl told me she thought I was mean (although that's not the exact word she used!) before she knew me, but when she spent more time with me she liked me and thought I was funny. I found it exasperating. I try to be aware of my expression, but even now, my daughter will catch me and say, "Why are you making that face?" I'll say, "What face?" and she'll scrunch up her eyebrows into a little scowl. It makes me laugh.

There are two lessons here. The first is to be aware of how we are communicating with our bodies and our faces. We have a certain amount of control over facial expression or posture. Just as we can choose fitting words to say, we can make some conscious choices about what our bodies and faces are saying.

The second and more important lesson is not to judge others by their appearance. We tend to make assumptions about people based on their bodies and body language. The media reinforces these stereotypes. In the movie of *The Wizard of Oz* Dorothy says to Glinda the Good Witch that she "thought all witches were ugly." Glinda laughs softly and says "Only bad witches are ugly." How often are heroines blond and blue-eyed and villains dark complexioned? A friend recently shocked me by referring to someone as a "blond, blue-eyed child of God." How do hair and eye color relate to being included as one of God's children? They don't, but in our culture we associate physical appearance with personality traits that have no connection whatsoever.

Personal Energetics

Our personal energetics are the subtlest way we engage others in the world. We sense people with our energy bodies as quickly as we sense them with our eyes. As we discussed in the last section, we each have an energetic personality, a unique way of showing up in the world and interacting with others. As we can learn to understand our own energetic personalities, we can begin to sense those of other people. We are interacting on a spiritual or energetic level all the time, although most people are unaware of it.

Have you noticed how some people fill up a room? We have various ways to describe that dynamic; we call them charismatic, dominant, or show-offs, maybe. People with that quality are often giving their energetic personalities free expression. That way of being in the world can be off-putting to those who hold their energy closer in. It can feel overwhelming. To the more energetically expansive person, the quieter one can appear cold, shy, or almost invisible. Just as we are responsible for our words and body language, it helps to understand our energetic personalities. When you come into a room, do you size it up quickly, place yourself in the most powerful position, and immediately start a conversation? Or do you hang back at the periphery and get a sense of the group before joining in? When you're mad, do you fume at everyone around you or do you hold the energy inside you? Do you jump in and express yourself fully, but maybe without thought for how you affect those around you, or are you overly concerned with not imposing yourself on anyone?

As a child of seven or eight, I was with my grandfather in a golf cart. Somebody hit a golf ball and it hit me hard in the chest. Grandpa was angry and tossed the ball back at him, saying, "You hit the kid!" As we drove away, I called after the golfer "Sorry!" I was actually apologizing for messing up his golf shot! I was startled by Grandpa's unusual show of anger and felt embarrassed that I was the cause. From my perspective now, I was overly concerned with not being a nuisance to anyone. He hit *me* with a careless shot and I was apologizing. Become aware of how you naturally relate to others on that level and make adjustments as you see fit.

We connect to one another through channels of energy, which often appear like cords or tendrils that join one body to another. These cords solidify relationships and can help bind us to one another psychically. They can also be burdensome when relationships are not entirely healthy, especially when one person is draining energy from another. These energetic connections manifest from the first moments of our lives. From birth, there is an "etheric umbilicus" that connects mother and child. As we make relationships, we form other connecting cords from our solar plexus region. When a relationship ends, these energy cords will often dissipate.[19]

In my early intuitive development work, my teacher had us take turns standing in front of the room in pairs. The rest of the class would watch and try to see how the two people engaged each other energetically. It was amazing. We could sense the distinct energetic personalities of our classmates in their relationship to each other. Just standing in close proximity incited a range of responses. Some people sent out many tendrils of energy right away, reaching out to the other person quickly and with their whole being. Others were more cautious, sending out an exploratory cord to see if they felt comfortable with the other person. If they did, they would send out more of their energy to mingle.

Our energetic personalities often mirror how we interact with people in our everyday lives. Introverts may tend to be slower in opening energetically to a person they don't know. Spunky, exuberant types may jump right in and send their energy out quickly. One way is not better than another, but they affect us differently. Our energetic personality affects the way we view the world and how we respond to other people who enter our lives. There are some people who just do not harmonize energetically, and will not be comfortable with each other no matter what they do. There are some people you're going to like or dislike right away. You may be sensing them energetically and picking up aspects of their personality that feel comfortable or uncomfortable to you. Consider accepting this energetic explanation, rather than finding intellectual reasons to justify your instinctual like or dislike.

As you pay attention to your own energetic personality, you can find balance with how you express your true self. Many misunderstandings begin at the energetic level. You meet someone for the first time and, because they are more reserved energetically than you are, you think they don't like you. We take our interactions with other people very personally, even when their responses have nothing to do with us. We translate other people's energetic personalities through our personal filters. When people have a very different style from our own, it tends to cause discomfort, at least initially. Instead of making quick assumptions about people, try to become sensitive to their energy. Once you are aware of these differences in energetic style, you can usually find ways to interact that feel safe and comfortable for both parties. When you look through shaman's eyes at the people around you, you pick up on subtleties often missed with everyday vision. Try to become sensitive to how you express yourself nonverbally and to how other people's energy personalities affect you.

Truthfulness and Politeness

In *Section 1: Your Self*, we talked about how crucial it is for you to be honest with yourself. Honesty is, of course, important in your relationships with other people. It is the basis on which we feel safe with one another. Has someone close to you ever told you a lie? It can feel like the rug has been pulled out from under the entire relationship. Everything good you have experienced with that person can come into question if you feel they speak or act falsely. The same is true for you.

When you misrepresent yourself, or tell a lie, you're sending a clear signal that you're not to be trusted. You don't value your relationship enough to treat it with integrity.

It can be hard to tell the truth sometimes. The truth can be painful, both to speak and to hear. There are ways of being truthful that are kind. It's not your job to tell everyone you pass on the street what you think about their haircuts or their outfits. However, when a close friend asks you your opinion about something, do your best to give it honestly, fairly, and tactfully. Truth and tact can usually coexist, but you must think and act carefully.

I have several friends who contact me regularly for advice. When they explain their current situation or dilemma to me, I answer their questions honestly. With one friend, I have a standing order to be brutally honest and tell her what I think, even when she isn't explicitly asking for my opinion. She values my perspective and trusts that I'm coming from a loving place. Conversely, when I ask a friend for the truth, I want them to be honest with me, kind but truthful. With other people in my life, I will respond when asked and mind my own business when not.

One Buddhist precept relates to using language responsibly. The basis of this precept is to refrain from doing four things: not telling the truth, exaggerating or embellishing, speaking with a "forked tongue" or telling two people opposite things, and using profanity or abusive language. This precept encourages us to speak truthfully and mindfully in order to retain our self-respect and others' trust.[20] It is more important to be truthful than to be polite. You create the "you" that the world sees. Your word, and what that word is worth, reflects on you and affects the way people respond to you.

I once had a client who was talking about an affair he had just ended. I genuinely liked this man and knew he was in a great deal of pain, and feeling guilty for the suffering he'd caused his wife. At one point, he talked about trying to protect his wife by seeing the other woman only at specific times in public to do certain activities. I stopped him and told him that he was deluding himself if he thought his motivation was really to protect his wife. He was disconnected from reality. I know it felt like a slap in the face to him, but at that moment it was important to be honest with him, rather than polite. I was careful to add some kind and loving words too. He came to me for an intuitive opinion, and no one would be served if I was too afraid of hurting his feelings to tell him the truth.

There are many situations where the idea of "telling the truth" gets challenged. What do you do if you are undercharged at the supermarket, a friend asks if you like her new boyfriend, or you really need a day off and consider calling in "sick?" You see your friend's wife out with another man. Do you tell him? Your boss tells a racist joke. Do you protest even though it might hurt your career? These are all situations where you need to follow your heart and your gut, determining for yourself what integrity means on a case-by-case basis.

Despite being awkward sometimes, choosing your words carefully and telling the truth is easier and healthier than negotiating your way through a series of half-truths. When we make mistakes we are often tempted to lie to cover them up. Trashing your integrity ultimately hurts you more than it hurts anyone else. It creates psychic holes in your constitution and saps your personal power. Peace comes from acceptance of what is. Honesty is that acceptance. Your inner divinity will guide you when you feel uncomfortable with the truth, and help you know how to respond. Create your own guidelines for what that means practically in your life. Does it mean going back and making amends for things you've done in the past? It may or may not. Find a way to live with integrity that feels comfortable to you now. When you have that peaceful feeling, and the increased personal power that results from living well, you will be living more harmoniously, more connected to your inner divinity.

COMPASSION

"He who has fed a stranger may have fed an Angel." The Talmud

When you find compassion in your heart, you find unity with all life. You enter a space of healing simply by extending goodwill to another being. Compassion can simply be an internal feeling, a wish that good things will happen to all people. Compassion can extend to action, a kind word or a helping hand. You affect the world around you with your sincere intentions and with your actions. You affect the world most fully when your compassion spans both your thoughts and your deeds.

It is difficult to get out of our own minds and see things from another person's perspective. It is virtually impossible to truly understand what it feels like to be someone else. However, by opening your heart and trying to connect to people in a compassionate way, you create an opportunity for healing relationships. We are all living, breathing, struggling, celebrating, and learning together on this planet. Our backgrounds and our outer appearances may be different, but in many ways we share the fundamental emotions and challenges of living with every person on this planet. Having compassion is understanding we are all interrelated. You want the people close to you to behave compassionately, kindly, and with patience towards you, right? We all do. When you're having a bad day, isn't it helpful to have someone who won't judge you or try to fix you, someone who will accept you and give you an attentive ear or a loving shoulder to cry on? That kind of gentle acceptance is nurturing for everyone. We all want it, but sometimes find it challenging to return it to the people in our lives.

Compassion is an important element of most spiritual practices. This consistent theme spreading throughout the religions of the world indicates that it's a higher truth. Buddha is often quoted as having said, "In separateness lies the world's great misery; in compassion lies the world's true strength." Jesus' teachings about relating to each other emphasize compassion. He asks his followers to care for one another and for the estranged or rejected members of their community: the sick, the sinners, and the poor. When we are harsh to one another, we bring harshness into our own lives. When we offer angry words more than nurturing ones, we are the recipients of that anger. When we speak and act lovingly toward each other, we create an environment of love that we also enjoy. To have compassion and love for each other is the ultimate way to express God's law on earth, treating all people as you wish to be treated yourself.

In addition to the religious conviction that compassion is the cornerstone of a healthy and happy society, science has been discovering that compassion actually facilitates healing. When we extend love to each other, we create space for healing. This subject is covered more fully in *Section 6: Your Health*.

UNDERSTANDING AND NURTURING YOUR RELATIONSHIPS

"Call it a clan, call it a network, call it a tribe, call it a family. Whatever you call it, whoever you are, you need one." Jane Howard

Family Models

As we move through our lives we develop many different kinds of relationships. Our first experience with relating to other human beings comes from our family. It is from within that family structure that we typically form our views about how relationships work. The examples shown to us by our parents, grandparents, aunts, uncles, and older brothers and sisters influence the way we behave. In some cases, children model their behavior on what their parents demonstrate to them.

In others, children rebel against their families by acting in opposite ways. In either case, the interpersonal dynamics of family life shape the way we relate to each other as adults.

To gain greater insight into the way you relate to other people, take a look at the dynamics of your family. Be as objective as you can. As when you became aware of your inner dialogue, you will see that the dynamic of your family has been a constant filter through which you view the world and engage in relationships. Just observe at first. It can be challenging to uncover the beliefs you have assumed for your entire life, just as it is hard to know the true colors of a garden if you have only seen it through tinted glasses. Disengage emotionally and take a look at the way your family members related to each other and to you. Make a list of the emotions that were expressed and how. For example, did your parents communicate openly, show affection to one another, and apologize when they were wrong? Did they pit one family member against the other? Did they argue by yelling and insulting each other, or by having a respectful discussion? Did they manipulate each other or support each other? Once you have a list of the ways your family related to each other, make another column next to your list and note all the areas in your life where you have behaved or are behaving the same way.

Be brutally honest with yourself. Your behavior may show up differently from that of your parents, but pay attention to the underlying emotions and dynamics. If your mother was insecure and gave or withheld her affection to have control over you, look to see if you may be doing that in your relationships. This is shadow side work. It is not necessarily fun, but can be amazingly revealing. Once you have insight into the way you have modeled your family's way of relating, for better or worse, you can consciously begin to choose which ways of being are healthy and create peace in your life, and which ways are destructive. Just as when you accept or reject your internal dialogue to create a nurturing environment in your head, you can reconstruct your way of relating to others to create more harmonious relationships.

Harville Hendrix is an author and counselor who works with couples to form healthier relationships. He is best known for his Imago theory, which asserts that we are attracted to mates based on an image of the ideal partner we've subconsciously modeled on our parents or primary caretakers. The down side, according to Hendrix, is that we are often more drawn to the negative aspects of our parents' relationship, because at some deep level we seek to heal our childhood wounds through reliving old dynamics with current partners. He also states that we typically seek partners who possess qualities we lack: an extrovert if we are shy, an ambitious go-getter if we are more laidback. But there is hope, he says! By becoming conscious of our instinctual choices in partners, and of our need to heal the past through our romantic relationships, we begin the journey to find deep and true love.[21]

Children

Children can be our greatest teachers. From us, they mostly need a safe space to grow and unfold. We have a tremendous influence over them; however, we cannot change who they are fundamentally. We may be able to influence their behavior, but not their natural temperament. By allowing children to be who they are, we help them keep their connection to their inner divinity. Many of us have had difficult childhood experiences: feeling unloved or abandoned, or experiencing physical and emotional abuse. Think about what you would have wished for yourself and do it for the children in your life. Usually it is love and acceptance. Engage your children; talk to them, express affection, listen to their thoughts, and respect their emotions. Let your children develop naturally. Think of planting a garden. When you plant flowers in the spring, you wish only to see them bloom. You aren't wishing the daffodils were tulips, or trying to change a sunflower into a rose. You partner with the elements in providing their care. Be the soil, the sun, and the rain for your children. Create a safe and sacred space for them to blossom, secure in your love and acceptance.

Those of us who have relationships with children have the power to mold their opinions of the world and of themselves. They will model you. Children learn from us, not who they are (that is deeply encoded in their being), but how to behave and often how to think. When we show respect for each other, children will too. When we show hate toward each other, children will too. I was happy to hear my young daughter saying good morning to the various creatures in our yard. "Good morning birds, good morning trees, good morning fish." I realized that is what I do. Connecting with the environment where we live feels right to me. As she gets older, she will determine how she wants to develop her own relationship, but for now I've planted a seed of respect for the earth's creatures.

Children are highly perceptive to emotions and energy. They can pick up what we are feeling even when we are not willing to admit it. They can sense anger and sadness, often more astutely than adults. When you're in the presence of a child, consider that they can often "read" you as you engage with them. "Are you cranky?" my daughter will sometimes ask, even before I realize myself that I am indeed cranky! The subtle signals our bodies and energetic personalities emanate are more tangible to children. Young children are typically more in touch with their core selves and have yet to unlearn how to connect to everything around them. Therefore, loving communication is all the more important when dealing with children.

Before babies learn a verbal language, they are in harmony with their mother's energy and body language. Babies are known to get peaceful when mom feels peaceful or to get agitated when mom is stressed. At that age it's pure instinct. As babies grow into young children, language becomes part of their toolbox for making sense of the world around them. If their primary caregivers are communicating that they are safe, loved, and accepted, children are more likely to develop confidence, self-love, and acceptance. If they are ignored, treated harshly, or disapproved of, they will incorporate those messages of worthlessness, ultimately feeling unloved. As a parent, I know that to be patient and kind all the time is a struggle. I certainly lose my patience. Sometimes I hear myself rushing my daughter through some transition (putting clothes on, going to school, getting to bed, etc.) and cringe at how I'm barking at her. I try to catch it right away. If I'm really out of line or am just too tired to be a good communicator, I stop, apologize, and explain to her why we need to get going or why I'm frustrated. That usually helps bring us back together as a team, instead of one of us being the dictator. As she's grown older she'll sometimes offer a hug or kiss "to make me feel better."

As in other relationships, it's important not to label your children. There is a big difference between telling children they are not *acting* nicely and telling them *they* are not nice. Distinguish your children's behavior from who they are when you talk to them. Many a time I have told my daughter she is *acting* unacceptably (throwing sippy cups, kicking, spitting, etc.), but I don't tell her that *she* is unacceptable. The thought of being truly unacceptable or unforgivable can be devastating to a child. I've ingrained in my daughter that I will love her no matter what she does. Now when she misbehaves she'll say, "But you still love me, right?" Even though she knows it, she wants reinforcement. You can help your children learn the boundaries of acceptable behavior—which vary across families and situations—knowing that they are always lovable and acceptable as people.

A child's energy personality is often more obvious than an adult's because children haven't learned to hide it yet. As adults, we must respect their unique natural tendencies. Forcing a shy or fearful child to do something they are apprehensive about is harmful. Certainly we should help a child explore new situations and overcome their fears, but we must be sensitive to their style of relating. My daughter can be a little slow to jump into a new situation, but if I help her to feel safe initially, she will usually branch out on her own. She's enjoyed taking a dance class, but was reluctant about performing in the recital at the end of the year. At the dress rehearsal, she had a chance to get on stage and see what it would be like to dance in front of an audience. She didn't like it. Instead of screaming at her, as several mothers were doing back stage, we went home. Dancing was a fun and optional activity for her. There was no need to create angst by forcing her. When she tried a new gymnastics class, she stayed close to me at first and then felt brave enough to jump in and play with the other children. She knew I would be there as a safe base and it created a sense of confidence in her to explore on her own.

Let them play. Even with young children, there is a tendency these days to schedule kids as if they were adults, shuffling them between classes, music lessons, sports, etc. A friend recently told me of one six-year-old who had fourteen different lessons a week in addition to school. Although a full life can be wonderful and engaging for children, be careful to allow time for play. We need it as adults and we need to learn the skills of play as children. The ability to throw yourself into something for its own sake and not for any production value or specific outcome is unusual in adulthood. The ability to experiment and lose time in the creative process is a rare luxury in most workplaces. How often have you watched children build a tower with blocks only to find that knocking it down and starting over is the best part? My daughter loves to paint and finds great pleasure in experimenting with ways of applying paint to paper. Once they are done, she gives them to us proudly and promptly forgets about them. She creates worlds of animals inside her mind. Once, at three, she said, "I'm going to pretend I'm fighting alligators, OK?" She hopped up on the bed and wrestled the pillows. She had flocks of rainbow colored "air" chicks and kittens that followed her around. I admit I'm slow to get down on the floor and play. Playground duty can feel torturous for me. There always seems to be so much to do and I get antsy. But when I see the look on my daughter's face as we play horses and trot to the bedroom, or hear her peals of laughter when I agree to make "silly words," I know play is good medicine. Spiritual counselor and author Saundra Cortese explains the importance of allowing our children to play. She asserts that playing is a learned skill. When play is not a part of a child's early development, she can grow into an adult who is uncomfortable with enjoying herself, fearful of looking foolish or wasting time. This lack of playfulness can "break the spirit."[22]

Treat the children in your life with respect. Tell them the truth. Answer them when they talk to you. Explain to them what's going on, what you're feeling, or why something is necessary. Give a hug when they need it, and stand by supportively to let them try new things. In many ways it's no different than how we should behave in a relationship with an adult. The difference is that we need to adjust our communication so a child can understand us, and we need to be particularly sensitive to a child's still-forming communication skills. They've come in as spirits in tiny bodies. Our job is to help their spirits to express themselves freely while they are learning to be conscientious members of society.

Ancestors

Most of us know our ancestral line back only a few generations; however, geneticists have concluded that all humans alive today are descended from a single man who lived in Africa around 60,000 years ago.[23] In cultures around the world, ancestors who have passed on are still considered an active part of the family. They are remembered and included in the family through rituals to honor them. In Western culture, we tend to lose touch with past generations. You would not be alive if it were not for your ancestors. It's an obvious statement, but let it settle for a minute. Without each person in a long line of past generations, you would not exist. From the fundamental physical level of existence we owe a tremendous amount to those who lived before us. Their bodies became our bodies, and indeed, we carry our ancestral line inside our bodies, both physically and spiritually.

As you look to create more harmony in the relationships in your life, remember that those relations spiral backward in time, as well as forward. By nourishing your children, you create the possibility that they will in turn care for future generations tenderly. By offering your thanks to your ancestors, you infuse your past with an energy of love and appreciation that percolates back up into the present. Your offerings can be quite simple. Try hanging a picture of one of your ancestors where you can see it and offer your silent thanks each day. Each year at least once, and always at Christmas, we honor my paternal grandmother by cooking something special that she used to make for us. I look forward to the delicious results of our work, but also cherish the memories of her that it triggers. I remember her hands covered in flour working the pasta dough and flicking small pieces with her fingers to make the cavatelli shape, or pouring honey over my all time favorite Christmas breakfast *struffoli*. In teaching my daughter how to make some of her dishes we pass the love and appreciation we have for Nana on to the next generation.

Make peace with your ancestors. Some of us have had difficult relations with our parents or other elders in our family and blame them for what they were not able to provide. As an adult you're now able to acknowledge your forbears for what they have given you. If their gift is simply life, offer your thanks for that.

There are many lessons to learn from those who came before us. Most of us do not have much personal knowledge about the generations who lived long ago. Recently I was watching a movie that depicted a family living in pioneer times in America. I was struck by the physical exertion required to simply survive. From my vantage point, life then seemed brutal. The heroine cut wood every day to make a fire in order to feed her family and keep them warm. She tended to the sick and injured in unsanitary conditions. I was also reminded of how many people live under similar conditions today. I felt an overwhelming sense of gratitude to the ancestors who came before me, and appreciation for the relative luxury of my life. Over thousands of years people struggled and worked hard to survive and provide for their children. We are those children.

Managing Change

One common way of sabotaging our relationships is by boxing people in. When you define someone early in a relationship, you are setting yourself up for disappointment. When you label someone, summarizing the traits you believe they embody, you reduce them to a set of characteristics. This can feel comforting in the beginning, as it gives you the illusion of understanding the other person. If you understand who they are, then you often feel you can predict or control how they will behave in the future. Nothing remains constant in the universe, least of all people. The most reliable and consistent person can one day have a period of growth or change and become spontaneous and moody. They didn't necessarily deceive you into believing they were someone they were not, but they changed, or they began expressing a different aspect of themselves. We are complicated beings and in order to have fulfilling relationships, we need to understand that the people we love are evolving each day. Limited definitions of your loved ones, and inflexibility in relating to them, can cause you to feel as if you don't really know them.

Staying in the moment is critical. In relating to yourself, you've learned that staying in present time allows you to deal with reality, as the only true reality is happening now. When you are tied strongly to the past, your perceptions are skewed, filtered through what you believe happened. The past is always open for interpretation. I'm amazed at how often my husband and I will be part of the same conversation and at the end we'll realize that we came away with two very different interpretations of what we each communicated and even what happened physically. When we start arguing about the past, or bringing up things from the past as items in the current conversation, we tend to get nowhere. We can't change the past, nor can we really understand it. We can learn from it, but need to allow each other the space to be who we are now in this moment, in relation to one another.

As we grow individually, our relationships need to adapt in order to stay healthy. In many ways the parent/child relationship models this. Parents expect their children to grow and change. Sometimes parents continue to hold outdated opinions about their children, but often they allow their offspring the freedom to develop into adults as they did themselves. When we meet as adults, this dynamic is harder to accomplish. We are used to thinking of adults as fully formed beings who retain their characteristics as they age. This is not necessarily the case. Some people become even more entrenched in old patterns and beliefs as they get older, and others change. If you are committed to being in a long-term relationship, allow your partner, and yourself, to evolve and grow.

Change can feel threatening. If your partner begins to develop new interests or seems to be engaging the world differently, a typical first reaction is to fear being left behind. The flip side is also true. As you grow and develop you may find your partner feeling insecure with the "you" you are becoming, fearing there is no place for the familiar "us." There are several ways to address change in a relationship. The first is to simply acknowledge and be prepared for the likelihood of it happening. If you enter a relationship with the understanding that it is not static, that all relationships are dynamic, then you will be less surprised or disappointed when you, or your partner, change. Accepting change as a natural and inevitable part of your relationships allows you to engage more gracefully and less fearfully with the people in your life. I'm using romantic relationships as the primary example here, but what I'm saying applies to all kinds of relationships. Although we tend to feel insecure when change becomes apparent, it can actually be a wonderful opportunity to deepen the connection you have with your partner. If your relationship stayed the same, you would ultimately become bored. You would likely become so accustomed to the routine interactions you wouldn't even think about them any more. Your relationships might become like a play, where the actors know the script by heart and don't have to think or feel to play their roles.

Allowing your partner to grow while supporting and nurturing each other in that process allows you both to stay focused on creating a positive future. Another aspect of letting relationships evolve is to encourage each other in the process. Relationships are a fluid dance where each person is affecting and being affected by the other. When one person changes enough to create a shift in the dynamic of the relationship, it is often an appropriate time for both people to reassess where they are in their lives as individuals, as well as in their partnership. If you can have open dialogue, you can help each other in the process, or at least allow each other the flexibility to explore inwardly. No one feels comfortable being forced to fit an old mold of themselves. How would you feel if people treated you as if you were the same person you were at twelve? How would it feel if you were excited about exploring new avenues in life and others discouraged you because they were not the same things you were interested in ten years ago? You'd probably feel trapped and limited. Your life, and your partner's, is about creating infinite possibilities, multitudes of different ways for you to express your true nature. Through exploration and growth you will find the path that brings you to a place of inner peace.

Some relationships naturally come to an end. People can change and evolve to a point where they can no longer relate to one another as partners. Ultimately, this may be the best thing for all involved. Accepting change is about living your life fully and in the present moment. If you relate to others with kindness and honesty, and with the knowledge that you are evolving, you will be connecting to your inner divinity, and helping them connect to theirs.

Another way of coping with change is to stop taking everything personally. If you and your partner enjoyed Chinese food and ate it a lot, and then he got tired of Chinese and wanted to go out for pizza, it is no reflection on you. If you liked to make love in the mornings, and then one day preferred the afternoons, it is no reflection on your partner. We can be so sensitive in relationships that simple, innocuous changes can be interpreted as a threat. To create healthy relationships, stay on the same side. Consider your individual needs, and the needs of the relationship, without feeling antagonistic towards each other. We all get angry or frustrated sometimes, but if we want to be in the relationship we need to consider ourselves as players on the same team. Work together to come up with solutions that feel comfortable to both parties. Listen to what your partner has to say without jumping to the defensive. Conversely, when talking about your needs or complaints, wield your words wisely. Instead of using language that will make your partner feel attacked or inadequate, choose words that describe how you feel in a respectful way. Remember, the goal is healing and evolution. When one partner feels condemned, it's hard to follow that up with a collaborative plan of action. A friend of mine was having some serious disagreements with her ex, the father of her young daughter. Her ego wanted very much to make him miserable, and she was considering various actions to take against him. I pointed out that if he was miserable, he surely would make her miserable as well. She was much better off contributing to his happiness by finding some compassion in her heart and coming back to her center. From that place she knew what the right actions were. Especially in our immediate families, we benefit personally from treating each other well and considering each other's feelings. When you're happy, are you more or less likely to be kind? How about patient? Generous? If the people around you are happy and are attaining a level of inner peace, that energy will affect you for the positive. What you do to another person, you ultimately do to yourself.

Acceptance

Acceptance is not resignation. It is not giving up because you feel powerless to control a situation or to make it better. Acceptance is allowing what is to be. It is acknowledging the current state of things, be they circumstances or people. Accepting the people in your life as they are can be frustrating and difficult. No one is perfect. For all the things we wish were different about our partners, they have things they wish were different about us. However, we need to love each other as we are. When you get to a level of acceptance where you are not lamenting another person's character flaws, but working with them as they are, you set the stage for healthy change. The things we find the most difficult about the people close to us can turn out to be where we have the most to learn ourselves.

One way to increase the health of a relationship is for each person to focus on the positive elements of the other. When you feel criticized and rejected, aren't you inclined to withdraw or find fault in the other person? When you feel loved and appreciated, aren't you inspired to be more loving and appreciative? Which dynamic do you want to create in your relationships? Be an example of what you want to receive. When you create a positive energy in your relationships, you draw others into your life who are ready to operate in a similar fashion.

When you start from the premise that the people in your life are basically good, you can approach relationships from a healthy starting place. Many people have been so wounded it is hard for them to remain in the present moment with the person they are with. They constantly rerun past relationships and filter current partners through the screen of failed relationships and disappointing interactions. It is difficult to build on such a pessimistic framework.

Psychotherapist Carl Rogers put forth the idea that a therapist must have a positive outlook toward patients on which to build a healthy therapeutic relationship. He called it "Unconditional Positive Regard." Essentially, it means you honor the inherent dignity and value of each person in the moment and act toward them in positive ways that support their strengths and help them overcome the effects of their weaknesses.[24] The same applies to our personal relationships. When we're able to accept our loved ones as they are, we create space for them to grow and develop. When we're constantly seeking a change in them we limit who they can become naturally and in their own time. No matter how flawed someone may seem, they carry the spark of divine perfection. They carry the potential to manifest that divinity outwardly, but that expression must come from them.

BOUNDARIES AND PSYCHIC PROTECTION

"Let us not look back in anger or look forward in fear, but around in awareness."
James Thurber

We communicate with each other all the time, engaging each other's bodies and energies. Setting boundaries on that energetic contact can be challenging; however, limiting the degree to which you allow others into your energetic space can be crucial for your mental health. People, especially sensitive or empathic people, often have difficulty separating themselves from others, once their energies have mingled. If you are sensitive and don't make an effort to protect yourself from other peoples' energy, you will pick up thoughts and emotions from everyone you are near—either physically or emotionally.

There is a time and place for this type of connectedness. In an intimate relationship it can be bonding. In a therapeutic relationship it can yield positive results through deeper understanding. But allowing strangers or more casual acquaintances to have such an impact on your energetic system can be unhealthy. A clear sense of what it feels like to be you—alone, inside your body—is important. If you have this baseline conception of yourself, it can help you understand why you feel certain things at certain times. If you're an easy going person when you're alone, but after spending the afternoon with a friend who is more edgy and uptight you come away feeling nervous, you can separate that person's feelings and characteristics from your own. This is one reason why spending time alone is important. Emotions are easier to pick up than a cold if you're sensitive. Just being around others can become overwhelming for sensitive people who haven't learned to set up boundaries. Half the battle is simply acknowledging that you *are* picking up other people's energy. If you can identify that influence, you can choose who you want to let that close and when. It's not always that easy, but once you have a clearer idea of who you are alone and are aware of the effect of other people on you, it is much easier to bring yourself back to your own center and release the energies from other people that attach to you.

I once had lunch with a friend who was feeling very sad. I love her dearly and wanted very much to help her. My empathy allowed a transference of emotions and for the rest of the day I was miserably sad. Even though I'm aware of this dynamic, it took me more than a day to shake an emotion that I'd clearly picked up from her. Our deep connection and my willingness to listen and be supportive were helpful, but it wasn't helpful to either one of us for me to become sad too.

The goal is to be able to consciously choose to experience another person's energy and then to clear that energy away from your own. In a personal relationship, close connectedness can help you see a person's perspective more easily. It can help you be sensitive to their needs. It can help create an atmosphere of understanding and empathy. In a professional capacity, you want to be able to connect closely to a person in order to give them a helpful counseling session, or to be able to understand what expectations they have in your business dealings. But you need to be able to return to your identity relatively clear of anyone else's. This can be hard, but it gets easier with practice.

Essentially, there are three phases of psychic protection. The first is *preparation*. The second is the *time during an encounter*. And the third is *cleansing afterward*. In the preparation phase, you work to consciously choose your boundaries. On an intellectual level, you increase your awareness of your interactions with others and make some decisions. If someone is difficult for you to be around, pushes your buttons, or engages you in power struggles, you know you need to prepare before being with them. It's a good idea to think about how you will react if they say something hurtful or try to get you to do something you don't want to. Have a strategy for keeping your center. On a spiritual level, you work on your "shield," by developing a strong energy body. In a meditation, visualize yourself surrounded by a cocoon of white light. Pay attention to the quality of that light and see if there are any holes or gaps in the cocoon. If there are repairs needed, put your hands in that spot on your body and visualize white light flooding into the space and filling the gaps. Keep this visualization up until the cocoon feels strong and unbroken. Practice this periodically. Tune into your luminous egg of light briefly throughout the day to keep it strong and energized. It never goes away, because it is your energy field, but you can nourish it with attention in order to strengthen your ability to set boundaries.

In the second phase, during the actual encounter with someone, you can work to control your communication and stick to your healthy plan of action for dealing with them. By controlling your energy shield, letting it expand or pulling it back, you decide how much of your energetic self you wish to share and how much of the other person's energy you wish to experience closely. If you feel someone slipping into your personal space, simply strengthen your light cocoon and make its surface even more impermeable. This is a mind/body technique. It may feel like you are making it up at first, but it works. Imagination is a powerful tool, not just "make-believe." By visualizing things, conjuring them in your mind, you affect reality all the time. If you're feeling invaded by another person's energy or want to separate, visualize cutting the cords of light that connect you, so that your light cocoon is strong and unbroken. You can picture negative emotions coming at you like aliens in a video game and bouncing off your light shield, or whatever imagery works for you. What's important is to see the light and the unbroken surface of your luminous egg.

The third phase is cleansing. Once you're alone again after being with other people, you need to release any energy you might have picked up. It's not only the energy of people who are close to you that "sticks," but even people you stand next to in a check-out line, or who work in the next cubicle. By using visualizations and purification techniques, you can rid yourself of unwanted energies. The most literal example is water. Wash your hands frequently; use water as a literal and metaphorical cleansing agent. Have you noticed that a hot shower refreshes not only your body, but often your mood? If you can't get to a shower, simply create one in your mind. Imagine a warm cleansing shower washing away any energetic residue that's on your body. I also love the imagery of waterfalls. Imagine a waterfall cascading over you, or a "lightfall" of golden light purifying your body and soul. Rituals are helpful as well. Simply state your intention to separate from someone's energy. Release any hold you have on them and ask to be released from any hold they have on you. Light a candle, use a drum, or rattle to shake off the energies. Smudging is a traditional ritual of purification that involves burning sacred plants and letting the smoke flow over your body. Sage, cedar, sweet grass, and lavender are common plants used in smudging. Smudge sticks can be bought in many alternative bookstores or gift shops today. With any ritual the power is in the intention you hold, not in the mechanics of the steps involved. Experiment with what feels right to you and what gives you the best results.

Use your creativity and your increased awareness of energy dynamics to prepare your psychic boundaries. Know you're strong enough to hold those boundaries when you need to and that you have a choice about whom you invite into your soul space. Just as you clean your physical body, you need to refresh your energy body and cleanse periodically. You will become more sensitive to the energetic dynamics around you. You will hear your inner voice and sense with your inner body more consistently when there isn't the static of stray energy broadcasting around you. You will feel emotionally and physically healthier when the energy you carry around is primarily your own. By clearing out energies that don't belong, you're making space for your inner divinity to shine more brightly and more purely.

Remember these three phases when you are entering a situation that you know can be stressful: prepare, protect, and cleanse. If you will be spending the holidays with a difficult relative or need to meet with your disgruntled ex-spouse, build up your energy field, picture it strong and unbroken while you are in the situation and then do a cleansing ritual as soon as possible afterward. This is an active process. Don't be afraid to assert your will. I recently had a client who worked in the same small office as her mother-in-law in her husband's family business. She felt attacked by her mother-in-law and trapped by the situation. She knew about surrounding herself in a ball of light to build her field, but when she felt the psychic attacks coming she cowered and felt powerless. I saw that she needed to put out a clear, forceful message when she felt her energy being drained by her mother-in-law's negativity. Internally, she needed to yell "Stop!" When you feel someone stealing your energy or throwing psychic sludge on you, stand up for yourself. Your strong will and clear intention will protect you.

FORGIVENESS

"And be ye kind one to another, tenderhearted, forgiving one another, even as God for Christ's sake hath forgiven you." Ephesians 4:32

Forgiveness is not about condoning despicable behavior, or minimizing the hurt inflicted. It's not about being a coward and letting someone use you as a doormat. It's not about the other person at all. It's about you.

In moving through our lives, we inevitably cause each other pain. Releasing each other and ourselves from the grip of that pain involves forgiveness. When we amass grievances against one another without clearing the decks periodically, we doom our relationships to failure. Forgiveness is not about condoning—it is about releasing. You don't need to assess whether a person deserves to be forgiven, you simply need to forgive for your own well-being. Forgiving releases you from the poisonous energy of resentment.

In attempting to relate to others in a healthy way, so much comes down to treating others as we wish to be treated. We all make mistakes. I've made some huge ones. Fortunately, I've had people in my life who were willing to love and accept me despite my failures, despite the hurt or disappointment I caused them. When you make a mistake, how do you want people to treat you? I was not inspired to be a better person by being berated or frequently reminded of my mistakes, but by forgiving myself and being grateful for the support of those around me.

We are all accountable for our actions, and those around us should hold us accountable. However, there is a difference between accountability and forgiveness. When someone else makes a mistake, they decide how they will handle it internally, just as you react in your own way when you make a mistake. You cannot control someone else's response to their own transgressions. You can only choose your own behavior and thinking when you need to forgive yourself, or someone else. In many ways, forgiveness is about disconnecting your reactions from the other person. You may wish the person who caused you harm would come forward with a heartfelt apology, but whether or not that happens need not determine whether you forgive them. You are in control of your own state of acceptance and forgiveness. Step out of the victim mentality. Recognize your power to bring healing into your life by releasing the hurts of the past. When you let go of past hurts, you can live in the present moment. When you are struggling with pain whose source is in the past, you pull that pain into your life, each moment, each day. You carry it with you, preventing yourself from living fully and clearly now. When you hold a grudge, you bind yourself to the target of your resentment. When you release that grudge through forgiveness, you release yourself from that unhealthy connection.

In your relationships, consider apologizing when you're wrong. It sounds simple, but for many of us it is difficult. It can be humbling or embarrassing, certainly uncomfortable at times. Yet it helps to harmonize your relationships. The unity that can evolve when one person is willing to express remorse or acknowledge a mistake lays the groundwork for a healthier relationship in the future. It expresses the willingness to act in partnership, to step aside from your ego when necessary, to be kind. My father and my daughter had a tiff when she was five. While playing a game, my daughter spit on my father. He got angry and left the room. She apologized quickly and he forgave her. Later he was inspired to call and apologize to her for how angry he got. He explained to me later that she had said, "Everybody makes mistakes, even my mom and dad." My father was not raised in such an openly communicative way and I was proud of both of them for working together so kindly.

At least one study shows that forgiveness can be taught. The Stanford Forgiveness Projects have been working to determine how forgiving can be learned and how the act of forgiving affects the forgiver. Professor Frederic Luskin has determined that people can be taught how to forgive. The projects used real cases of "unresolved hurt" to test the effects of forgiveness on those who had learned the forgiveness techniques. The studies demonstrated that forgiveness increases mental and physical health and vitality and the willingness to forgive in the future and decreases a sense of hurt feelings and the physical symptoms of stress (backache, sleeplessness, headache, stomachache, etc.).[25]

In his book *Forgive for Good* Dr. Luskin outlines nine steps to forgiveness: know exactly how you feel about the event and be able to articulate it, do what you need to feel better, shift from a standpoint of blame and take the experience less personally, change your perspective to recognize that your pain is coming from how you are perceiving the event now, not what offended you or hurt you in the past, practice stress management techniques to calm your body's flight or fight response, release your expectations of other people, look for other ways to get your needs met than through reliving that which has hurt you, live well and focus on the love, beauty, and kindness around you, and change your "grievance story to remind you of the heroic choice to forgive."[26] Consider following these guidelines for moving through the hurtful moments of the past and into a future with the potential for inner peace.

When we judge, we create disharmony. We create separation. When you're judging another person, you're not seeing them as a whole being, an intricate expression of divine creation. You're reducing them to a specific action they committed, or belief they hold, and rejecting them based on your opinion. I've experienced judgment and felt the pain of rejection. We have all been judged in our lives. God knows we all judge! I often catch myself doing it. It creates a barrier around me. It stops the flow of love: outward when I judge others and inward when I judge myself. We cannot expect everyone to follow our own moral codes, to hold the same opinions, or to have the same ideas about right and wrong. We *can* focus on our own lives and disengage from judging others. In doing so we set the stage for honest, healthy interactions.

You can create an atmosphere of healing in your relationships around hurtful incidents by doing two things: offering sincere apologies and extending forgiveness. These two actions work in a cyclical fashion, apologies inspiring forgiveness and forgiveness inspiring apologies; however, remember that your reactions are not contingent upon another person's. Forgiveness often increases harmony in relationships with others, but the focus is on how *you* relate to your world. At its core, forgiveness is an act of personal healing.

Conflict Resolution

Conflict is part of every long-term relationship. It is how you manage conflict that determines the health of the relationship. There are many different styles for dealing with disputes, depending on the personalities and energetic dynamics involved. Here are some guidelines for managing conflict in a healthy way.

First, deal with conflict right away. Don't let hurt feelings fester, or anger stew. That hurts you in ways we are just beginning to comprehend and poisons your relationship in the present. When you harbor resentments you view your partner through a filter of disapproval. You taint their interactions with you by withholding your true feelings. Have respect for yourself and the people you care about: deal with conflict in a timely manner.

Second, instead of making accusations and putting the other person on the defensive, talk about how you are feeling and why, using language responsibly. When we're disgruntled the tendency is to use black and white language. You are wrong, I am right. We place each other in opposite corners of the ring, when what we're truly searching for is a place of acceptance and reconciliation. With your words you can create space for healing, or force a more spiritually violent outcome. Your emotions have power and can affect others. By speaking carefully and with awareness of the spiritual aspect of your communication, conflicts can often resolve peacefully and without lasting damage.

Third, offer some ways the situation could have been handled that would have caused you less pain (anger, frustration, etc.) Many conflicts arise from misunderstandings and differing expectations. If you can be clear with each other about what you need and what you are able to give, you can sidestep conflicts in the future. We are each capable of modifying our behavior to live cooperatively in a relationship; however, if you are seeking to change who your partner is on a fundamental level, you will be disappointed.

Fourth, remember that conflict usually involves more than just the two parties most embroiled in the situation. The effects of an interpersonal conflict spill over into the community: children are affected by their parents' fighting, co-workers suffer when there is strife among people in the office, neighbors are asked to take sides. Traditional cultures often recognize the effects of interpersonal conflict on a community level and look to the community to help resolve them. Often the whole tribe is involved in rituals of peacemaking.

Myron Eshowsky, a shaman and educator with extensive experience in peacemaking, describes an African ritual of conflict resolution used by the Dagara people. The community creates sacred space within a circle of ash, which symbolizes protection. The two people who are in conflict explain their grievances and then step into that circle. They are free to vent their feelings and even to yell at each other, but without physical violence. The community witnesses and supports them as they express their emotions. To the Dagara, water symbolizes peace and life. The participants will hold water in their mouths, eventually spitting it out as there is a catharsis and the release of the grudges held by either side.[27]

These particular rituals may seem odd to the Western reader. However, the intention behind them is universal. Conflict between individuals and groups affects the greater community; therefore, it can be helpful to involve the members of that community in providing a safe and mediated space in order to resolve conflict among its members.

Fifth, agree on changes of behavior for the future, or compromise if possible. If you know a particular behavior or situation causes conflict, try to agree on changing it. For example, if it drives you crazy to get last minute requests at work, set up a system with your boss, where you actively check on the status of new assignments so you can prepare. If your spouse has a hard time paying the bills on time, help design a system to keep the bills organized and up to date. If a friend has difficulty keeping your conversations confidential, ask them to respect your privacy, and if they don't, stop sharing personal information with them. Avoiding conflict through active management of your interactions is preferable to trying to heal a relationship that has been damaged.

CLOSING

"If you would learn the secret of right relations look only for the divine in people and things, and leave all the rest to God." J. Allen Boone

Though we sometimes wish we could, we cannot isolate ourselves from the other beings with which we share the planet. Given that so many of us coexist on the relatively small living space of Earth, it makes sense, even purely out of selfishness, to try to live together harmoniously. We are affecting each other constantly, not only with our words and deeds, but also with our energy. Awareness of our intangible natures, and those of others, sets the framework for healthy interactions.

Imagine for a moment some of your life's biggest lessons. How many of them involve a direct interaction with another person? Whether in a one-time meeting or a long-term relationship, the people whom we encounter provide opportunities for tremendous growth and increased self-awareness. With each connection we make with another being, we create the potential for new experiences, ideas, insights, and beliefs that might not have been possible without that meeting. We can do harm or good in our relationships, we can inspire and we can deflate. By using our personal power responsibly—communicating thoughtfully and truthfully, forgiving easily, and loving generously—we contribute greatly to the spiritual health of those around us. As we are all interconnected, we contribute to our own spiritual health as well.

We are all made from the same list of "ingredients." Which of those ingredients are actually used and in what amounts determines the recipe for the unique creations we each are. We all hold similar potentials and capacities within us, whether they lie dormant, surface only if certain circumstances occur, or become an integral part of who we are in our everyday lives. We all have the capacity for cruelty and kindness. When children are tended lovingly, the odds decrease that they will grow into cruel adults; when they are raised on abuse, the odds increase that they will find someone to abuse. We all have the capacity for fear and bravery. When children are taught that the world is a cruel and dangerous place, they will learn to cringe at living, waiting for the inevitable blows life deals out; when they are taught to realize their own power and worth, they develop the courage to stand up for themselves and what they believe in. We all have the capacity for open-mindedness and for prejudice. No child is born with an inherent hatred toward other people. We teach through our relationships, and not only children. As adults we're still learning who we can be and who we want to be in this world.

A contractor who worked on my home paid me a lovely compliment. Although he is an active Baptist, and we come from very different perspectives spiritually, we've had some good conversations about spirituality and found we share some core beliefs. He said that in watching me deal with some difficult situations through the course of our project, he saw that I always tried to be kind, and it made him want to be kind, too. Now, this is a man who is already kind and doesn't need my help in expressing it, but my point is that I inspired something in him by how I related to other people. I watch the way my daughter's preschool teacher engages each child with such consistent patience and gentleness, and I feel ashamed of myself sometimes, as I reflect on cranky moments when I've been impatient and gruff with my daughter. She inspires me to be a better person and a better parent. I've watched my husband show generosity to people in dire need, engaging them in conversation and being willing to help, when others lowered their heads and walked quickly past. He inspired me to see every person as spiritual kin, and as a child of God. We are all divine beings. When we start treating each other as spiritual equals, we begin to create a world that will support us all. Start making graceful ripples in your world. Let your tiniest acts of kindness, your healing thoughts, and your loving words radiate from you, knowing that they will grow and expand.

EXERCISES FOR SECTION 2: YOUR RELATIONSHIPS

Refer to the *How To Use This Book* section in the *Introduction* if you have questions. Relax your body and clear your mind before you begin, be open to the information you receive, and write down your experiences when you are finished.

Communication: The Power of Words

* ✳ Pay attention to the words you use. Are they nurturing or hurtful, well thought-out or rash?

* ✳ Meditate on the Buddhist precept described by Thich Nhat Hanh.

  * ○ Do you tell the truth?

  * ○ Do you exaggerate or embellish?

  * ○ Do you gossip, or speak with a "forked tongue?"

  * ○ Do you use abusive language?[28]

Communication: Listening

* ✳ Practice listening with your whole body. Let your concentration fall solely on what is being said and formulate your response after the other person is done speaking. Ask questions to help understand what the other person needs from you.

Communication: Body Language

* ✳ Experiment with your body language. For example, change your posture, your facial expression, or the way you greet people, and pay attention to the way people respond to you.

Communication: Personal Energetics

* ✳ Pay attention to how your body responds energetically in different situations.

* ✳ Meditate with the intention of becoming familiar with your energetic personality. Ask for guidance about how to express your natural energy in the healthiest way in each of your most important relationships.

Communication: Truthfulness and Politeness

* ✳ Become aware of the level of truth in your communication. If you find falseness, work to communicate more truthfully.

Compassion

* ✳ Meditate on sending compassion and love to specific people. Pay attention to how you feel when love and compassion are flowing from you.

* Experiment with sending compassion to groups of people, animals, bodies of water, and land.

Understanding and Nurturing Your Relationships: Family Models

* Make an informal chart of your family dynamics. How did your primary caregivers relate to each other and the rest of the family? Notice how you have been affected by their methods of relating. Consider which ways are working for you and which you want to change.

Understanding and Nurturing Your Relationships: Children

* Play like a child. Better yet, play with a child!

Understanding and Nurturing Your Relationships: Ancestors

* Meditate to receive a ritual to honor your ancestors.

Understanding and Nurturing Your Relationships: Managing Change

* Try to see the people in your life anew each time they walk in the door. Pay attention to how you feel about them when you let them be who they are, purely in that moment.

Understanding and Nurturing Your Relationships: Acceptance

* Practice honoring the divine in each person you meet or to whom you relate. Start your interactions with "unconditional positive regard," an acceptance of each person's inherent dignity and value.

Boundaries and Psychic Protection

* Practice the three phases of psychic protection: prepare, protect, cleanse.

* Psychic Boundaries Meditation
(*This meditation is included on the* Inner Divinity *companion CD. See the* Resources *section for more information.*)

  Close your eyes. Take a few deep breaths. Imagine yourself with a glow all around you. Light is emanating from you and surrounding you. A luminous egg is forming around you. It's a beautiful cocoon of golden white light. With each breath, watch it grow stronger and brighter. With each breath, you feel more and more comfortable in your beautiful light cocoon. It wraps around you, keeping you safe and protected. Once your luminous egg, your cocoon of light, is fully formed all around you, try expanding this light to a few feet around your body in all directions. With each breath the light gets stronger and brighter.

  Pay attention to the quality of the light and the wholeness of the cocoon you're enveloped in. Are there any tears or weak spots you can see or sense? If there are, take your hands and patch them by sending more light to those spots. Focus your energy there until the weak spots are strong and glowing. Just relax and enjoy being in your light. Examine it, making sure it is smooth and unbroken, a pure luminous egg of protection. This is a safe place where you can always go, a sanctuary.

Your light is always with you. The more you pay attention to it, the stronger it will grow. You're safe and protected in this light. Pull the light in closer to your body now, so it expands only about six inches outside your body. Keep taking deep breaths and pay attention to any weak spots in your cocoon. Focus your energy to make them stronger. Sense your unbroken, protective cocoon of light and take a few moments to enjoy this feeling of love, protection, and safety.

Remember that if you're in a situation where you feel uncomfortable or vulnerable, physically, emotionally, or spiritually, you can visualize yourself wrapped in your luminous cocoon. Take a few more deep breaths. When you're ready, open your eyes.

Forgiveness and Judgment

✳ After identifying someone you have not forgiven, meditate on these questions, "Why am I afraid to forgive? What have I gained from not forgiving?"

✳ <u>Meditation on Forgiveness</u>
Settle in and take a few deep breaths. Take a minute and pick one person you haven't forgiven for something. Focus on them for a moment. You don't need to relive a painful event, but remember it enough to see the possible lessons for you. Focus on your heart chakra, the center of your heart. With each breath breathe in a deep vibrant green. When you feel centered in your heart and can feel the energy from your heart radiating through you, extend that energy outside of your body. See a green light spreading outward from your chest to a few feet in front of you.

Picture the person you need to forgive. If you see any energy connection to that person that feels uncomfortable or negative, gently remove it. Just visualize it evaporating or retreating back into the green light. Repeat to yourself, "I forgive you and thank you for being a teacher for me." As you repeat those words, picture your green light getting stronger and brighter. Stay focused on this light and on the person until you feel you can forgive them. When you feel you have been able to truly forgive that person, release their image, pull your heart energy back in, and sit feeling the release. Feel the positive effects of forgiveness on your heart. Breathe deeply a few more times and when you're ready, open your eyes.

Forgiveness and Judgment: Conflict Resolution

    ✳   Choose a conflict you are experiencing and apply the following guidelines for conflict resolution to help bring peace to the situation. First, deal with the problem quickly. Second, talk about your feelings in a non-accusatory way. Third, offer some ways the situation could have been handled. Fourth, consider who else is affected. Fifth, agree on changes in behavior or compromise when possible.

SECTION 3: YOUR ENVIRONMENT
Creating Peace with Your Surroundings

Your relationship with your environment affects you every day. By becoming more attuned to your natural and manmade environments, you can make wiser choices about practical things, like where to work and live. You can also learn to exist in cooperation with what is all around you. By your "environment" I'm referring to nature (plants, animals, water, sun, air, etc.), as well as the manmade objects and spaces around you, such as your home, car, furniture, and clothes. There is certainly a distinction between these energies. The elements of nature are alive with their own creative life force, while manmade objects simply soak up the vital energies of animate beings, reflecting them back.

In this section we'll discuss how to create living space that feels more harmonious, and how to better attune yourself to the natural world. Many indigenous cultures knew how to live respectfully and in balance with their natural environment. We'll look at some examples of how they did it and apply them to your life now. Your environment can boost your personal power. It can feed your body and nourish your soul. It can support you or make you miserable: much of that choice is yours. Are you paying attention to what your environment needs from you? Are you treating the earth and the elements of nature with respect and care? Do you recognize the spiritual and energetic characteristics of your natural and manmade surroundings? Connect energetically to the land you live on, the water you drink, and the home in which you live. By opening to this connection, by giving to and receiving from your environment, you can create peace and happiness in your life.

LIVING IN THE MATERIAL WORLD

"More than society's messenger, more than a mirror of reality, the electronic communication media collect and concentrate the planet's woes and deliver them into our living rooms each night." Dr. Paul D. Klite

Assault of the Media

You are surrounded by the mass media. Everywhere you go, from your home, to your car, to the grocery store, you can tap into images, sounds, and information from around the world. Some programs are educational or inspirational, but many are highly charged news stories interspersed with advertisements that create insecurity.

According to Rocky Mountain Media Watch, a non-profit organization that analyzes local U.S. television newscasts, 40-50 percent of news airtime is devoted to violent topics, regardless of actual rates of crime. Consumers therefore develop an "exaggerated sense of the world as a violent and dangerous place."[29] We are being inundated with distressing energy. Even less overtly negative data, like commercials, are often carrying messages that are hard on our systems. By design, advertising creates insecurity and fear. Ads for mouthwash make us worry that we have bad breath. Ads for the latest car or clothes play on our desire to be popular and our insecurities about social status. There are ads for prescription drugs on television today that don't even explain what ailment they are designed to treat. They simply suggest you might need them, that you're somehow lacking or at risk without them, and urge you to ask your doctor for a prescription.

We can control our media intake. Some people choose to screen themselves from the deluge of information the media spins out. Others stress the importance of keeping informed about current events and welcome the easy access to information. You will need to determine for yourself what level of exposure feels right to you; however, I do recommend that you experiment. If you're a news junkie, see if you feel differently after a few days without it. Pay attention to the way your moods may shift after watching or reading the news, or simply watching a lot of commercial television. There are easy choices you can make to limit your exposure to the media. For example, when I bring my car in for service, the television is inevitably on in the waiting area. Typically it's turned to an exploitative talk show or a soap opera. I know I don't feel good after watching either of those, so I move into an adjacent space in the showroom and read or talk on the phone. Sometimes in the evening I'm tired and want to flop down on the couch and be entertained. Usually there is something to be found that fits the bill, but sometimes there is nothing on worth watching. There is nothing wrong with some mindless enter-tainment. In fact, sometimes the distraction is a welcome release to a stressful day. But if I find myself getting pulled into something degrading or disturbing, I turn the television off and go to bed. You digest and internalize the data you take in.

We also have a responsibility to monitor the level of violent and commercial imagery to which our children are exposed. Whether on the news, in a movie, or in the slew of video games that mirror the most violent elements of society, our youth are feeding from a "toxic culture." Director Peter Weir warns, "The terrifying result of exposure to constant violent imagery can cause young people to lose the capacity to discriminate between reality and unreality." Watch televi-sion with your children and screen movies to make sure what they are watching is appropriate. If you're with your child, you can answer any questions they have or contradict something you feel is wrong. For example, commercials for sugary breakfast cereals frequently say things like "part of a nutritious breakfast." From an early age I've told my daughter that those foods are not good for her body. Now she watches, but she doesn't necessarily accept everything that she hears on a commercial.

Be careful of what you may be watching without realizing a child is listening. It is our responsibility to explain what they see and hear in age appropriate ways. Although I shield my young daughter from news reports that contain violent con-tent, I try to answer her questions about the world. For example, when a tsunami hit Asia in December 2004, not only was it all over the news, but everyone was talking about it. I talked with my daughter (just four at the time) to explain what happened, but it would not have been healthy for her to see the disturbing images of devastation and dead bodies. Soon enough they will become aware of the world around them, they will know that violence exists. It is our responsibility to show them that there is also kindness, also compassion. It is our responsibility to help them make wise choices about how they spend their time and energy.

The energetic channels that crisscross and encircle you affect the way you feel. The more you see or hear bad news and anxiety-producing commercials, the more your mood is altered. Emotionally and psychically, the media can feel like a bom-bardment of the senses. In *Section 2: Your Relationships* I discussed methods for protecting yourself psychically from encounters with other people, and for cleans-ing yourself of energies that aren't yours. You can apply those exercises to this con-cept, as well. Create your own ritual to decontaminate yourself from the energy residue that sticks on you after experiencing a violent or depressing news story, or a demeaning or base television show.

Choosing Your Environment

We've already discussed how other people's energy affects you. A day with an edgy friend can pull you off your usually calm center, for example. The effects of other people's energetic personalities are offset when you are clear about what your own center feels like and have the tools to bring yourself back. The same concept holds true for different environments. Pay attention to the way you feel in different surroundings. Most of us have an instinctual preference for our larger environment. Do you thrive on the bustle and excitement of a city, drawing energy from it and feeling uplifted as you stride along the city sidewalks? Does stepping into a forest feel like coming home, your breathing becoming deeper and more regular as your cares and worries melt away? Or maybe the suburbs suit you best? I had a client from North Carolina who recently returned from a visit to New York City. She'd lived there in the past and was familiar with the city and its energy, but on this visit her awareness was heightened. She had spent time at home getting more in touch with her own true nature. She said that she could never live there again. Energetically, the city pulled her off balance. She felt dazed, overwhelmed, and bombarded with energy that overloaded her circuits. It gave her a greater understanding of why she felt how she did when she lived there years before. The energy of the city didn't feel good to her and, therefore, she had trouble finding peace within herself while she lived there.

Is the climate an important factor for you in choosing a comfortable space? I'm very cold sensitive. I simply don't feel at ease in the cold. One year, after a particularly cold and snowy winter, I realized I was dreading the next season's winter. It was only June! That was the last straw for me. After several years of thinking about it, and to the chagrin of my family, I moved with my husband hundreds of miles away, mostly to escape the cold. My daughter is the opposite. She is a little furnace, generating all the heat she needs, and complaining when it's warm outside. She gets very out of sorts when she is too hot—which is at about the same temperature I start being comfortable. For you it may be hot vs. cold, or dry vs. humid, or open spaces vs. shady forests. Your natural environment impacts you. The more you recognize what brings peace to your system and what brings discomfort, the easier it is for you to keep your center and find a place that suits you.

There may be places on earth that are particularly peaceful for you. You know these places—you walk in and somehow things click and feel "right." What makes these places special? Usually it's more than the objects in them, or even the people, or the landscape. In many of these places it is a combination of the setting on the earth, the manmade structures, the people, the care and placement of the objects, the animals and plants, and especially the spirit of the place. In our discussion of environment we must include the spiritual dimension. The spirits of a place, whether nature spirits or other spiritual beings, infuse a setting with their energy. Their presence and personality often factor strongly in your perception of a place.

There is a special place I've visited for a long time. When I step on the grounds I feel comfortable and connected. While I'm there, I feel in balance, I feel a kinship with the beings and land around me, my creative energies are inspired, and I have new ideas and insights. Sometimes I try to break down what is so special about this place for me. Is it the food, the trails, the family time, the gardens, the time away from ordinary life? Yes, it is all those things, but it is more. The spirit of this place feels good to my soul. The site has a long history, dating back to the Native Americans and early settlers who came because of the mineral spring's healing properties. In the 1930s Lou and Virginia Austin founded Capon Springs and Farms as we know it today. Mr. Austin had an unshakable belief that "no man walks alone, that his Maker is integrated with each human being in a living, working partnership."[30] I suspect this understanding of inner divinity greatly affected his relationship with the place, and therefore has helped infuse Capon with a gentle and loving energy. The relationship between the spiritual and material aspects of this place creates a sense of well-being in me. I'm at home in my skin when I'm at home at Capon.

Think about a place that is particularly soothing to you. Can you pinpoint some of the factors that make it harmonious? Is there something indefinable that makes it special? Whether specific places, like Capon Springs, or more general settings, like the beach or the city, try to spend time in those places in which you feel at home in *your* skin: content, energized, and peaceful.

Every geographical location emits its own energetic vibration or personality. Sometimes we crave the energy of a particular place or landscape. Many people are soothed by the beach. A trip to the ocean can satisfy an energetic need, as well as a need for rest and relaxation. Others are called to the mountains, or to particular places. I have a friend who yearns for Mt. Shasta, California. When she's there she feels as if she has found her physical and spiritual home. Every part of her being feels properly aligned and smoothly functioning. Sometimes we're called to places without understanding why. During one of my first meditation experiences, I envisioned that I was soaring over a high desert landscape. There were red rocks below and I swooped down into a gorgeous canyon, the likes of which I had never seen in real life. The walls were close and smooth and a clear stream ran over polished river rocks at the bottom of the canyon. I met a spirit teacher there, with whom I would work for years to come. I was especially moved by this canyon. Sometime later I was at home, glanced over at the television from the next room, and saw a man standing in a very similar place. I rushed over to see where he was. He was standing in Oak Creek Canyon in Sedona, Arizona. At the time I had never heard of Sedona, let alone the energy vortexes there, or the reputation it had garnered as a New Age mecca. I had to go, of course. A year or so later I took a trip and spent a few days in Sedona. It was glorious and just what I needed at that time. I think I was guided there to soak up some site–specific energy that my body needed.

You can enjoy visiting many places, but a smaller subset is energetically appropriate for you to live in. Find a place to live that feels comfortable to you. Many factors go into determining where to live—family, job, culture, climate, opportunities, etc. Ultimately it is an instinctual decision—you either feel at home in a place, or you don't.

Some people are strongly influenced by their environment. They are "field dependent." As I use the term here, field dependent people tend to be highly affected by their surroundings, sensitive to the energy of a place. They need to pay particular attention to the places they live and visit. Field independent people are less affected by their environment and tend to rely more on their internal perceptions and states of being to feel content. You may be able to live happily in many places and climates, finding that it doesn't really matter to you where you call home. You are probably field independent. If you find yourself on a quest for the ideal town in which to live, cringing at the tumult of the city or the bucolic drone of the country, or struggling to find that one perfect house, you may be field dependent. There is a continuum for field independence and dependence. We all fall somewhere along that line, not wholly one or the other. It helps to be aware of this aspect of your makeup. If you know you're highly field dependent, and your environs dramatically affect you physically, emotionally, and/or spiritually, it makes sense to choose your living spaces carefully. Take your time, do your intuitive research and find those place (cities, towns, countries, streets, apartments, homes) that help you feel the most at ease. This search is not about creating or defining yourself by where you live, but about locating places that allow your true self, your inner divine nature, to feel at home and blossom.

You also affect the environment around you. Everything exists in relationship. It's your job to sense what spaces feel right for you, but also to help create harmony in the places where you are. We can't always be in a place perfectly suited to us.

But we can live harmoniously each day. If you are not naturally comfortable in the woods, you still don't have to be miserable for each moment you are there. Some aspects of your surroundings are in your control and some are not. Recognize which situation you are in and either make the best of it or work to change it. If you are uncomfortable in a particular climate or town, you can move. You can create harmony from imbalance in your personal spaces with a little care and attention. You can be a catalyzing agent to either create or disrupt the peace of a place. The ripples of an angry outburst or a sincere smile reach far out into any place, touching people as they go. Ultimately the peace you have or lack comes from within you, from the expression of your divine nature in the material world.

CREATING SACRED LIVING SPACE

"Your sacred space is where you can find yourself again and again." Joseph Campbell

Your Home

Your home is rich with symbolism. It represents an outward reflection of your deeper self. It reflects your tastes, and expresses both your public and private selves. Whether an apartment, cabin, or house, your home is not simply an assemblage of wood, stone, or brick. Your home has a soul. Each living space has a unique vibration and spiritual identity independent of the residents. When a home is inhabited, its soul mingles with that of the people living there, creating a vibrant relationship. Some people consider their home as merely a place to sleep and eat. Others truly engage the spirit of their home and manifest a space that provides not only basic shelter for the body, but a haven for the soul.

You've probably walked into homes that felt immediately comfortable to you. It wasn't just the décor or the people inside, but something about the space itself that welcomed you. In earlier times and cultures, homes were often treated with a greater sense of respect and care, even considered deities. Homes were believed to have their own spirit that people acknowledged and honored. To show disrespect or neglect could bring conflict and suffering to the house and its inhabitants.[31] By connecting with your living space with this attitude, you create the basis for a serene mood in your home.

First, connect intuitively to feel what your home needs to be at its best for you. There are also established systems you can incorporate into this process. Feng Shui is the study of harmonious placement. It is an ancient system that describes how to create a peaceful and healthy space where your personal energy can thrive in balance with its surroundings. The practice of Feng Shui was first recorded around the ninth century and focused on the observation of natural forces and their energetic relationships.[32] Today there are many schools of Feng Shui. Each has specific methods of planning and organizing spaces and objects to create a beneficial flow of vital energy or *ch'i*. As you become more attuned to the vital force that flows through your body, heighten your awareness of the course of energy through your home. As you create or adjust your relationship to your most immediate environment, your living space, you may want to combine some Feng Shui techniques with your own ideas.

Obviously your living structure needs basic care and maintenance. If paint is peeling and bricks are crumbling, the energy of your home will be more ramshackle than serene. Therefore, your first task is to make sure your home is well cared for. Just as your body needs attention and nourishment to be healthy, your living space needs physical upkeep. This helps clean the energy of a place on a fundamental level.

Another way of clearing the energy of your space to allow for a smoother flow of energy is to clear away the clutter. Give or throw away what you don't want or need. Clean out your closets that haven't been touched in years. Inertia takes over and many of us wind up with packed closets and overflowing drawers with a minimum of usable items. For a while I gathered materials for projects I intended to do in the future. Although sewing an elaborate and beautiful quilt is a lovely idea, it simply was not going to happen in the foreseeable future, given the circumstances of my life. After several moves where I hauled bags of fabric, I gave them away. It was a relief. In fact, my interest had really waned. The raw materials were a sad reminder that I wasn't following through with the project I had once found inspiring. I had more space and unburdened myself of some outdated plans. Clearing out your space makes room energetically and physically for what is important to you *now*.

Second, you'll want to consider the functionality of your space. Too often, people choose furniture and live with it without really considering the most efficient and harmonious use of space. Walk through each room and consider what you do there. Can you move smoothly from one task to another? Are there pieces of furniture that jut out or that you repeatedly trip over or have to walk around? Much of this is common sense, but if you are busy, it's amazing what gets overlooked. Rearrange things with a new sensitivity to the energy that flows in and around them. Be silent and ask each object or piece of furniture where it wants to be.

Third, consider the aesthetics of the space. Does the wallpaper from the previous owners make you cringe? Do you hate that seashell lamp, but you keep it because it was a gift from someone you love? Keep what feels good to you and give away the rest. It would be better to live sparsely than surrounded by objects or colors that jar your energy. Use your instincts, intuition, and senses to create space that feels good to you. Consider each object, each room, and manifest a space that is truly your own, a reflection of your sacred self.

Sanctuaries

Consider creating a sanctuary, a space reserved for tending your spiritual self, for connecting with your inner divinity and the sacred energy all around you. Creating a sanctuary in your home fosters harmonious energy. Almost any place can become a sanctuary: a peaceful room or garden spot, or simply a nook or cupboard to which you pay special attention. There are many ways to create sacred space, but the most important is your intention. Set this space aside from your everyday space somehow. Keep it clean and spend time there in quiet contemplation, meditation, or prayer. Create your own rituals to bless that space and initiate it as a sacred spot in your home. Smudging with sage, rattling, or calling on the spirits or saints to bless your space are all effective ways of starting. Sanctuary space can be a haven for deep inner work, or simply a reminder to pay attention or give thanks.

Sanctuaries were created throughout the ages and across faiths. In the Jewish tradition, a mezuzah is placed on the doorposts. A mezuzah is a small case that contains a tiny scroll with a hand written blessing. The custom is to touch the mezuzah every time you pass. A mezuzah reminds you to stop and express love and gratitude to God.[33] Each doorpost becomes a small sanctuary. In a traditional Roman Catholic service, the priest offers mass from the sanctuary. This most holy place is set apart from the rest of the church. As the priest recites a prayer, he is filled with thoughts of God and the holy nature of the mysteries he is about to celebrate. Pagan sanctuaries were often centered around a spot in nature believed to have a special energy, like a spring or a grove of oak trees. The image of the Buddha himself is often the focal point of Buddhist shrines. A sanctuary is created for those who meditate there, as Buddha embodies the sacred energy of enlightenment.

For the Ancient Greeks, gods and goddesses were everywhere and occupied different positions according to their strengths and personalities. Hestia, goddess of the fire and hearth, was especially important to the home. The hearth was her sanctuary. Each time a fire was lit, the occupants of the home would pay their respects to

Hestia. If you have a spiritual being you feel strongly connected to, you may want to devote an altar or sanctuary to that spirit.

Traditionally, sacred spaces had specific purposes, like a specific form of prayer, or the honoring of a particular god or goddess. For Catholics, praying at the stations of the cross is a time to meditate specifically on the time surrounding Jesus' sentencing and ultimate death. Each of the fourteen "stages," typically distributed around the perimeter of the inside of a church, represents a period in the process of Jesus' death, from when he was condemned to die, to when he was laid in the tomb. As parishioners move through the stages, they stop at each and meditate or pray.

In Japan, Shinto shrines are common sanctuaries. They are typically built to honor nature or ancestral spirits. Followers of the Shinto faith believe ancestral spirits hold tremendous power to protect and support the living members of their families. Therefore, they are paid special attention with frequent offerings of incense and food. Your ancestors can be remembered and honored simply by hanging a cluster of pictures on one wall. Each time you pass that wall and see the images of your forebears, you will be reminded that they gave you life.

Your sanctuary can even be a place you take with you, a portable altar. A portable altar can contain photographs, objects that represent nature, or reminders of your spiritual mentors. The benefit of having a portable altar is that you can keep your sanctuary with you even when you're not at home.

The place you set aside for fostering and engaging your spiritual self, as well as the spiritual aspect of your living space, will grow in power over time and especially with use. The room where I do my spiritual healing work and meditation has grown perceptibly more soothing as time goes by. At first it was an ordinary room and I wasn't particularly excited about moving my office there. Once I placed the material objects, furniture, drums, and artwork in the room, I liked the way it looked and it felt more conducive to the work I do. Now, after years spent with helping spirits present, people comment frequently about how serene the room feels. For me, just entering the room is a trigger and I start to slip into a more meditative space. The more I use it, the more the sacred energy of the space grows and helps create an atmosphere where healing takes place.

You can use any sacred space as a model for your sanctuary, but do create your sanctuary intuitively. Choose a spot that feels right to you. If you love to be outside in nature, and feel most peaceful there, carve out a niche among growing things and bird sounds. Consider incorporating the elements, by adding a fountain for the tranquil sound of water, or growing a flowering hedge to provide some privacy, or adding stones. If you're most at home inside, a special table in the corner of your bedroom may suit you. Add a candle, pictures that have meaning for you and trigger a meditative or spiritual focus, and other objects that symbolize your inner spirit and the spirit world around you.

Consider making your sanctuary multi-sensory, engaging as many of your senses as possible. Incense has been used in many religious traditions around the world in sacred rituals. In shamanic cultures it is believed that the scent of incense entices the spirits. Sound is used consistently as well: the chime of a bell in a Catholic mass, the peaceful drone of a Tibetan bowl, the vibration of a singing voice. Visual images, silky fabrics, or rosary beads to touch add sensory dimension to your sanctuary. These are just some examples of ways that sacred spaces are created to engage your physical senses as well as your spiritual ones. This is not necessarily a public space, so freely express yourself. Use your creativity to design sacred space that most reflects your inner divinity.

The purpose of a sanctuary is to help you turn inward. It is a touchstone, a place of worship, a place that reminds you of the divine all around you and within you. Sanctuaries can help you make that connection quickly, but you don't need an external object to open yourself to spirit. Seek peace, compassion, love, and wholeness from the haven of your sanctuary. Put out what you wish to receive back. The power of a sanctuary comes from the energy with which you imbue it. Nourish your sanctuary and allow it to nourish you in return.

Blessing Ceremonies

Performing a blessing ceremony can help make any space a sanctuary. It would be lovely if your living space had the same effect on you as a dedicated sanctuary, helping you to feel safe and connected to the source of divine love. Call on helping spirits, angels, and saints. Engage your sacred self through the power of your intention to bless your surroundings. You can design your own ritual or use methods already in practice. Consider performing a blessing ceremony for your home or your land. Following are some examples of how to do that.

Walk around the periphery of your land with offerings of whatever is meaningful to you. In some traditional Native American cultures, corn and tobacco were considered sacred. Use lavender or rose petals. Find something that is special to you or create something new. Walk your land with intention and leave your gifts.

Give thanks for the support you receive from your home ground. Ask for blessings from the earth and from the spirits who inhabit the land.

Use the technique of smudging in your home. Burn some sage or cedar or simply a candle. Go from room to room with the intention of cleansing, blessing, and asking for help. Welcome a partnership with the spirit of your home in each room. Be open to what may be communicated to you during your ritual and allow for the mysterious or unexpected to take place. Let the smoke flow into each corner of the room, gently spreading your intention throughout your home.

Stay in your heart. This is a process of remembering how to connect with your surroundings in a respectful and loving way. If it feels right for you to rattle, do it. Sing to each room, drum, use a chime or a Tibetan bowl, or just hold silence as you process through your home. The items you use in a ceremony help you focus your intention, engage your senses, or call on the spirits. The power of any ritual or ceremony lies in the power of the intention of the participants. There is not a magic formula. Let yourself be creative. Craft ceremonies that speak to you. With your ritual, weave a brilliant web of light to nourish you and support you in all aspects of your life.

NATURE

"I have been to the end of the earth. I have been to the end of the waters. I have been to the end of the sky. I have been to the end of the mountains. I have found none that are not my friends." Navajo proverb

Nature speaks to us if we stop and listen. Shamans of all ages knew this. They developed ways to relate to their natural surroundings, to understand what happened around them. Understanding what happened around them allowed them to better understand what happened within them. We cannot detach ourselves from the natural environment. It surrounds us and permeates us.

The natural environment is a sanctuary. By spending time in nature you connect with the cycles of life and the seasons. You gain perspective on your own place in the ecosystem and you open the door to relate spiritually to all that surrounds you. Being in nature reactivates your connection to your source. It reminds you of your animal nature and of your divine nature. Being in nature helps break down the barriers your ego has created. It allows you to shift more easily to a receptive state where you can hear your own instinctive voice as you hear the wind in the trees. The warmth of the sun on your face rekindles the knowledge that you're not alone in the universe. Being in nature makes it easy to look through our shaman's eyes, to see the interconnection between all beings and the larger patterns at play. Nature creates a space where we can find union with each other and with God.

We can easily walk through the day forgetting to appreciate the abundance of nature all around us. On a recent walk in my neighborhood park, I passed by the playground equipment and found that the beings playing there were not children! There was a flock of vibrantly colored bluebirds. They flitted around the swings, the slide, and the jungle gym, gliding away and landing again. I was thrilled to find so many of them together. I said hello and walked past. A hawk swooped down from a low tree, just a foot or two off the ground. She has a nest in the park. As I walked the path, the bluebirds shifted in a mass and moved, sometimes in front of me, sometimes flying away. These birds are spectacular. I feel lucky to have this park nearby.

The work of readjusting our relationship is as much about the mundane as it is the profound. Sometimes we need a reminder to shift our perspective into our ordinary lives. We've got to *live* this state of mind. We don't need huge break-through moments or visions or spirit visitations as much as we need to pay attention, to walk around every day open to the natural world around us. Personally, I've gotten caught in a trap of feeling like I want more of something. For me it's often about having a beautiful, natural setting right where I live. I've been guilty of not fully appreciating the land and the creatures right around me in my small suburban neighborhood. To pine for a mountain range out my window while forgetting to walk across the street into this beautiful little park is foolish. I'm able to walk into a flock of brilliant bluebirds, stroll past hawks, and sometimes hear the owls call at night. I can get caught up in feeling I need to have the wilderness, but I have nature right here.

Once I was telling my father about how I craved a piece of land for solitude, and to be surrounded by nature, he looked at me in surprise and said "But Mara, you're in nature all the time." It was a profound statement. We can't escape it. Whether you are living in Manhattan, or the Amazon, or anywhere on this earth, you are in nature. Seek out the natural things that can be found even in an urban environment. Remember that each little creature, being, plant, or tree is a microcosm for the larger whole. Maybe I can't walk in pristine wilderness today. I see houses around, I hear trucks emptying the dumpsters from the restaurant nearby, and I'm walking past a playground, but it serves my purpose and I try to serve it in return. I need to respect and cherish the bits of nature all around. As our generations unfold we will have less and less nature to cherish, and if we do not appreciate our immediate environment we're going to miss an opportunity to nourish the small doses of nature all around us and in turn to be nourished by them.

A friend of mine recently told a story about her garden that I found inspiring. Diane lived in a small house with very little front yard. She felt exposed to the steady stream of people walking past on the sidewalk and wished to create a private space for herself. She turned to gardening. Her passion for plants would help her create a barrier from her neighbors, she thought. She planted beautiful flowers in her front yard. She created a harmonious and lovely place on her small plot of earth. Her neighbors began calling to her and commenting on her beautiful flowers. She realized much later that the garden she had intended as a barrier from her neighbors was actually a gift to them. They were not gardeners themselves, so especially appreciated the bursts of color in Diane's yard. Her effort to create beauty and peace for herself by escaping through nature became a perfect way to create harmony in the environment all around her.

Walk outside. Breathe fresh air. Stop and admire the fall leaves, the ice crystals coating your window, or the tiny bud of a spring crocus. Enjoy nature physically and you will be engaged spiritually. Indulge in the feast for your physical senses, and you will find a bounty for your sacred senses as well. Nature embodies the power of the universe. Draw on that power to ignite your divinity, sparking the power already within you.

Spirits of Nature

Our beautiful earth and the living things on it are more than physical beings. Shamans were keenly aware of the spirits of the places they lived in and engaged them often. The land itself is often in need of healing. The spirits who live there appreciate our help and often offer their support to us. If at this point you can't relate to the idea of spiritual entities inhabiting nature, don't worry. Think of the natural environment any way that feels comfortable to you, as long as you recognize its vital importance and acknowledge our debt to it. Remember, no one has ever seen wind. We see the wind affecting other things; quivering leaves, ripples pushed across a pond, undulating fields of grass. Wind is a tangible force in the environment which is invisible. It is not too far fetched to imagine other invisible forces with equal power to touch the objects and beings they encounter.

A short while ago I was going out into nature to try to connect with the spirit of the place I was in. I went out to embrace nature and to be embraced by nature in return. I opened my senses, my eyes, my ears, and my heart, to be present and express my gratitude. It was beautiful outside, clear skies, a crisp New England fall day. I walked over to a small bridge crossing a stream. I closed my eyes for a few moments to appreciate the sound. In our overstressing of the visual, we tend to forget how much impact sound can have on us. I was simply appreciating the sound of the water and the breeze in the trees. After a few moments I sensed a presence behind me. These encounters are not usually dramatic for me. I had a feeling in my gut and an image in my mind's eye of someone there with me, someone very leafy. It was a spirit of that place who had answered my call for communion. For the rest of the week that I was in that space I felt that spirit around me frequently in a loving and calming way. When I returned months later, this spirit sought me out and we reconnected.

In most traditional cultures there is a meaningful and active spiritual connection to the earth spirits. Native people often foster a healthy relationship with the spirits around them by engaging animals and plants in a respectful way. North American natives hunted deer for meat, but thanked the spirit of the deer for allowing itself to be sacrificed to feed the people. They showed their reverence for life by killing only what was needed to survive and using as much as possible of the deer: meat for food, hides for clothing and shelter, bones for cutting implements.

In early Japan, Shinto rituals and celebrations focused on creating harmony among deities, human beings, and aspects of nature. This philosophy of balance and unity is still a significant attribute of Japanese religious life and art today. The Celts also worked with the spirits of the land, called the "little people," leprechauns, fairies, and nature devas. In many traditions these spirits were attended to in some way. Some were placated so they didn't create mischief. In Iceland these spirits, or "hidden folk," are taken into consideration when building new construction. Planners are careful to avoid the "little people's homes." When these spirits have not been consulted regarding the construction company's plans, the jobs tend to become difficult, with equipment failures or sick employees.[34]

In other cases the spirits were simply honored, by leaving out a plate of food, for example. Today, flowers or incense are placed on many altars of different faiths. Some token of appreciation is made to bridge the gap between the physical and the spiritual beings. Of course *we* are spiritual beings, you and I just happen to reside in a physical body at this time. Try to connect to the spirits of nature where you live and work and you may find that you can call on them for support.

In recent times, people have worked directly with the spirits of the land to get advice about growing food. In the Findhorn community in Scotland, they tend not only to the physical aspects of the gardens, but to the spirits that inhabit them. By working with the devas or angels, they've had incredibly bountiful harvests from relatively inhospitable soil. Cabbages that typically grow to four pounds grew to forty! Dorothy Maclean, one of the founders of the community, discovered the spiritual aspect of pea plants. To her amazement she found herself communicating with an intelligent being, what she called the angel or deva of the garden peas. Each species in the garden seemed to have an angel. Dorothy spoke with them all in order to find out what they needed to improve the harvest. [35]

Even in the principles of Feng Shui, practitioners recognize the spirit of the tiger and the dragon and the energies they represent. They observe the physical formations of the land to understand which spirit resides in that place. Then they are able to build structures in a way that creates harmony and doesn't cause disruption in the energetic lines of that site.

Once I had an interesting encounter with a woodchuck. I was at a retreat center and I saw him near my cabin. He was eating plants and flowers, showing a distinct preference for the yellow ones. I admired him and talked to him a little bit. When I went to bed that night, as soon as I turned out the light, I heard scratching in the walls of my cabin. I've heard mice and squirrels in the walls before, but this was definitely a larger creature. Although the sound was coming from inside the walls, it sounded like someone was sitting on my bed and eating a carrot! It was very loud. I thought it was probably the woodchuck. That first night, he kept me up on and off all night long. I kept turning on a flashlight to see if he'd managed to eat through the walls and into our bedroom! The next night he started chomping again. I went to bed and called on that leafy spirit I'd met earlier in the same trip. I called on my helping spirits and focused on my heart. I tried to communicate silently with the woodchuck. I said that I wanted to be in good relationship with him. I didn't want to ban him from his cozy spot, I just really needed a good night's sleep. Would he mind either moving to another spot for the evening, or just being quiet so I could sleep? Immediately the noise stopped. It didn't come back for the remainder of the trip.

Seek out the spirits of your land. Be open to different ways of perceiving them and communicating with them. Thank them, honor them, and let them into your life. See what miracles happen.

The Elements: Water, Earth, Air, Fire

We are dependent upon certain basic elements of nature, particularly the fundamental aspects of water, earth, air, and fire. We cannot exist without those four elements. They are the building blocks from which all life sprang and continues to spring. Our adult bodies are up to 70 percent water. Our bodies need nutrients from the earth to function. All life relies on the warmth of the sun to survive. We need air every moment of every day. We often forget our own dependence on these elements, and are polluting them. We are polluting the air that we take into our lungs every day. Have you ever had an experience where you were not able to breathe? If so, you have renewed appreciation for air. If you have to go without food or water for an extended period of time, you have a renewed appreciation for the plentiful nourishment most of us take for granted. Try to engage your environment in a new way. Try to see the connectedness between yourself and the beings and elements around you.

Traditional cultures revered the natural elements, and were more cognizant of their dependence on them than most of us are today. The four directions, north, south, east, and west, are typically incorporated in daily rituals, as are the four major elements of air, earth, fire, and water. The elements are recognized as significant sources of power. Mongolian shamans refer to "gol," the true source, the "center of all existence." Their words for fire and river both derive from this root source, symbolizing the generative and fundamental power of fire and water.[36] Many meditation practices, including Zen, often involve focusing on the breath, as it is the connector to the true essence of life. These methods help release you from extraneous concerns and allow you to concentrate on the very basic act of bringing air in and out of the body. Most pagan rituals, especially the Beltane rituals, celebrate the earth and her gifts to us, honoring our mother both physically and spiritually. The Hopis prayed to the sun, as a source of power, but also as a partner in personal enlightenment and evolution.

There are some exercises you can do to help understand your relationship with the elements. Start simply by paying closer attention to the way earth, air, fire, and water function in your life. Notice the solidity of the ground under your feet, the sweetness of a breath of fresh air, the warmth of the sun on your face, and the cool relief of a drink of water. Notice and nourish your relationship with each element.

Next, consider the classic shamanic method of merging with the elements. Sandra Ingerman describes this in *Medicine for the Earth*. You can journey, meditate, or simply use your own instincts and do this exercise as you wish. I suggest you take ten or fifteen minutes. Your intention is to merge with water in some form: it can be rain, a lake, a river, a cloud, whatever appeals to you. What does it feel like to be water? Even though we're made so much of water, we have become intellectually disconnected from that aspect of ourselves. Repeat this exercise with each of the elements over the course of time. What does it feel like to be earth? Experience yourself as soil, rock, or sand. Experience yourself as air, maybe as a tornado or a gentle breeze, or simply the air in your living room. Experience yourself as fire, a candle's flame, a warm campfire, or the sun. See what information those elements have to share with you and express your appreciation to those elements for sustaining your life.

Weather

Weather is a source of fascination for us. Today we're able to indulge our cultural obsession with weather with twenty-four-hour television stations dedicated to the fronts shifting above the earth. We take weather quite personally. We get angry when it rains during a picnic or wedding. We complain when it's too hot or cold. We revel in the sun during a temperate summer day. We are deeply connected to the weather patterns where we live. We react emotionally and physically to weather, and possibly affect the weather more than we know. In traditional cultures it was often believed that the state of weather reflected the state of the community and vice versa. Today we tend to see weather patterns as impersonal and oblivious to human beings.

We have a complicated relationship with weather. It's a universal condition, a safe topic of conversation for those sharing space and place, yet weather is an aspect of nature with which we have a most intimate relationship. Unless you live in a community where you can walk from your home to your work place to the grocery store without going outside, weather touches you. The sun, the wind, and the cold touch you. They govern your choice of clothes and often your mood. Pay attention to your relationship with weather.

I heard a newscast a few nights ago. We'd had about ten days of glorious, sunny weather. The weather person had a short teaser to get you to watch the six o'clock news. She said something like, "More sunshine? Let's see if we can get some rain in the forecast." Her tone suggested that we hoped to get rid of this sun and finally get some rain. I hear the inverse more often. When can we get rid of this annoying rain? Whatever the weather is, we often have some complaint about it. Today is a beautiful, rainy, dark day. It was preceded by ten days of blue skies and sunshine. Now the earth is soaking up the water and the flowers and the plants are happy and getting a nice long drink. It's good and we should appreciate it. Enjoy the variety of weather if your community has it. If not, enjoy the consistency. But whatever weather you have, as much as you can, try to just appreciate it and accept it for what it is.

Obviously, weather can be destructive. Do what you can to make peace with what the climate of the earth is doing around you. We're all human and if it rains for days on end, sometimes that gets dreary. Or if it's too dry we worry about the plants and the animals. But try to have a balance about accepting what is. There is so much extreme weather these days; massive wildfires, earthquakes, and tornadoes. In Asia in December 2004 a huge tsunami wreaked havoc. Five indigenous tribes on the Indian archipelago of Andaman and Nicobar Islands are believed to have saved themselves because of their astute and profound relationship with the environment around them, the elements, and the forces of weather. They moved to high ground before the tsunami hit. Anthropologists and government officials suspect that their ancient knowledge of the ocean, wind, and birds may have saved their lives. "They can smell the wind. They can gauge the depth of the sea with the sound of their oars. They have a sixth sense which we don't possess," said Ashish Roy, a local environmentalist and lawyer.[37] These tribes have maintained their harmonious relationship with their environment. Even though the land was dramatically impacted, their ability to anticipate and adapt to changes, even sudden ones, preserved their lives.

Severe weather, such as the tsunami, is another indication of how out of balance we are as a planet and as a culture. David Corbin and Nan Moss are shamanic practitioners and teachers. They write about working with weather from a shamanic perspective, working with the *spirits* of weather. They invite participants to consider the spiritual aspects of the elements of weather that we're so used to thinking about as neutral or lifeless phenomena. Moss and Corbin write, "the principle of reciprocity: as above, so below; as within, so without; is real and operative in our world and lives, independent of our conscious understanding."[38] By creating harmony in your inner world, you can help create harmony in the physical world around you.

One wonderful way to engage weather is simply by watching clouds. It's something you probably did as a child. Lie on your back in a grassy field or on the sand at the beach and watch the clouds drift. It's remarkably meditative. You may see images. You may be able to ask questions and get answers from what you see in the clouds. Or you may simply appreciate the ephemeral patterns. For the beauty of cloud watching from the comfort of your own home, you can get a set of the exquisite *CloudDancing* cards that Nan and David have created. See the *Resources* section for more information. One of my favorite moments is when I'm on an airplane flying above thick cloud cover and I'm looking down at the soft blanket gently covering the earth, or seeing patches of fluffy clouds and the shadows they cast on the earth from that elevated perspective. It helps me shift and see that weather is really all around us. Our perspective can be limited as we usually see clouds above us. Remember the way it feels when you've been in a misty place, to know you are *in* the clouds. It's magical when the clouds descend and you are enveloped inside them.

Some people may even be able to influence the weather. Shamans were called upon to serve their communities by using rituals to gain the cooperation of the spirits of weather. One ceremony is used to manifest rain. In 1998 a devastating fire ravaged a portion of the rainforest of Brazil. Yanomami shamans performed a ritual to bring rain. Rain fell the next day, after six or seven months of drought.[39]

When I was a young girl, maybe six or seven, I remember taking a walk with my Grammy. She is my maternal grandmother and an inspiration to me in many ways. At that time in my life I loved to get out in nature with her because she'd make it so interesting. She appreciated all the tiny creatures and growing things and showed them to me with a sense of wonder. One day, on vacation in West Virginia, we set off on a walk. It is quite a short walk now to my adult eyes, but then it was an adventure. We'd walked about half way up the mountain when thunder boomed ominously. Very quickly the skies opened and it began to rain. I was scared. Without missing a beat, my Grammy said something like, "Don't worry, I'll make it stop." She reached down, picked up a branch, raised it over her head and turned it like a faucet. The rain stopped. I was quite impressed. But that was just my Gram. It always felt like magical things were possible when she was around.

Gregg Braden talks about his experience with a Native American friend "praying rain." The mountains of northern New Mexico had been experiencing a long and severe drought. Rain was desperately needed, but not in the forecasts. Gregg's friend brought him to a place in the desert where "the skins between the worlds are very thin." The ancestors of his community had placed stones in a detailed pattern on the ground. I'm reminded of the labyrinth, as he describes his friend moving gracefully through the stone medicine wheel without disturbing a rock. After completing a circuit and standing silently in prayer for a few moments, the friend indicates that he is done. That afternoon, the rains fell heavily in the area, pooling in the desert and quenching the earth's thirst. Even the weather maps showed an unusual shift in the air mass, bringing moist air to the region. He explained to

Gregg later that he used a special prayer to *experience* the rain. Instead of praying to remedy the drought, thereby focusing on the *lack* of rain, he shifted his focus to the experience of being in rain and to offer thanks for the rain.[40] We'll talk more about this form of prayer in *Section 7: Your Future*, as it holds tremendous potential for manifesting, for creating the life experience you desire.

In traditional cultures aspects of weather like lightning were thought of as alive, as having a spirit. Some elements of weather were used in shamanic cultures as a way of harnessing power, sometimes to gain power over rivals, but also to employ the power of nature for the good of the community. In Norse mythology, Thor was the god of thunder. He was believed to protect both humans and gods from the forces of evil. Lightning flashed whenever he threw his hammer. Ancient Greeks and Romans connected some of their gods and goddesses to the forces of weather. They believed there was a divine energy behind weather. The supreme gods Zeus and Jupiter had dominion over the sky, the rain, and especially the power of thunder and lightning. The Etruscans revered Tinia, The Thunderer and Sky-Father, ruler of all weather and climate manifestations.[41] These ancient cultures acknowledged the life force behind the elements of weather, by personifying them as gods. Think of the spirits of weather as co-creators of our ecological reality; not necessarily as objects of worship or fear, but as fellow beings to acknowledge and respect.

When you're willing to consider that everything has life, everything is connected and related in some way through the vital force that flows through us all, an amazing world opens to you, and vast potential is created. When you're willing to look at the world in that light, it changes you. You understand that one word can affect someone for years to come. You understand that the loss of one species can change the ecosystem from that point forward. You understand that weather influences us all and in turn we influence the weather. It's a powerful concept to contemplate. Allow it to expand your consciousness if it is something new to you. If you've already become aware of it, explore it more deeply. At the end of this chapter I've made some suggestions for exercises to connect more deeply with weather and the web of life itself.

Labyrinth

There are many ways to connect to the elements around you. An ancient tradition that blends introspection with outward awareness is the walking of the labyrinth. Following a "unicursal" path that alternates in a clockwise and counterclockwise circuit, labyrinths always provide one way in and one way out. The labyrinth is a symbol that has been traced back to over 3,500 years ago to locations all over the globe. Labyrinths are created in myriad ways: on the earth with rocks or sod, carved into stone, painted on floor tiles in cathedrals, and woven in baskets. The image of the labyrinth has been relatively consistent across time.

The intentions of those who walked the labyrinth centuries ago are not entirely known to us now. However, we do know that fishermen in Northern Europe walked labyrinths near the shore to "entrap bad weather before fishing expeditions." The Chartres Cathedral in France has a large labyrinth set in the floor. For Christians worshipping there, the center symbolized arriving in Jerusalem. The labyrinth thereby acted as a short pilgrimage.[42] The labyrinth was also used as a form of walking meditation.

Today, the labyrinth has become a tool for connecting with nature as you connect with yourself, for engaging your body on a physical journey toward the center, while your soul journeys inward too. It can be used simply for relaxation, to develop the ability to stay present in the moment, or to seek guidance. The labyrinth helps people of all ages connect to the earth they walk on.

In Durham, North Carolina, Jill Over is bringing the ancient practice of walking the labyrinth to elementary school children. She works from an environmental perspective as she guides children through the construction and uses of a labyrinth. She engages them in a dialogue with the earth around them as they learn about the four directions (north, south, east, and west), and experience being outside in a peaceful and focused way. "With proper preparation and simple instructions, the labyrinth can be used to teach children (and adults) to 'slow down,' to become more aware of themselves and the present moment, to observe the details and beauty of nature, and to experience playfulness and spontaneity. With a little effort, children can be taught to look inside themselves, as well as explore their relationship and reactions to the external world."[43]

Jill has a remarkable labyrinth at her home. It winds through trees and rock formations and is abloom with tiny treasures to discover; crystals, seashells, and stones. I brought my daughter there as a three–and–a–half year old. I was inspired by her ability to shift her pace to a slow walk and really engage what she saw. The bark of a tree was appreciated and petted. A crystal orb perched atop a seashell was carefully examined and then replaced, exactly as it was. She watched her own steps as she carefully navigated the path, careful not to step outside the rocks that guided us through. I've found the most peaceful energy in an outside labyrinth walk. The sounds of the birds become more noticeable, and I fall into a natural rhythm with the earth below my feet and the elements all around me.

When walking a labyrinth, allow your senses to open to what's happening around you, as you pay attention to the energy within you. As labyrinths are typically walked slowly and silently, you're able to pay attention to the details often missed as you go through daily life. Permanent labyrinths may be available in your area. Sometimes they are painted on large cloths and brought to churches or other spots for people to walk. You can construct your own labyrinth if you like. There are even miniature labyrinths that you can "walk" with your finger. Any of these provide a way of focusing your energy and connecting with the natural world around you.

WEB OF LIFE

"Whatever befalls the earth, befalls the sons of earth … the earth does not belong to man, man belongs to the earth … all things are connected … man did not weave the web of life; he is merely a strand in it … whatever he does to the web, he does to himself." Chief Seattle

Native cultures around the world express the belief that as individuals we are parts of a whole, and what we do, think, say, and feel impacts the other parts. This interconnectedness relates not only to humans, but to nature as well. In fact, to many traditional thinkers, living in harmony with the natural environment is one of the key elements of living a virtuous life. This harmony is essential for the health of our bodies, our spirits, and our land. Most Western cultures have become detached from the common sense notion that our actions alter our environment. As creatures dependent upon the environment for sustenance on all levels, we will ultimately be altered by the way we live in relation to that environment. We don't seem to be making the connection between the desecration of the land, air, and water and the deterioration in some significant areas of our health. And when we do make the connection intellectually, it seems extremely difficult to make the necessary changes as a society to bring the relationship back into balance, to care for nature as we'd like to be cared for ourselves.

Where modern society has taken a wrong turn is in viewing nature not as a home, but merely as a supplier of raw materials. In order for true personal and planetary healing to occur, this attitude must change. We must accept that being in harmony with nature is as vital for healing as being in harmony with ourselves. Given that the notion of *personal* harmony affecting health is not an accepted principle in many allopathic practices, we have a long way to go.

In the Navajo tradition there is a phrase called "walking in beauty." For the Navajo, beauty equals harmony. It means that for life to be beautiful it must be balanced; people must relate in a respectful way; people must show reverence for all aspects of the world, the physical and the spiritual, from the leaf on a tree to Spirit itself. Religion and medicine merge, as they believe sickness is caused by losing one's balance, wandering off that spiritual path of beauty and harmony. Traditionally, Navajos make great efforts to live harmoniously with everyone and everything around them.[44]

Shamanic cultures, and some other traditions we've discussed, believe that everything in the universe is not only connected but made of the same source. Tom Cowan eloquently describes the Celtic idea of the web of life. "If both God and the human soul are to be found in the ocean, a lake, a flame, a spark of light, the Celtic mind (viewed) creation from a shamanic perspective, namely, everything in the universe is alive, conscious, accessible, and power-filled. The Creator/Spirit and the human soul are ultimately one, made of the same substance, the same divine energy."[45]

We are accustomed to thinking of ourselves and the objects and beings around us as existing in empty space, props and actors moving through the void of the stage. However, the spaces in between are active and charged too. When art instructors teach drawing and painting, they often instruct their students to look at the spaces around and between the objects they are rendering. This is called negative space. Pay attention to the negative spaces around you. Awareness of these spaces creates a richer understanding of the relationships between things. For the art student, it helps to sense how the objects of a still life or landscape relate to each other in space. For example, the negative space between a blue vase and a yellow teapot standing next to it holds the energy of each of those objects. The air between the two may be colored by a mixture of their colors. Noticing the shape of the negative space itself helps the artist to draw the objects accurately in relation to one another. In a similar way, you can perceive your environment more astutely by being aware of the subtle spaces between everything, as well as the tangible objects around you.

In Buddhist thought, the illusion of separation is believed to be the root of all suffering. By awakening to the true nature of life, enlightenment is possible. One of the fundamental truths in Buddhism is the interconnectedness of all things.

This profound realization is the turning point from which you can live your life in unity with yourself and your environment. You begin to understand that each action, thought, and word has an instantaneous effect on both you and your environment. We share a common collective consciousness and energy, as described by people such as Carl Jung, and we share a common field in which we exist and interrelate. We share biological, psychological, and spiritual origins. We are indeed a family.

When she was four, I took my daughter shopping for a Halloween costume. She was thrilled to find a Sleeping Beauty dress and crown and some fancy, sparkling shoes. On our way home we stopped to pick up some dry cleaning. The cleaners has a drive through. They come out to get your dirty laundry and put the clean laundry in your car for you—it's very decadent. A young man came out to put the clothes in our car. As soon as he opened the back door, my daughter launched into a description of her costume, where she was going to wear it, the sparkling shoes, her best friend, etc. He was very kind and polite to her. He smiled and was sufficiently impressed with her story. As soon as he closed the door she said, "He was my brother, when I was a different girl with Ally." (Ally is someone she talks about a lot. We don't know who she is in ordinary reality.) I kind of mulled that over for a while and then I said to her, "Really we all are brothers and sisters with everyone on the planet, because we're connected." She said, "I know that!" emphatically, as if I'd said the most obvious thing in the world. Sometimes children seem to know things instinctively that we adults have to learn all over again.

Scientists are beginning to understand the interconnectedness of all life on another level. They see the ramifications to the larger environment of altering parts of the ecosystem. Environmental scientist Peter L. deFur explains what he has observed about the natural world's mysteries, he echoes Chief Seattle's words, "all things are connected," because he has witnessed evidence of the connections. He sees the effects on the watershed when wetlands upstream have been lost. In addition to the physical changes and adaptations in nature, there is another ineffable relationship that he detects "as life adapts and forms patterns. Call it a life force or spirit. The web of life is only partly understandable on an intellectual, i.e. scientific level. Another part of the web of life is understood on … a spiritual level."[46]

The divine energy of the universe is contained within us. Human beings are not the only vessels for that holy energy. Remember your inner divinity, and also be aware of the divine energy all around you.

Flow

Being in the "flow" is acting in partnership with the universe to allow your life to unfold as it should. Being in the flow is showing up and doing your inner work and then allowing life to happen without trying to control too much. When you allow spirit to work with you for the highest good instead of your personal desires, you are letting things flow. Dance with the light of the universe and alternate who leads. Make way for the spirits to help you and for miracles to happen. Happiness is kindled when you live your life in the flow. Hippocrates said "There is one common flow, one common breathing, all things are in sympathy."[47]

We take part in the flow of life on many levels. There are the small patterns of energy that swirl around us as we move from room to room, or are generated as we read something or have a conversation. Larger patterns in our personal lives play out more slowly: the development of important relationships, the progress of our careers, the unfolding of our true selves and inner passions. In communities there are still larger flows: cities evolve, nations make war and peace, cultural standards shift. The flow of nature can be felt on all levels, from a tiny procession of ants to the vast patterns of weather. All of these systems flow to different rhythms, they interact with one another and their flows are altered, merged, and recreated.

Most of us have forgotten that we're affected by the energetic characteristics of our environment, including other people, unseen spiritual forces and natural patterns. Remembering is not hard; you simply need to pay attention. When was the last time you walked into a building and felt sick to your stomach? Unless we have a rational cause to justify such a reaction, most of us ignore it. Many of us are so used to ignoring our own bodies' communication that we aren't even aware of our stomach hurting. There are many potential reasons why we react physically to certain places. Places hold the energy of the people in them, especially their emotions. Maybe the building is filled with unhappy or stressed people. You might have been picking up on that energy, even though to the casual observer everything looked fine. There may be toxic substances in the building that you are intuitively picking up on. Or the space might simply be vibrating at a frequency that is uncomfortable for you. When was the last time you met someone and felt like you'd known them for a long time even though you'd just been introduced? You may have felt intuitively that their energetic personality harmonized with yours. Their presence was comfortable. Your movement into physical structures or personal relationships affects the flow and you are affected in turn.

Each day has a particular energetic flow as well. In astrological terms, when Mercury is retrograde people report difficulty with communication and transportation issues. If you know in advance which days hold the potential for difficulty in these areas, you can plan accordingly. It doesn't mean that the pattern of the stars has to dictate your actions and decisions; however, it allows you to be sensitive to the nature of that day's energy and to recognize that there are larger dynamics playing out. It will serve you well not to fight against them. You don't have to know the exact dates of astrological movement to be sensitive to these patterns. Just use your instincts. Your gut and your heart are often the best instruments for measuring the energetic tone of a day, a place, or a person. If you wake up one morning and everything feels off, you burn your toast and stub your toe on the door jamb as you rush to an almost forgotten appointment, there may be practical reasons for the chaos you feel.

Step outside and look up. Gaze at the sky and see what the energy conveys to you. Get quiet for a moment in the morning and ask what kind of day you should be prepared for. You don't have to know why each day is energetically different to make the best of it. In recognizing the potential hazards of an energetically off day, you can remind yourself to think before you speak, to double check the details of your schedule, and to put an extra pair of pantyhose in your purse! In other words, being sensitive to the energetic flows all around you provides an opportunity for you to adapt. It allows you to flow with the wave instead of getting knocked over and washed up bedraggled on the shore.

A Taoist legend illustrates this point. An old man is swimming in a rushing river. The current is very strong and suddenly he disappears. Some followers of Confucius were watching from the shore and ran to save him. Before they could get to him, the man reached the shore without their help. They were shocked, and asked the old man how he had survived. He replied that he let himself rise and fall with the currents. To live most harmoniously develop flexibility of body and mind, until they are at one with the currents of the world without.[48]

The expression "as above, so below" illustrates the idea that the state of the macrocosm is reflected in the state of the microcosm. If the larger organism is in chaos, the beings that exist within it will feel personal chaos. The inverse is often true. If we feel chaotic, our world mirrors that sensation. Work in partnership with what's around you to create space that supports you. Create an internal environment that you want to be reflected back at you through your external environment.

CLOSING

"Place yourself in the middle of the stream of power and wisdom which flows into your life."
Ralph Waldo Emerson

The big picture can be difficult to see and harder to understand. In my own life, I don't always know the ideal course. That's why, when I'm praying or journeying to ask the spirits for help, I usually ask them for what's for the highest good rather than what I am specifically desiring. Sometimes we lack the perspective to know what is best for us. All we can really do is try to foster harmony rather than discord in our actions and our words.

In your life, you may not be able to see what's going to happen, but you do have choices every day, smaller choices about how you treat your loved ones, or your neighbors, or a stray animal. You choose how you treat your environment in the smallest way. Are you going to recycle your cans or are you going to litter? Will you create a home that's serene or unwelcoming? These choices add up. The positive ways in which you relate to other living things add up to living in right relationship to the world. "Skalalitude" is a Salish word from the Pacific Northwest which explains the possibilities when we relate to nature cooperatively, "when people and nature are in perfect harmony, then magic and beauty are everywhere."[49]

Many of us don't see these interrelationships, and over time come to feel we're alone as individuals. In society today, there's often less of a sense of community and of the "safety net" of the family. Some teenagers find acceptance in gangs. We've become a more mobile society with nuclear families being distanced physically from their older generations. We typically don't get together as a community and have a barn raising any more. (Although a friend recently offered to "go Amish on me" and swap help renovating our bathrooms!) There certainly are churches, organizations and families that do inspire a sense of community, but it seems to be harder for people to find. Our sense of isolation has grown. It can be lonely when you feel disconnected and completely responsible for yourself. It makes it easier to act out of fear, with an attitude of taking what you want regardless of the impact on others. That creates imbalance and discord in our individual lives, as well as in the greater community.

Everything in your environment is alive in some way, having energy or a spiritual aspect. This is one of the fundamental tenets of shamanism; everything has a spirit. When we relate to our environment while acknowledging that life force, we create a partnership. Once we become aware of this dynamic and multidimensional world we live in, we can take active steps to create harmony in our immediate environs and for our planet as a whole.

Dorothy Maclean of Findhorn teaches others how to connect with the natural world and the spirits that inhabit it. She suggests we reflect on a time when we were larger than ourselves, out in nature during a beautiful sunset perhaps, when our consciousness was expanded. She explains the interrelationship between the inner divine and the outside world. "When I put myself in the right attitude—of love, peace and joy—and bring this attitude into all that I do, the information is here. All the answers are right here. If we approach our questions with the right attitude, we will find the right answer. When we need help, we can go inward and reconnect with our inner divinity, that feeling of joy and unconditional love, and see the external situation differently. When one is able to link with the unconditional love of God, everything on the outside changes."[50]

Practically, consider how the media affects your psyche. Experiment with it. Pay attention to how you choose where you want to live. Make choices that feel good to your body and your spirit. Attune to the natural world. Just go sit outside. You don't have to do anything; it doesn't have to be productive time. Simply sit outside and see the richness of life around you. Maybe experiment with some new ways of engaging, like taking a labyrinth walk, or merging with the earth and seeing what the earth has to say to you. Create a sanctuary for yourself and for the land that you inhabit.

There is a unity of life. Remember the divine power of life flows through all of us. We choose how we engage the energy that flows in us, around us, and between us. Allow this time of opening in *your* life to be a time of opening to *all* life. Allow your inner divinity to radiate out. Jesus asked his followers to let their light shine brightly into the world. As you do that, what you will see reflected back at you is the sacred and exquisite light of the divine.

EXERCISES FOR SECTION 3: YOUR ENVIRONMENT

Refer to the *How To Use This Book* section in the *Introduction* if you have questions. Relax your body and clear your mind before you begin, be open to the information you receive, and write down your experiences when you are finished.

Living in the Material World: Assault of the Media

* Experiment with your exposure to the media. Try leaving the television and radio off for a day, or a week. Take some notes about how you feel before starting your "media fast." Pay attention to how you feel during and after that time. Are you more centered and peaceful? How does your body feel?

* Create a ritual to cleanse yourself of the energetic residue that may stick to you after experiencing certain types of media.

Living in the Material World: Choosing Your Environment

* Through quiet meditation, get a sense for your level of field dependence. Are you strongly influenced by what is around you or more self-aligned?

* Take an inventory of the kinds of places (climates, topographies, urban or rural environments, etc.) that feel good to you. Sit quietly and envision yourself in a series of different places. Experience each place with all your senses. Note which help you to harmonize with your environment and which feel irritating.

Creating Sacred Living Space: Your Home

* Talk to your home. Recreate your relationship by listening to what the spirit of your home has to say to you. Simply sit and relax or take a journey to the spirit of your home. Ask if it needs anything from you that you haven't provided. Thank your home for the safety and comfort it provides.

Creating Sacred Living Space: Sanctuaries

* Create a sanctuary. Meditate or journey for advice, or simply begin. Find a space in your home that speaks to you and create sacred space.

Creating Sacred Living Space: Blessing Ceremonies

* Create a blessing ceremony. Design a ritual to bless your home and land. Engage your inner divinity as well as the spirits with which you share space. Work cooperatively to make your living spaces holy.

Nature

* Sit outside and simply observe your natural surroundings. Pay attention to all your physical senses, as well as your inner senses. Simply let yourself *be* in the natural world.

* <u>Connecting with Nature Meditation</u>
  (This meditation is included on the Inner Divinity *companion CD. See the* Resources *section for more information.)*

  Close your eyes. Take a few deep breaths and relax. Imagine yourself in a sunny meadow. The grass is soft and green and sprinkled with wildflowers. Use all your senses to experience this tranquil place. Smell the air, hear the birds singing, watch the clouds drifting by, touch the tips of the grass, and taste a tender clover flower. Pay attention to the physical qualities of this place as well as the energy or life force that fills it. Relax and spend a few minutes soaking up the energy and connecting with the life of the meadow.

  Now, walk to the far side of the meadow and enter the woods you find there. Feel the cool air fill your lungs as you inhale the fresh pine scent. Evergreens tower above your head, the needles making a soft carpet underfoot. Open your heart and your senses to the beauty and wisdom of this forest. Spend a few moments here in peaceful connection.

  Now, walk along the forest path until it opens onto a rocky shore. Hear the rhythmic crashing of the waves and the calls of the gulls. Step carefully over the rocks and onto the sand. Walk slowly along the shore. Feel the cool water lap at your feet and the warm sun shining on your face. Take a few moments and explore this ocean landscape and feel what it is like to be a part of it.

  Now, picture yourself in your own special place in nature, whatever landscape suits you. Relax and soak up the energy in your ideal natural environment.

  When you're ready, take a few deep breaths, bring your awareness back to your body, and open your eyes.

  After you've finished this meditation, reflect on the way these different places in nature affected you.

Nature: Spirits of Nature

* Journey to meet the spirit of the land. You can do this for your own land, or for a place you are drawn to. Clearly state your intention to meet a

101

"helping spirit of the land." Simply meet them at this time and introduce yourself. Make clear your intention to be in harmony with the land.

❋ Find something in nature that appeals to you, a tree or a rock, for example. Sit near it and make a connection. Does it have anything to say to you?

Nature: The Elements

❋ Practice merging with the elements: water, earth, fire, and air. Journey or meditate. Introduce yourself to the element in whatever form comes to you (i.e. a raindrop, a grain of sand, a star, a breeze). See if there is anything the element wants to communicate to you. Be open to ways of communicating other than language. Ask permission to merge with the element. Experience your union with that aspect of nature and yourself.

Nature: Weather

❋ Cloud watch.

❋ Go outside in different weather and simply experience it.

❋ Observe the way your mood may reflect the weather of the day and vice versa.

Nature: Labyrinth

❋ Find a labyrinth in your area to walk.

Web of Life: Flow

❋ Practice sensing the energy of the day and allow yourself to ride it like a tide rather than fighting it.

❋ Pay attention to how you can harmonize yourself with your environment.

SECTION 4: YOUR INTUITION
Tapping Your Inner Knowing

Intuition is "the spontaneous knowing of something that one has no way of consciously knowing."[51] Intuition is a gift and also a birthright. Your intuition can be developed and perfected with intention, training, and practice. Natural talent is important, just as it is in the arts or sciences, but more important than an innate ability is the focus and discipline involved in learning a new skill. The word "intuition" stems from the Latin word *intueri*, which means "to look within."[52] In this section we'll discuss how your inner knowing, what I call sacred intelligence, can help you in all aspects of your life. You will learn how it works and strengthen your own skills. I'll take you step by step in adjusting your life to hear your intuitive voice, in practice exercises for letting information flow through you, and in understanding ways of being that foster or block your intuitive sensing.

You perceive the world through more than just your five physical senses. Listening to your intuition helps you create a satisfying life. Your personal power increases when you understand that you contain all you need to make sound decisions and to face life's challenges. Your sense of peace increases as you come to trust the messages your body and spirit send to you each day. This inner calm grows as you learn to work in partnership with your own spirit, to accept, interpret, and act on the information given to you. As your levels of peace and power increase, so does your happiness. Accessing your intuition helps you get in touch with your deepest dreams. You must take the practical steps to live those dreams, but your inner divinity is a wise guide. Because your essential nature is sacred, you have access to universal sources of information and guidance.

My first formal introduction to the unseen senses came from Karen Webster, a gifted author and teacher. Karen confirmed my budding experiences with my own intuition and taught me how to use intuition effectively. She even predicted that I would become an intuitive consultant. At the time it felt farfetched, but exciting. She helped open a new door through which I could find a life that inspired me.

What do you want out of life? Although each of us has a unique answer to this question—a job working with animals, a house in the country, financial independence—most of us are looking for essentially the same thing. We seek a sense of peace and contentment in our lives; a feeling of balance, a healthy body, mind, and spirit. In order to reach that place of peace you must find your own path, your unique way of seeking and achieving that goal. For example, you may need excitement and change to feel whole and content. Or you may need comfort, stability, and companionship. Our paths are as distinctive as we are. There is no one blueprint to follow to a harmonious and happy life.

Sometimes we fall into the trap of accepting a path that isn't our own in an attempt to find peace. For example, there are many messages in the media today telling us that if we have money, the right car, the right clothes, and are thin and beautiful we will be happy. Some people obtain those things and are still left hungry for a sense of contentment. You must look inward to find your personal path. Fortunately, you have the skills to communicate with your deeper self and discover what you need to be happy. Reconnecting with inner sources of wisdom and with spiritual guidance can help create a healthy life. Since we are spiritual beings as well as physical beings, we need to tend to our energetic or non-physical bodies with as much diligence and care as we devote to our physical bodies. Cultivating your intuition, your ability to sense intangible things, is a great way to nurture your spiritual self. For many people, the intuitive sense has withered from disuse, but fortunately it responds well to a little attention.

In my spiritual healing practice, I've seen many people reconnect with their inner sense of knowing. One woman began to connect on a deep level with her creativity. She realized she needed to change some aspects of her personal life, including her sleeping patterns, in order to allow her writing to flourish. After making those changes, she started writing prolifically. These insights impacted her life significantly, both personally and professionally.

One client recognized she had been trying to fulfill the expectations of her family, especially in her career. She'd concentrated on being a success, was driven to the extreme, and overly focused on her work life. She'd forgotten what her own interests really were and had pushed herself so hard that she developed a stress related illness. That illness was a wake-up call. After doing some intuitive and healing work, she realized she needed to get her life in balance. She took some time off to think about what she truly wanted for her life and considered starting her own business. She is no longer suffering from her illness.

Another young woman felt guilty about the advantages she had in her early life. Guilt was instilled early on by her parents and some zealous religious teaching. As an adult, she chose work that drained her physically and emotionally to the point of exhaustion. She believed she had to give to others at the expense of her own needs to somehow compensate for her good fortune. After getting in better touch with her own intuition and sense of what was healthy for her, she committed to taking time for herself and looking for a new job that didn't drain her so much. She realized she needed to care for herself with as much love and attention as she cared for others.

Having a well-honed intuitive sense can help you find a parking space and it can help you find a life partner. It can help you pick the foods your body needs and it can help you make wise career decisions. According to a Global Intuition Survey, 92 percent of the female executives interviewed said they had experienced a "flash from subconscious levels."[53] Intuition often helps you to tell a good decision from a detrimental one. This ability alone can have a profound impact on your life. Studies have shown that business people who score high on intuitive ability tests tend to make more sound business decisions than low scorers. Likewise, nurses who are the best in their field have been found to apply their intuitive instincts as well as their clinical knowledge to patient care.[54]

Being intuitive doesn't make you infallible, but it gives you another skill set to apply to living connected to your divine nature. Have you ever looked back on a choice with regret and realized you ignored a gut feeling that was a warning at the time? Developing your intuition is learning to pay attention to yourself and your surroundings in a new way, learning to sense with your gut and listen with your heart. Intuition is primarily about two things for me. It is practical and useful in everyday life, and it is also recognition of my inner divinity and the spiritual dimensions of my life. I can explain how intuition works for me, but it won't really sink in and be meaningful to you until you experience it.

Everyone has an intuitive sense and uses it to varying degrees. It is like a muscle—it develops the more you use it and focus on it. When ignored it will atrophy, but it is very receptive to a little attention and practice. Intuition does not always increase steadily and incrementally. There is no guarantee that if you do X, Y, and Z you will have clear intuition. The process differs for everyone and often works in confusing, sporadic ways. Fortunately, there are many ways to heighten your intuition, so you can pick from a wide variety of techniques. If the desire and effort are there, you can improve your intuitive abilities.

The way intuition feels is difficult to explain. It involves using senses that we don't have adequate words to describe. Intuition is sticking your hand into the unknown. Often you can't see, but can only feel. Information comes to each of us in different ways. Not only do we have to create a new way of perceiving, but also a new way to integrate those perceptions into our everyday lives. Delving into the innate power of your own intuition may be a new realm, a foreign place that is mysterious and maybe a little daunting. It may feel like a long lost home to which you've been yearning to return. In this section I'll give you specific suggestions to help you experience the way your inner divinity expresses itself through your intuition. Author Lou Austin describes how we can access universal information. He refers to his divine connection as "Partner." "The important thing that I learned in the beginning was that my Partner could speak to me, if only I got quiet enough to listen. Years later I came across the Biblical promise: 'Behold I stand at the door and knock. If a man hears my voice and opens the door, I will come into him …'"[55]

ACCESSING YOUR INTUITION

"Most people search high and wide for the keys to success. If they only knew, the key to their dreams lies within." George Washington Carver

There are some basic practices that help you connect to your intuition. Your sacred intelligence develops as you use it. Your intuitive sense, like any other sense, can be heightened through discipline. The steps I list here are not necessarily the only ones that will benefit you. They are a good place to start building a foundation for the growing structure of your intuitive abilities.

Silence

Silence is a healing balm for your senses. It cleanses your mind and washes your energetic body. Simply adding time in your day to be silent can bring about deep shifts in your consciousness. Periods of silence are practiced in all faiths. Silence strengthens our bond with the divine, simply and serenely. We can hear our own inner voices more clearly when external noises are minimized.

Make time in your day. Find a quiet place. Turn off the phone. In order to have a dialogue with your intuition, you need to clear a place. Most of us live hectic lives. Your senses are inundated with information, from television and radio, other people and places. You are constantly filtering energy, information, and emotions through your systems. It is easy to be overwhelmed with this level of stimuli. Sometimes you feel it as a mental sensation, intellectual overload. Your brain calls a time out. Words become hard to find, and clear thinking eludes you. Sometimes you feel it emotionally, as sadness, anger, or fear. Your emotions go a little haywire and you get weepy or anxious for no ascertainable reason, cranky at the slightest provocation. Sometimes it actually manifests physically. Your body has had enough and "talks back" in the only way it knows how. You develop headaches or stomachaches, high blood pressure, or muscle tension. To protect ourselves we often try to shut parts of ourselves off, sometimes intentionally, and sometimes subconsciously. We become a little numb. But when we become numb to the outside world, we often become numb to our inside world, as well. Silence reconnects us to both.

In order to allow your intuition a chance to be heard, you need to give yourself a time and place to be silent. Rarely is your intuition going to scream loud enough to be heard above the din of daily life. As you develop your intuition and learn to recognize its voice, you can distinguish it more easily from the other information you perceive. However, especially in the beginning, you need to give it that peaceful place in your life. It needs to be respected and given your complete attention, even if only for five minutes. Silence creates the space where communication from your higher self can be heard.

Meditation

A client recently asked me if I thought it was important to meditate. I told him that I did, but I define meditation pretty loosely. You don't have to spend an hour a day in the lotus position to gain the benefits of meditation. The main premise of my advice to meditate is not based on achieving enlightenment or another end goal, but to help you live more connected to your life, your body, your breath, in each moment of the day. If you're able to take a five minute walk on your lunch break and devote your attention to your breath and your feet touching the earth, that is your meditation. If you're able to find ten minutes of silence after you step out of the shower and before the kids find you, great. Meditate as often as you can, in whatever form you can manage. Meditation is a time to shift your attention inward and still your thoughts. It is more beneficial to integrate short periods of time into your day than to try for longer periods that are unrealistic. Be honest with yourself about what you can do, and then have the discipline to do it.

The important thing is to create the time and the silence to connect to your deeper self. As much as possible, try to still your thoughts. Slow your internal dialog. Not thinking is exceptionally difficult; be gentle with yourself. If you're meditating and you realize you have been thinking about your bills or plans for the weekend, don't worry about it. Gently still your thoughts, bringing your mind back to center.

I describe a variety of meditations in the exercise section at the end of this chapter. One form is mindfulness meditation, which involves watching your thoughts without engaging them. This can be helpful in learning about your inherent tendencies, fears, and biases. Ironically, paying attention to your thoughts allows you to gain a level of freedom from them. Another form is concentration meditation, paying attention to an object in your mind's eye with your eyes closed, or a material object with your eyes open. You simply maintain your attention on that object and exclude everything else from your field of thought. Another choice is to center on one of the chakras. For example, the third eye meditation, where you hold your attention on the space between and slightly above your eyebrows, is helpful in opening your intuitive senses. You can focus on all of your chakras in turn, moving from the root chakra at the base of your spine and ending with your crown chakra at the top of your head. Yet another way is to focus on relaxing your body, moving from your toes to your head and relaxing each part of your body completely. Or simply be still. Most importantly, just make the time and don't get frustrated. By cultivating the ability to bring your mind to a quiet place, you are making room for intuitive information to be heard when you ask for it. Meditation helps break thought patterns and puts you in a receptive state of awareness. Let your meditation practice take any form you want. If you haven't meditated before, experiment with different methods to see what suits you.

A symbol can provide an entranceway to your intuition. A visual or sensory guide can act as a portal. As you close your eyes and seek intuitive guidance, try visualizing something to step through. It's reminiscent of shamanic journeying where you are transported into the spirit worlds through a tunnel in the earth or an opening in the sky. We are creatures of habit and can be easily trained. Triggers help you enter certain states of consciousness quickly. Pick an image that works for you, such as your favorite tree, a beautiful circle of light, or some other image that comes to you when you ask for it. When you are meditating, or seeking intuitive guidance, visualize your portal symbol. Over time you will become attuned to that portal image and be connected quickly to your source of intuitive guidance. If you enjoy art, try drawing or painting the portal image. Your portal can be a sound or a tune. Shamans use song extensively to shift their consciousness to perceive the spirit world. Your portal might be a movement, or a smell that you conjure. Experiment until you find something that works for you. Using a portal can rapidly put you into a receptive state, shedding the cloak of your everyday life and shifting your consciousness to perceive the intangible. Earlier, I mentioned that my office acts as a trigger for me. More specifically, I'm transported when I imagine a hollow bone or a black velvet field, smell lavender, or hear a drumbeat. One symbol I also relate to is an image of a solar eclipse. It visually conveys the idea of emerging, birthing from the void, tapping the universal power.

Intention

Intention is power. Author Denise Linn says, "Where intention goes, energy flows."[56] What is your intention for connecting to your intuition? Think about it, and understand your motivations, so your intentions can be clear. Then you will bring focus and power to your intuitive practice.

Clearly formulate your intention and ask. Usually, you have to ask to receive. Stating the intention that you are welcoming intuition and higher sources of guidance into your life is incredibly powerful. Say it silently, say it out loud. Repeat it daily. Ask for something—clarity, guidance, information—whatever you truly want by increasing your intuition. Start by using one of the techniques explained later in this section. Ask and then let go and be open to what you receive. In whatever style suits you, ask for the connection to your intuition. Intuition is a tool to access universal information.

I typically set an intention for my work, whether with clients or for myself. I close my eyes and take a few deep breaths. I relax into my space and focus on the work I'm about to do. I ask that the work is for the highest good. I invite guides and spirit teachers of the light who are willing to play a part in bringing healing into the world to participate.

Be clear and specific about the energies to which you wish to connect. Don't just ask to connect to "a spirit." Use some of the techniques from *Section 3: Your Environment* to create a blessing ritual to use. Your intention regarding safety and creating a sacred space in which to work is as important as your intentions regarding what you want to receive from connecting to your intuitive knowledge.

Observation

Engage all your senses and just pay attention. Stilling your body and your thoughts and perceiving from a place of stillness is key to "hearing" what your intuition conveys to you and to "seeing" the visions of your shaman's eyes. Learn to be passive for a few moments. Many of us are used to taking charge, processing information quickly, judging it, and acting on it. There is great value in simply observing and then waiting a while to do the processing. Let yourself digest the information you receive. Reserve judgment. You may receive guidance you don't believe. That's okay. Don't close down. Take in all the information you can, record it, and distill it. Don't judge your experiences while they are happening. Decide later how you feel about them. Be a sensory sponge for a little while, and just accept what comes to you.

We often have trouble accepting intuitive information. Usually information begins to flow quickly, and just as quickly we begin to rationalize it away. We don't trust ourselves. We think we're making things up or deluding ourselves in some way. It is a challenge simply to receive, to accept what comes at first without allowing your left-brain, rational side to intervene. Observation without judgment at this stage is important.

You do not need to share this information with anyone. Especially if you're in the early stages of learning to trust your intuitive sense, I recommend you exercise caution in sharing your insights. It is hard enough not to judge yourself at this stage, so be particularly careful about sharing this type of experience with people who may judge it harshly. The judgment of others, particularly people who are close to you, can freeze your budding intuition. If possible, find someone you trust who is open-minded with whom you can share. Or find a group of people who are exploring intuition too. It is helpful to have support in the process of connecting to your sacred intelligence.

Trust

Believe in yourself. You *are* intuitive. Trust that you can receive wisdom from your higher self and from God. Expect that guidance. Trust your voice and acknowledge intuition as a sense, like any of the five physical senses, which can be used to perceive things more clearly. Author and psychic Sonia Choquette says there are four important things to tell your subconscious mind: you are open to psychic guidance, you expect psychic guidance, you will trust psychic guidance, and you will act on psychic guidance.[57]

Sometimes people deny the validity of their intuitive or mystical experiences. I've known people who have very clear psychic visions who brush them off by saying "I'm not psychic," as if having a vision or getting a piece of information intuitively was out of the realm of possibility for them. Intuition is not a gift bestowed only upon a few people, but an innate ability. You have the right to hone your intuitive skills as much as possible. You contain the spark of divine knowledge. You don't stop using your muscles because you are not an athlete. You don't stop singing in the shower because you're not performing at Carnegie Hall. Let's demystify intuitive experiences, bringing them into the realm of ordinary life. Intuitive perceptions can be unusual, and certainly clear intuition is a gift, as an athletic body or a beautiful voice is a gift, but intuition is available to us all. It's important to accept intuition as a natural part of yourself, a sense you can use and develop as much as any other.

Of course it is helpful if, in addition to trusting your voice, you also pay attention to it. I recently had an incident where my inner voice spoke loudly. I heard it, thanked it, and then immediately forgot it. I had my checkbook in my hand along with several other things, a pile of papers for recycling, something for the trash, etc. As I walked about twenty feet from my office to the kitchen, my inner voice boomed, "Don't throw your checkbook in the trash!" I noted it and went about my business. I wasn't about to throw my checkbook in the trash! Of course, the next day I couldn't find my checkbook. I remembered hearing the voice so I wasn't particularly worried because, obviously, I had been careful not to throw it in the trash with the other papers, right? Wrong. I looked around for a while and then decided to check the trash, which had already gone outside to the big can. It was in the trash! I couldn't believe it. I'd been told, I'd heard, and I thought I'd heeded the warning.

How does your intuition speak to you? The booming voice is infrequent for me. In my daily life, more often it's a subtle feeling. A whisper, "Take the umbrella." or "Don't wear your favorite shirt because you will spill blueberry juice on it." I'm beyond feeling smug when I listen and the voice is right, but always kick myself when I don't pay attention. Expect that intuitive insights are available to you, and when they come, act on them. When you act on your hunches and are correct, your skill is reinforced and your confidence builds. You listen more carefully and therefore hear more clearly the next time. As with any skill, the more you use it with good results, the more faith you have in your abilities, and the more proficient you become.

Also remember to trust your abilities in general. What you believe about yourself affects what happens to you. If you believe you are capable of running five miles, even if you can't now, it will fuel you to do the work necessary to reach that goal. If you believe you can *never* run five miles, you will have no reason or will to try. Intuition is similar. It takes work, but the work pays off. There is an element of faith at play. For me, there are two aspects to receiving information: the first is having confidence in myself and my abilities, and the second is letting go and having faith in God, the universe, my spirit guides, or whatever divine source is helping me. I trust I'm capable and *also* that I'm receiving a tremendous amount of help and couldn't do what I do without it. It's an integrated partnership.

Patience

In the words of Veruka Salt as she fell down the bad egg shoot in the movie *Willy Wonka and the Chocolate Factory*, "I want it now!" We all want it now. We want everything now. Expect your intuition to evolve and grow, but don't expect it to happen in a bolt of lightning. Don't rush the process. Do your inner work, be disciplined in your personal spiritual practices and be gentle with yourself. Let this process unfold in a natural way. Don't hinder the flow of energy by getting caught up in impatience, doubt, or judgment. Know that all is as it should be. You have what you need now, and will develop what you need in the future. Enjoy the process of exploration and the small pleasures of each moment of discovery. Breathe and stay present.

Also remember that you may get non-specific information. This may be helpful and frustrating at the same time. I can think of two instances lately where my mom (who is my partner in much of this work, and a gifted intuitive and healer) had an uneasy feeling the day before something happened in my family. They weren't momentous things, fortunately; one was a minor car accident and one was a problem with a contractor. The day before each of these events she had a sense of uneasiness. She didn't know exactly what it was about, other than she knew it was about two trips and two locations. She had an inkling that it was about a visit to this contractor and a visit home to Connecticut, but she wasn't sure exactly what it was going to be. That information helped her prepare psychologically for a challenge. It allowed her to stay centered, but it didn't allow her to do anything to change the situation.

Writing it Down

Buy yourself a notebook and write it all down: your intentions, your meditation experiences, your intuitive "ah-ha" moments, your state of mind, your dreams, the synchronicities of your life. Don't hold back or wait until later. Write things down as soon as possible after they happen. Sometimes you get amazing information that makes perfect sense when you are experiencing it, but when you look back on it, it doesn't make sense anymore. Dreams can be like this. Conversely, sometimes you'll get strange messages that you can't figure out while they are happening, but they make sense afterwards. This often happens with premonitions or when the material you received was a metaphor for your conscious mind to untangle. It is important to write your experiences down right away, so they don't fade into the mist. Looking back at your notebook can provide you with a key to your intuitive code—the way your intuitive voice communicates with you.

Intuition often works in symbols and images. Over time, you may develop a symbol dictionary of sorts. If you consistently find that when you get a tingle in your left knee something wonderful is about to happen, you can learn to expect it. If seeing a spider in a meditation heralds a complicated situation, you can prepare yourself. Your symbolic system is unique. Archetypal symbols that are part of our collective unconscious can appear in your personal dreams and visions, but look first to your instinctual impressions rather than to a generic book to interpret your experiences.

Years ago I had a series of dreams about losing my shoes. After I had documented these dreams for a while, I realized that shoes represented my life's path, big choices I had to make about who I wanted to be and what I wanted to do. Thereafter, when I dreamed about forgetting or losing my shoes, or having a mismatched pair or only one, I knew I had to examine choices that affected my life in a big way.

When I work with clients, I always ask them to let me know if something I describe doesn't make sense. Usually I'm seeing a symbol and can then translate metaphorically instead of literally. Sometimes intuition speaks in strange voices. Sometimes it's funny. Sometimes it's formal. Sometimes it sounds just like your own voice. Write it all down, no matter how weird or stupid or embarrassing it may seem to you. Keep track of the content and of the nuances associated with your experiences.

TYPES OF INTUITION

"Intuition isn't mystical. It's a sort of background sense of how things should work; it's facts hidden in the brain." Dr. James D. Watson

Intuition manifests uniquely for each person, tailored to our personal energetics, body states, and levels of receptivity. It gets through to us as it can. According to Dr. Mona Lisa Schultz, the brain is the "chief interpreter and processor of intuition." She describes the right hemisphere as controlling the image based, non-verbal, macro-level processing that allows the intuitive spark to ignite. The left hemisphere provides the translation, allowing us to convert images and symbols into language we can understand intellectually. The temporal lobe is the main highway for auditory and visual data, as well as for dreams and memories.[58] Given that we each have a distinct pattern of brain functioning and a unique balance of left and right brain dominance, our intuitive strengths manifest differently. Or from a non-scientific perspective, God just made us differently. Recently, I asked my daughter where she got her nose. I was joking, because her nose doesn't look like her father's or mine. She told me that the earth made her nose that way. However we come to be who we are, we are distinctly individual in the way we experience the world. Our senses are developed to differing levels and our thought patterns are as unique as our fingerprints. One style of receiving instinctual information isn't better than another. It is simply helpful to be aware of some different ways that it might manifest for you.

Clairsentience

Clairsentience is a sense of knowing through physical sensation without logical data to back it up. It may be felt as a tickling sensation or the hair on the back of your neck standing up. When you perceive clairsentiently, your body is receiving energetic signals for you to interpret. It is a somatic translation of intuitive information. We are all familiar with "gut feelings." When you experience a hunch as a gut feeling, you are picking up information as a clairsentient. Clairsentients will often develop a key to their sensory readings. For example, your heart races for no discernible reason when danger is present, you suddenly get cold when a fight is about to ensue, or your eye twitches when someone is not telling you the truth. Over time you learn to correlate your sensations with the information they represent.

Pay attention to the way your body feels as you are working intuitively. If you have unusual sensations or a certain feeling in your body, it may be an indicator of what kind of information you are getting, or if you are receiving accurate information. I get a tingling feeling, almost like the hair on the back of my neck standing up, or goose bumps up my spine, either when there is a discarnate spirit present that wants to convey information to or through me, or when I have something really important to tell someone. Sometimes I get that shivery feeling and sometimes I don't. It is an indication to me that I am touching on something important. For you it might be an itch on your cheek, or a sensation in your stomach. Pay attention to your body.

Your body can be a very good indicator about how you feel about a decision you're going to make. Practice sitting down, getting calm and centered, and telling yourself something that you know is absolutely true and see how your body feels physically and take note of it. Then tell yourself something that is absolutely false and see how your body feels. You can use that as a gauge. When you're unsure of a decision, if you've practiced this "true-false" method, when you sit down and say "I want this job," or "I'm going to move to Chicago," or "I can trust so and so," or whatever you're trying to get information about, your body can help you with some physical sensation that you have learned to associate with a positive/negative, true/false response.

Clairvoyance

Clairvoyance is perceiving intuitive messages as images or visions. It may be precognitive, tapping into the events of the future, or it may concern the past. Edgar Cayce, one of the most famous medical intuitives, was clairvoyant. Our society is highly visual. Many people have subconsciously developed their visual sense more than their other senses, so clairvoyance is often easier for people to accept than some of the other ways of working intuitively. When I see clients I will often see them in a future state that represents health on all levels. I recently saw a woman who has an office job outside in a garden in the sun with her arms all dirty wearing a big straw hat. It turned out that she loved to garden and had been craving more time outside where she felt a deep sense of peace and happiness. This inner sight may contain literal or symbolic information, so be aware that even though you see a very clear image, it may represent something quite different in ordinary reality.

Clairaudience

Clairaudience is receiving information through your sense of hearing. Sometimes the voices or sounds seem to be coming from inside, and sometimes they seem to be external. Of course many psychotics hear voices. A difference that cannot be overlooked between psychosis and intuitive receptivity is staying balanced, healthy, and clear on who you are and what you are doing, keeping your realities straight. Shamans do this all the time. They enter non-ordinary reality through journeying, but are able to navigate back to ordinary reality and can function in both. A psychotic can't tell the difference. Joan of Arc was probably the most famous clairaudient. She heard the voices of saints from an early age.

Inner Knowing

A sense of inner knowing is my most developed intuitive sense. When asked a question, I simply "know" something. It can be combined with some visuals, or sometimes words form in my mind. This is a common form of intuition, the simple knowledge of the truth of something without any data to back it up. Sometimes this manifests behind the scenes. It can be subtler than other intuitive communication. My clients will sometimes say, "How did you know that?" and I won't have a concrete answer, I just knew.

As someone with inner knowing, you may go through life without really being aware that you are intuitive. Inner knowing can feel like your thoughts. For this reason, if inner knowing is your strongest sense, make sure to work to distinguish your thoughts and emotions from intuitive transmissions. See if messages repeat over time. Consciously center yourself with your breath and ask for clear intuitive information to compare. Sometimes you will find yourself just knowing what to do or say.

Sometimes we can't be sure how information is picked up. During lunch one day my daughter said, "Mom, can we go to the museum today?" I asked, "What museum?" We do have one in town, but she's never specifically asked to go and we hadn't been in a long time. I said that we weren't going that day. Five minutes later a friend's mom called and invited us to go to the museum. We did go to the museum that day after all. This may have been inner knowing, or telepathy between my daughter and her friend.

Telepathy

Telepathy is the transference of information directly from person to person without speech or body language. It can happen over long distances. We've all heard stories of when people knew their child was in trouble, or felt the need to call a friend, only to discover the person had been thinking of them strongly, calling them psychically. This happens with my mom and a good friend sometimes. I'll call one of them, only to get voice mail because she is calling me at the same time. Myron Eshowsky, a shaman and faculty member of the Foundation for Shamanic

Studies, describes how when he's teaching he often hears people speaking to him before they actually ask their question.

As my daughter's sixth birthday approached, many details about her presents and party were running through my mind. One day, I was brushing my teeth and she was getting herself ready too. I was planning my day silently, thinking that I'd wrap her presents while she was at a play date that afternoon. I never watch television in the daytime and decided I'd see if Oprah was on while I wrapped. I like Oprah but very rarely have the opportunity to watch her show, and certainly have never mentioned her to my daughter. After a few seconds my daughter said, "O … Oprah." I spun around and asked, "What did you say?" She replied, "Oprah." "What is that?" I asked. "I don't know," she replied. This was one of the clearest instances of telepathy I've experienced. It was direct transmission from one person to another, when no conversation was taking place and the person receiving the information had no idea what she was picking up on. It also gave me shivers. I know my daughter is intuitive, but having her read my thoughts was a little unnerving!

METHODS FOR WORKING INTUITIVELY

"Trust yourself. You know more than you think you do." Dr. Benjamin Spock

Working intuitively involves opening your energy. It is helpful if you have done some of the practice exercises from *Section 1: Your Self* that deal with opening and closing your energetic field. When asking to receive information, open your energy outward. When you're finished, bring your energy back in, sealing the integrity of your energy body. There are many ways to work intuitively. You will likely find you're good at some and not as good at others. I have definite preferences for the way I work, although I also like to experiment. The methods I list here are suggestions only, not a definitive list.

Learning how to "read" is about tapping your sacred intelligence, opening your connection to universal sources of information, and getting out of the way. You can read via any object. I can get information about your love life by looking at your navel, or at the lint on the carpet. I can do it, not because I'm brilliant, but because the tool you use to read is not important; it's a way for you to distract your conscious mind. Tools can help you concentrate and focus. Information is intangible and humans often need something tangible to focus on.

Practice different ways of receiving information and see what method is strongest for you. Do you feel things in your body? Are you reminded of other things that contain relevant information to which you make analogies? If you get stuck, switch the method you are using. You can use your imagination; it is an excellent tool to let information flow. Remember the typical ways people perceive intuitively: clairsentience, clairaudience, clairvoyance, inner knowing, and telepathy. Use these ways to remember your options, but don't limit yourself to them.

Setting a Blessing Intention

Bless the work that you do. Set an intention. How you craft the words of that intention is entirely up to you; however, I think it is a good idea to include some specifics about what kinds of spiritual assistance you are looking for, and what you hope to achieve with the work. Here is a sample blessing that I use before I start working:

> I know I am safe and protected in this space.
> I ask that spirits of the light who wish to join me to bring about healing, harmony, and joy do so at this time.
> I ask that my work is for the highest good.

I will typically smudge my workspace, as well. Here is one intention I use frequently:

> Thank you, spirits, for helping to create a sanctuary in this space.
> I bless this room, knowing it is a safe place for healing to take place.
> May this space foster peace and balance.

Frequently I will use shamanic rituals. I will "rattle in the spirits," facing each of the four directions (east, south, west, and north), the sky, and the earth in turn. I will honor the spirits of those directions and ask them for help. I acknowledge the presence of my personal helping spirits, ancestral and descendant spirits, and the spirits living on the land I am working on.

Create some blessing rituals that feel right to you. They can be very simple, as you see from my examples. The important part is to create a base of sacred energy from which to work. The power of your ritual is in your intention, not the mechanics. Use your intention to align your inner divinity with the divine forces of the universe.

Intuitive Readings

When I work intuitively, I sit for a moment, state my blessing intention, and wait for a sense of flow up my spine. That sensation is my cue that I'm prepared to receive information from a non-physical source. Once I'm ready, I ask a question and then clear my mind. I prefer working without tools. For me, intuitive information tends to flow like a conversation. Sometimes I receive direct messages, words, or sentences that appear verbatim in my consciousness. Often I sense a dynamic or a mood and need to translate the essence I feel into language I can understand.

Periodically, I write down the information I receive, or make a tape to review later. I avoid predictions. The future is a fluid place. I prefer to focus on how I can best create the future I want, rather than making pronouncements about what will and will not happen. If you've created a portal image for yourself, it can be helpful to use it before starting, or to refocus during a session. Simply let the guidance flow.

There are some good ways to practice receiving intuitive information that don't involve personal questions about you. These methods can be used to receive information for someone else, but in this case I'm suggesting them as ways to practice receiving information without the emotional attachment we feel when asking questions about our own lives. These methods should only be used with the person's permission. Ask a friend to give you a name of someone they know. Make sure the person is willing to be a guinea pig for your intuitive explorations. Knowing nothing but a name, sit, get centered, and write down all that comes to you. You can confer with your friend later to see where you received accurate information. You can also use photos for this exercise. Gaze at a photograph and let yourself sink into a state of receptivity. Delve past the superficial details of the person and their surroundings. Open yourself to feel what you can about them.

Psychometry

Objects are often imprinted with information. The energy of the owner can be present. The object can provide a gateway to getting information. Even owners long past can leave their mark on an object, allowing an intuitive person to get a glimpse of them. The more important an object was to a person, the stronger the energy held there. Some intuitives like to hold a piece of their client's jewelry when doing a reading. You can experiment with this in a similar fashion to the name and photo readings. Find a partner who will lend you an object, maybe something belonging to a relative or friend. Simply sit holding the object, center yourself with some deep breathing, and listen to what the object speaks to you.

Automatic Writing and Drawing

Automatic writing and drawing are two good ways to tap into your creative and intuitive self. Automatic writing can work in a couple of different ways. Sometimes the pen will actually be moved by your subconscious, feeling like it is being pushed or pulled. This is quite rare. Usually it feels more like a stream of consciousness exercise, where you write or draw whatever comes into your head. The difference between automatic writing and stream of consciousness work is that with automatic writing, you are trying to cleanse your mind of conscious thought. It's helpful to do some deep breathing to center yourself before you start. Clear a quiet place to work. Often I will light a candle. Relax and write or draw whatever comes to you. For me it usually feels as if things just pop into my thoughts; a word, sentences, color, shapes, concepts, or images. Do not edit. If you hear or see nonsense words or images that don't make sense to you—put them down anyway. If the words sound like your own voice, that's okay. The tone varies from person to person and it may vary from session to session. Let it flow and don't hold back. If you feel blocked, just start writing or drawing anything—lists of words or shapes or letters—just don't fixate on *not* writing or drawing. It's easy, and you can't make a mistake if you relax and let it happen. The abstract expressionist artist Mark Rothko employed this technique for his paintings. He asserted that "art is of the spirit" and often employed "psychic automatism" as he allowed the brush to move paint instinctually on the canvas without conscious interference.[59]

The reason for trying both the writing and the drawing is that one is language based and one is image based. Experiment with how information comes through to you. It may be easier for you to open to colors, shapes, and pictures, or it may be easier to receive words. Both are good ways to receive information, literally and symbolically. Practice and see which speaks to you more.

Dreams

Your dream state is a fertile place to reap intuitive information. Some people are naturally gifted in this area and find that they remember their dreams and use them in their daily lives. Dreams may be precognitive, showing you something likely to happen in the future. They may help you decipher your choices in the present by showing you different scenarios. They may help you in your work. Billy Joel said many of his songs come to him first in his dreams. Dreams may communicate in personal codes and symbols. A friend of mine has a snake dream every time there is someone in her life who is untrustworthy. She's learned to pay close attention to those dreams, and apply what they are conveying to her waking life. Paying attention to your dreams and writing them down is a vehicle for accessing your sacred intelligence.

Dreams have historically fascinated us with their unbound sense of possibilities and richness of experiences. Ancient civilizations placed great credence in the messages delivered through dreams. Rulers often had dream interpreters whom they would consult to unravel the symbolism of their nightly journeys. These dream interpreters advised them on the status of their futures and the soundness of their decisions. Ancient Greeks journeyed to the temple of Aesculapius at Epidaurus, where healing dreams were sought that revealed cures for diseases. These and other ancient cultures believed that the gods visited them during the dream state, providing access to the spirit world in ways unavailable in ordinary consciousness.

Some of our egoic security systems are on high and our inner voices need to search around until they find an opening through which to speak to us. Dreams often provide that gap in security. During our waking hours we're often so focused on physical and intellectual sensing that intuitive sensing is ignored. Ironically, your brain is actually more engaged, more "awake," when you are asleep. When awake, only about 10 percent of the brain is firing in a given moment; while sleeping it lights up completely.[60] We all dream each night, even if we don't remember the dreams upon waking.

Sigmund Freud made dream interpretation famous. He tended to interpret dreams as relating to sexuality or other primitive drives. When you start decoding the symbolism of your own dreams, pay attention to recurring themes and images. Often these are the messages most pressing for you to understand at a given time. Dreams can work in puns and metaphors. Don't take everything literally. Once I had a dream of wandering around a city. I asked an unseen presence where I was. The answer that boomed down was "Providence." I can be a little dense, but that one I understood when I woke up. It wasn't about the physical town of Providence, it was about the state of divine synchronicity, or providence, that I was experiencing at that time.

Other dreams are clear, literal glimpses of something yet to be. I had a dream once many years ago that I was very sick in a blue room. It was a distinctive blue. A few months later I traveled to Europe. We went to Nice, Monaco, and Paris. Nice was lovely. Monaco was lavish and Paris was ... well, I can't tell you how Paris was at that time because I spent three or four days desperately ill in my hotel room. It was a lovely blue.

You may already feel a strong connection to your dreaming self. If you aren't engaged in a dialogue with the dream world at this time, you can begin one. Start going to bed with the intention of waking up after a dream is over so you can record it. If you find that too exhausting, or disturbing to a partner, intend that you will remember the most important dreams when you wake up in the morning. Keep a notebook and pen by your bed. It is amazing how quickly dreams vanish. Once our conscious mind takes over and the demands of the day come to the fore, memories of dreams, even those that seemed important at the time, dissolve quickly and often irretrievably. By writing them down, you can tap back into the energy of a dream and even revisit it sometimes.

Lucid dreaming is a method of even more deliberately engaging the dream world for information. Lucid dreaming involves becoming aware that you are dreaming while still inside the dream. Don Juan, the shaman in Carlos Castaneda's books, advised Carlos to look down at his hands while dreaming to develop the ability to dream consciously. Sometimes lucid dreams happen spontaneously and sometimes they occur when you seek them out. Experiment with your dream life as a way to tap into the rich sources of information contained in your inner divinity. Your connection to the sacred realm is strong and direct through dreaming, when your intuitive senses are unfettered with the limited consciousness of daily life.

Connecting to Your Inner Guide

Discerning a direct connection to the divine being within you can help you feel supported and guided. I call this source the inner guide. It doesn't matter whether we call it an inner guide, our higher self, a spirit, or an angel. For now, we're working on making contact with a wise and loving source who is willing to share useful information with us. Some people perceive their inner guide as a presence in human form, some see it as an animal, some hear words, and some sense it simply as a presence.

In order to work with your inner guide, you need to welcome it into your life. Ask for its help. Make lifestyle changes if necessary in order to show you are serious and willing to do your own inner work. This path—the path of perceiving more clearly, of living more fully connected to spirit—is not always an easy one. It has some of the most effortless and blissful moments, but it requires work, some of it practical, like making space and being disciplined, and some of it internal, like changing attitudes and fears. When you're willing to work and put out the message that you're ready to accept help and welcome the help of guides, that help will become available to you. It may not present itself in the way you expect. In the exercises at the end of the section I've included a guided visualization to assist you in making contact with your inner guide. Try to engage all your senses during this exercise. Look, listen, smell, and feel. Also engage your extrasensory perception. Feel through your gut and through your heart; don't limit your experience only to senses that you have words for. It is often very difficult to describe intuitive experiences because we lack adequate language to describe intangible experience and knowing.

ENCOURAGING AND DISCOURAGING YOUR INTUITIVE SENSE

"The intuitive mind is a sacred gift and the rational mind is a faithful servant. We have created a society that honors the servant and has forgotten the gift." Albert Einstein

The way you approach life and the nature of your internal dialogue are the field from which your intuitive sense grows and develops. Your attitudes, thoughts, and beliefs encourage or discourage the development of your intuitive sense. The following are some guidelines to help you become aware of which internal ways of being foster your sacred intelligence and which disable it.

Blocks to Intuition

Giving away your power. Believing in an external authority which holds all the answers can block your intuition. You have the ability to connect directly to the power of the divine and sources of universal information. If you place your faith in another human being, or system, to determine what truth is, you have hobbled your intuitive horse. Religious doctrine can sometimes create a sense of powerlessness and distance from the source. You can certainly be intuitive and religious, but maintain a level of independent thought, faith, and confidence in yourself and your connection to truth. Wise advice from others can be helpful, but you don't always need an intermediary to translate for you.

Egoism. Although we hate to admit it, and often aren't even aware of it, most of us are very attached to our egos. It is human nature to want to be right and to be accepted. We like to hold ourselves in high esteem. When you let your ego have too much power over you, you can become opinionated and arrogant. This creates psychic rigidity and distances you from the sources of your intuitive wisdom. Don't take yourself too seriously and don't worry too much about what others think of you.

Intellectual hyperactivity. When you are unable to shift out of a logical left-brain mode of thinking, you suppress your intuitive voice, which operates from a fundamentally different place. Still your mind through meditation. Practice new ways of perceiving and processing information, for example, "see" a situation with your heart. Instead of using only hard-line reasoning to analyze your life, be flexible in your thinking and you won't stifle your intuition.

Doubt. Stop second-guessing yourself. A certain amount of self-monitoring is valuable. Check your motivations, keep on top of your responsibilities, and do what you say you are going to do. Once you've done those things, move forward with confidence. Do the best you can in each moment and be flexible enough to adjust, then you can move through life with poise and self-assurance.

Judgment. When you judge others harshly, you disconnect from the divine source, which loves and accepts all beings. Being judgmental is not the same as holding strong opinions. Being judgmental is believing in your superiority. Often we are judgmental about trivial things, the way someone talks or wears their hair. Perhaps you define others by their level of education or their weight. Catch yourself, and counteract that distancing energy with one of acceptance, knowing that we are all connected.

Chaos. When you are disorganized and in a rush, fleeting intuitive communication tends to get lost in the shuffle. Order brings serenity for some of us. I feel at odds when my surroundings are in disarray. You don't need to color code your sock drawer or arrange your CDs alphabetically to have order, but when you can't keep appointments straight, or find your W2s, or you need to search through a pile of clothes to find your favorite blouse at the bottom, your energy is distracted. Some people thrive on a little chaos. If you don't, or if you are uncertain, get the mechanics of your life organized, so your energy goes into something other than frantic searches and last minute crises. Find the level of order that feels harmonious to you. If it is more annoying to you to keep a filing system than it is to search through towering stacks of paper, that's okay. Be aware of how chaos affects your life and your ability to tap into the calm place where intuitive insights originate.

Tunnel vision. Our opinions, attitudes, and beliefs are shaped as we grow up. We all have biases and filters through which we view the world and other people. Many of us are not aware of them. If you believe your worldview is the only correct worldview, you are limiting your ability to tap into truth and wisdom from universal sources. The depth of your insights is limited because the information flowing through you has to go through so many filters. What makes its way into your conscious mind has been changed to fit your belief system. This happens to some extent even when we are aware of it, but awareness is the key. Be open to new perspectives and opinions and your intuitive sense will open as well.

Fossilized memories. Memory serves you well in many ways, but can hinder you in receiving intuitive information. One of the main barriers to hearing and interpreting intuitive information is the inability to live in the moment. We tend to run information, particularly non-logical information, through the database of our memory. Have I tried this before? Did someone react badly when I did this? Was I hurt by doing, saying, or feeling this? In many ways it is a valid process. We learn from experience. If a child burns her hand by grabbing a pot from the stove, the odds are she won't do it again. The problem is not remembering and learning from past experiences; the problem is getting stuck in the past, viewing everything through the tainted lens of the past. Release your past. Take what you need from the moments preceding this one and move forward.

Drama. Emotions are a natural and important part of our human experience; however, going to the extremes of emotional experience on a regular basis isn't helpful. Allow yourself to experience your emotions, but do not let them rule you. Life has enough drama; there is no need to create more. The highly charged energy of intense emotions can easily pull you off center and out of earshot of your intuitive voices.

Support for Intuition

Many supports for intuition reflect back to what we discussed in *Section 1: Your Self.* When you create a healthy relationship with yourself, you foster a well-developed intuitive sense. When you are living in harmony with your divine nature, you are naturally more attuned to your instinctual abilities.

Listening and Responding. Believe you have access to what you need and trust the information you receive. Listen to what your intuitive voice says. I saw a client recently who was debating about whether to take a trip or not. She had initially been excited about the trip, but for various reasons she had lost her enthusiasm. Her heart was saying, "I really don't want to do this." Intellectually she was questioning her change of mind and doubting her motivations. I told her to give herself permission to listen to what she truly wanted. She said, "Thank you. Those are exactly the words I needed to hear." She needed to give herself permission to do what she instinctively wanted. This happens often. We get into an internal struggle between our intellect and our intuition. The mental voice can be so loud that the quiet voice gets drowned out. If your inner voice is consistently telling you something, even if it's soft or subtle, pay attention to it.

Detachment. Take a few steps back to gain perspective. We are naturally invested in our lives and the outcome of our decisions. We are so surrounded by our circumstances that detachment is a challenge. Let go of your attachments to particular outcomes and life can flow more freely. Be committed to the process, not your expectations, and see what happens. Sometimes the most unpredictable scenarios are the most helpful and fulfilling. When you are so focused on what you want that you can't see what is available, you are limiting your opportunities.

Love. When you accept who you are, you can step aside from your ego and your personality. When all your focus is on yourself and what you need to do or change to be acceptable, you become self-centered. It is hard to be self-centered and develop a high level of intuition. When you filter intuitive information through a screen of self-hatred and disapproval, you receive tainted information. Be loving. Start with yourself.

Silence. Silence allows your intuition to be heard. Stillness creates space for you to notice your fleeting intuitive impressions. Silence is a salve for your senses and a key to recognizing your own intuitive voice.

Clearing your mind. Actively clearing your mind so you can passively receive guidance supports your intuition. Practice turning away from external stimuli to a quiet inward focus. Use the portal image from earlier in this section to help you turn from the outside world to the inside world. Practice meditation to still your mind for progressively longer periods of time.

Staying centered. Apply the balancing and grounding exercises from *Section 1: Your Self.* Much of preparing yourself to be a good intuitive is in preparing yourself to be an emotionally, psychically, and spiritually healthy person. Use your breath to bring calmness into your body. Use the earth as a partner in keeping your energy harmonious. When you are centered, your instinctual intelligence can work without dodging the energetic land mines that surface when you are hyped up or spaced out.

Staying in the moment. Intuition is based in the present. We all think about the past and the future at times; however, your attention needs to be in the present to pick up intuitive information. Things can change from one moment to the next.

If you are oblivious to the present, obsessing about the past, or worrying about the future, you aren't living as connected to your sacred intelligence as you can be.

Imagination. Many respected scientists have recognized the value of imagination and intuition. Albert Einstein's famous quote "Imagination is more important than knowledge," reflects the idea that flexible thinking, and a balance or communication between the left and right brain, helps advance us, as individuals and as a society. It is not solely technical knowledge that leads to scientific breakthroughs, but imaginative thought, as well. Pythagoras, Jonas Salk, and Thomas Edison are among important scientists and inventors who cite intuition as a valuable tool in their work.[61] Knowledge is important, but the ability to push the borders of convention, to question accepted theories of reality and to delve deep within to tap our highest human potential stems from accepting imagination as a vital partner.

ETHICS

"The first step in the evolution of ethics is a sense of solidarity with other human beings." Albert Schweitzer

There are ethical issues when working intuitively. These guidelines apply to living your life as an intuitive person, as well as getting intuitive information from other people. Intuitive ethics are clear in a number of ways. You should not attempt to get intuitive information about other people without their permission. Don't become an intuitive voyeur. It's akin to reading someone else's mail, diary, or medical records. It is an invasion of privacy. I make exceptions for situations that directly impact me, such as tuning in on whether I feel safe leaving my child with a particular babysitter, or if my mechanic is telling me the truth. I don't then try to get other information about that person just out of curiosity.

Invading someone's privacy, finding other people's weaknesses, gaining advantage over someone thorough knowledge, and letting your ego dictate your decisions are a few examples of clear boundary violations. There are also shades and nuances in working ethically. During intuitive consultations, clients often have questions about their relationships. People want information about those who are close to them. Here's the guideline I follow: if the information I can provide about another person is directly related to my client and will help them to understand and manage that relationship better, then I'm willing to provide it. If my client simply wants to know what her husband is thinking or wants a prediction about someone else's life, I'm not going to seek that information. My practice is not about uncovering people's secrets.

Occasionally, without soliciting it, you may receive very personal information about the person standing next to you at the bus stop. Information may come to you spontaneously in fleeting glimpses from a stranger on the street. What you do with that information is your choice and responsibility, but usually it is inappropriate to tell them. Imagine how upset you'd be if a stranger came up to you and said, "Oh by the way, I think your husband is having an affair," or "Better get your brakes checked," or "Have you been to your doctor lately?" Typically I counsel silence when dealing with strangers unless strongly guided otherwise. Check with your heart and check with your spirit guides and do what feels right to you.

One of my first intuitive experiences occurred when I was a teenager and attending church. I was drawn to a man sitting in the section in front of me. For the whole mass it was as if I couldn't see or hear anything else. I was receiving intuitive information from him. There were very few details, just an overwhelming feeling of emotional pain. I felt his suffering and I felt helpless. I didn't get any information that I thought would help him. I sensed his pain had something to do with his daughter, but mostly it was just an overwhelming emotion that I experienced in my body. I wanted to rush over and give him a hug and tell him everything would be all right. It was confusing for me at the time. I recall almost feeling guilty for not coming forward to help him, or at least acknowledge his suffering; however, it would have been inappropriate to do that there. Part of learning to use your intuition responsibly is learning when to step in and when to step back.

People frequently misunderstand the intuitive sense. When I tell someone what I do, sometimes a strange look comes over their face as they wonder if I can read their mind. Other people try to get me to do so, like a parlor game. Intuitive people are not all knowing. If you go to someone for a reading who claims they can tell you everything, all the time, with 100 percent accuracy, walk out the door. We have access to different information at different times. Being intuitive is collecting data in new ways, not being right all the time. Once a woman approached me at a Health and Healing Expo. I had just scheduled an appointment for a man in my office at a later date. She felt compelled to tell me that she thought I was in danger seeing him. I didn't get a bad feeling from him, but I took her warning seriously. My husband arranged to be home during the time of the appointment. I brought an intercom upstairs so that I could call for help. We had a productive and peaceful session and the man became a long-term client. The woman did what she needed to do. I respected her for that and I was glad she was wrong.

Know your motivation when receiving intuitive information. Keep any information you receive from someone else confidential, particularly when intuition is involved. This rule should apply to all personal conversations. Unfortunately, I find that it often does not.

CLOSING

"What lies behind us and what lies before us are small matters compared to what lies within us." Oliver Wendell Holmes

Your sacred intelligence is the key to accessing all the information that you *should* be able to know now. You can tap that help and guidance, because it is in you. You simply need to remember how to retrieve it.

You won't go wrong if you make your best decision in the moment, based on what you perceive with your inner senses. It doesn't mean things will always turn out the way you planned. Be flexible when thinking about intuitive information. Pay attention to the way your body feels when you pose a question. Be honest. Open yourself to help from the universe, the spirit world, and nature. I don't know what will happen in my life in exact detail. Sometimes I've been blindsided, but frequently I've been prepared.

Have faith in your intuition. Being in touch with your instinctual sense is potentially the most empowering thing you can do for yourself, because it applies to everything you do. It doesn't mean you won't be confused, surprised, or simply wrong sometimes; however, the more you listen to and trust your intuition, the stronger it will become, and ultimately the happier you will be.

Many of us look to outside sources for love, acceptance, and direction, and for validation of our beauty, intelligence, and competence. Instead, look inward to create your life and then let it unfold in outward reality. Choose what you want to wear, not what a fashion magazine tells you to wear. Choose a profession that's interesting to you, not because your mother told you what you were most suited to. Have friends who make you feel good when you are around them, instead of friends you think are the most popular or useful in some way. Follow the voice of your intuition and it will lead you to a life of peace, power, and happiness.

EXERCISES FOR SECTION 4: YOUR INTUITION

Refer to the *How To Use This Book* section in the *Introduction* if you have questions. Relax your body and clear your mind before you begin, be open to the information you receive, and write down your experiences when you are finished.

Steps for Accessing Your Intuition: Silence

  ✳ Third Eye Meditation
   During this meditation, focus on your third eye or sixth chakra. After getting into a comfortable and relaxed state, clear your mind and focus on the place between and slightly above your eyebrows. If any thoughts come up, gently push them away and return your awareness to the space on your forehead.

  ✳ Concentration Meditation
   During this meditation, focus on an object or internal image. Choose an internal image to focus on: a specific place on your body, a quartz crystal, or a spiral, or pick an external physical object. Relax and let all of your concentration focus on the object that you choose. When your mind wanders, gently bring your attention back to that object.

  ✳ Mindfulness Meditation
   Mindfulness is simply observing your thoughts and emotions with detachment, letting them be what they are. Don't judge or engage your thoughts, simply make a note "I feel angry," or "I feel sad." It is like watching yourself in a movie, except you are watching the movements of your mind, instead of your body.

   The goal is still to have a calm mind and peaceful heart, to be in a receptive state. In the concentration meditation, you pushed your thoughts aside; but in this meditation pay attention to your thoughts, note them, but do not become consumed by them. Keep an objective viewpoint as if you are watching something that is not you.

Methods for Working Intuitively

  ✳ Reading of person only by their name

  ✳ Reading of photos

  ✳ Psychometry: object reading

✳ <u>Automatic Drawing</u>
Sit quietly for a moment, clear your mind and wait. Set the intention that you are open to any communication from God, your guide, or your creative source. There is no right or wrong. Don't force anything; just relax as much as possible. Don't think of something to draw beforehand; don't worry if you can't draw a straight line. This is not drafting, it's feeling color and shape as communication from your inner divinity. Let yourself be guided, free from expectation.

✳ <u>Automatic Writing</u>
Begin the same as with the automatic drawing exercise, by clearing your mind and setting an intention. If any words come to you, write them down; if your hand starts moving, let it go. Do not judge or edit what you are getting. Just write down what comes.

✳ <u>Connecting to Your Inner Guide</u>
(This meditation is included on the Inner Divinity *companion CD. See the* Resources *section for more information.)*

Close your eyes. Picture yourself on a beautiful sunny beach. Take several deep breaths, inhaling the salty, clean air. You're walking slowly along the edge of the water. The sun is warm and the breezes are gently caressing your skin. The cool water rushes over your toes and your feet sink a little into the warm sand. As you walk along you see a path that veers off the beach and up a hill. Take this path. Walk along the path a short way until you get to a cloudy place. It's a light misty fog that is cooling and soothing to walk through. As you pass through it, the air clears again.

You hear the surf pounding in the background as you keep walking along the path. Walk along the path until you see a house in front of you. Go up to the door and go inside. It is your home. Not necessarily the home you live in now, but your spiritual home, a place where you feel truly at home, truly safe and comfortable. Spend several minutes looking around, exploring this place. Look around and take it all in. If there is an upstairs, go up and explore the rooms; if there is a basement, go down and take a look if you want. Just explore, and remember to ask your inner guide to visit you.

As you're looking around, there is a knock on the door. It's someone you have invited to be with you. Someone you've been waiting for for a long time. Make your way to the door. As you reach to open the door, sense the presence behind it. Feel the positive, supportive energy and love radiating from this being. Open the door. This is your inner guide, come to help you receive the guidance and wisdom you need in this life. Invite your guide into your home. Ask if there is anything you should know now. Take a few moments to receive an answer and just experience being with your guide.

When you are ready, say good-bye and thank you to your guide. Get ready to return to the beach. Trace your steps back down the path, and through the cloudy place. Follow the path back down to the beach. Walk back along the beach in the direction that you came from. Feel the sun on your face again and the warm sand under your feet. Take several deep breaths and when you're ready, bring your attention back to your body and open your eyes.

✳   Dreams
As you go to bed at night, set an intention. It may be to receive an answer to a question, to experience a lucid dream, or simply to remember your dreams when you wake up. Keep a dream journal by your bedside.

SECTION 5: YOUR SPIRITUAL SUPPORT

Building Your Spiritual Foundation

Your spiritual support is a well from which you nourish your soul, and a foundation upon which you build your ideal life. Spiritual support encompasses the many ways we seek solace and connection. It is finding a safe haven for your spiritual self. You can find support within yourself and all around you. Spiritual support can come from a connection with another person, someone who relates to you as you need during a spiritual crisis. There are also celestial beings, nature spirits, ancestral spirits, and other spirit helpers who offer their compassion and support when called upon.

The problem is not that we lack spiritual guidance, but that we often feel disconnected from it. We cannot be disconnected from our god-source, as we all originate from the same creative life force. Unfortunately, many of us have accepted a belief system that doesn't serve us. Shamans say we are dreaming the wrong dream. We are dreaming a life of separateness from the spirit world, the natural world, and each other. This illusion of separation is at the root of major problems in modern society. Our disconnection from our environment has led to the destruction of the very elements that sustain us.

The web of life includes humans, spirits, and the natural world. In many cases, we've elevated our individual needs above the needs of the collective well-being of this planet. That has caused a rift between human beings and the environment, and also within us as individuals. Often we feel isolated, not just from other groups of people, but also from ourselves. Many of us live disconnected from what we feel and who we are. Seeking out different types of spiritual support helps us reconnect to our true natures.

There is a world of support available to you, which you may be unused to sensing. Make the first move. Reach out to the spirit world around you. Spiritual assistance appears in many different forms, often in the unexpected. Your image of how spiritual assistance looks may get in the way of perceiving that assistance when it actually appears. I recommend you enter this process without preconceived notions or expectations for a particular outcome or experience. Be patient and receptive and see what happens. As you open your mind and your heart to the spirits, the veil between the spirit world and your everyday world is lifted. When you invite Spirit into your life, Spirit makes itself known and supports you.

You don't need to have a particular belief system or use specific terminology to try the exercises in this chapter. You just need a willingness to consider the mysteries of the world. Remember what I said in the introduction: I'll use different terminology when referring to Spirit, such as God, angels, universal life force, power animal, or spirit guide. Please substitute any word that feels right to you.

WHAT IS GOD?

"They say that God is everywhere, and yet we always think of Him as somewhat of a recluse." Emily Dickinson

What is God to you? Do you believe in a universal source of life? Do you accept the existence of helping spirits? There is no right answer. There are as many ways to celebrate your spiritual life as there are definitions of God. Give some thought to your sources of spiritual support. There is no definitive method, no right way, or only way. Consider your own definition of God (or the lack of God). Do you see God as peaceful or vengeful? Is God interested in and knowledgeable about you personally, or is God removed from the activities of individuals? Does God intervene in the course of history, or does God watch from a distance? Is God's existence a creation of the human need for hope or a universal fact? One of the main premises of this book is that God resides within you, a divine spark connecting you to the greatest spiritual force in the universe. Although many of the major religions describe this idea in their sacred texts, they also refer to God as an external being, a sentient, omnipotent source that is distinctly separate from the human race. Does God exist within us, outside us, or both? Stay in a receptive state of mind and see where those contemplations take you. Add some questions of your own. The goal is not to come up with a definitive answer, but to allow the mystery of the questions into your everyday life.

I have great faith in human beings. We are capable of creating beyond our expectations, of loving beyond reason, of fulfilling all we are meant to in our lifetimes. We can witness miracles. We can see the results of prayer manifesting in our lives. We can sometimes see or hear spiritual beings. However, I'm not convinced we have the capacity of mind and spirit to comprehend God fully and completely. For this reason, I work to keep an open mind when trying to define God for myself. My personal goal is to have an awareness of God in my life, whether it manifests as spirit helpers, uncanny synchronicities, intense feelings of love, or the awesome natural world. My definition of, and relationship to, God has evolved over time, and will continue to evolve in the future. We love to wrap up the loose ends, creating neat little packages for what we believe. Then we stop thinking. It is not easy to engage the world fully all the time. It can be tiring to consider new ideas and adjust your beliefs on a regular basis. Just as we limit our relationships when we define our loved ones and expect them to remain static and predictable characters in our lives, we limit our relationship with the spiritual world when we label it and file it away. It can even be dangerous to stop thinking about God, to settle on a definition and cling to it.

As you live your life and learn from others, you may discover that you hold a few pieces to a vast puzzle that is the map of the spiritual world. Allow God, or Spirit, into your life and into your mind. I encourage you to draft a working definition of what God or Spirit means to you. Be cautious about convincing yourself that you are right. Let your thinking evolve over time.

American poet John Godfrey Saxe based a poem on a story from India about six blind men trying to describe an elephant. Each one touched a different part and described it to his friends, sure he had the answer to what an elephant really is. The first man touches the side of the elephant and deduces it is like a wall. The next feels the tusk and likens the elephant to a spear. The third holds the trunk and describes it as a snake. Feeling the leg, the fourth pronounces the elephant to be like a tree. The fifth man touches the ear and decides the elephant is like a fan. And the sixth holds the tail and proclaims it is like a rope. Each man had his own opinion of the true nature of the elephant, but it was based on their very limited perspectives. They were all correct in their descriptions of what they perceived, but ultimately fell short of providing an accurate definition of an elephant.

The blind men's search to understand the essence of an elephant is a metaphor for our own search for God. It is paradoxical to hold specific beliefs and remain open to new ones, to see something and simultaneously accept that it may not be the complete picture. The essential nature of the spiritual world may be elusive to us, but we should engage and explore it to our full capacity anyway.

You experience the world through the filter of your beliefs. Once you settle on a set of viewpoints and rule out all others, you limit how you perceive the world around you. There is a Taoist expression, "The Tao that can be spoken is not the ultimate Tao." Pema Chödrön cautions, "As soon as you begin to believe in something you can no longer see anything else. The truth you believe in and cling to makes you unable to hear anything new."[62] Don't limit your experience in this world. There are vast possibilities and potentials available to you, if you are available to them.

When you think about something too much it often becomes elusive. Have you ever seen a bright star at night out of the corner of your eye, but then when you turn to look at it straight on you can't find it? The area of the eye that covers peripheral vision is more light sensitive. You can often see more light and dark contrast when you look out of the corner of your eye, than you can with the more color-sensitive parts of your eye that are engaged when looking straight ahead. You need to discern what kind of "vision" is best suited to your task. If you're looking for hard, concrete facts, maybe head-on is the best approach. When you're searching for something elusive, glittering, and mysterious, maybe a subtler and gentler vision will yield better results. Respect its ephemeral beauty as you seek it. Accept that all is not knowable in the intellectual sense. Even as your mind fails to find proof, your soul can find peace, basking in the twinkling starlight of the divine. Diane Schoemperlen says "… the opposite of knowledge may not be ignorance but mystery; … the opposite of truth may not be lies but something else again: a revelation so deeply imbedded in the thin places of reality that we cannot see it for looking: a reverence so clear and quiet and perfect that we have not yet begun to fathom it."[63]

SOURCES OF SPIRITUAL SUPPORT

"If we could see the miracle of a single flower clearly, our whole life would change."
Buddha

Internal Sources

Your spiritual support can come from internal sources, external sources, or from a combination of both. Internally, you can develop ways of being that allow you to shift your perspective and connect with your higher self, or a broader state of consciousness. If you have developed the ability to transcend your ego somewhat, you're more likely to be able to rely on your instincts and intuition to guide you wisely through times of spiritual crisis. You can sustain yourself in a way that would be unavailable had you not been practicing that shift. That shift from an egoic state, from being completely immersed in your body, intellect, and emotions, to a state where you're able to step aside from those things temporarily, allows you to perceive your life, yourself, and the world around you from a different and often illuminating viewpoint.

Sound and vibration can help you snap out of your ego temporarily. Tone or sing a power song to disengage from the physical and summon spiritual power. Experiment with singing and toning with abandon and see if you can achieve a state of distance from your usual internal dialogue. I am not a gifted singer, but have found moments of deep connection by singing or chanting.

Your "higher self" is another aspect of internal spiritual support. Many people believe that each individual has a higher self, a complex being that encompasses your individual spirit. You are able to shift your consciousness to make contact with that expanded level of your self, which is typically too subtle to perceive as you go about daily living. By reaching out to that outer level of yourself, you can tap into guidance to help you stay on the healthiest course. See the end of this section for a meditation to help you connect with your higher self.

Faith is an internal way of being that can brace you in times when you need something to lean on. Faith is an underlying field of support, a place that holds your latent possibilities and opportunities. Its nourishing soil, combined with your careful tending, helps the seeds of those potentials to spring forth into reality. Faith is an intangible conviction in something; it might be in the balanced ordering of the universe, the power of love, your own abilities, or any combination of other beliefs. Your faith may simply be in humanity or in nature itself. Your happiness may even be influenced by your faith. Various surveys have shown that a strong sense of faith positively affects people's self-reported levels of happiness. An article called "A Road to Happiness" in *Psychology Today* cites a survey showing that one of the factors in achieving happiness is "a faith that entails communal support, purpose, self-acceptance, outward focus, and hope."[64] Faith need not be in a particular religion, but some form of faith is at the heart of all spiritual practice.

External Sources

In some ways the distinction between "internal" and "external" structures of support is a matter of semantics. Spiritual energy is all around us. God, or whatever word you use instead of God, conveys that there is something more to this world than the physical. Spiritual support can take many external forms: a religious or spiritual community, a structure of practice, going to a church, temple, or mosque, or a pattern of prayer, to name a few. A routine of spiritual practice, be it meditation, shamanic journeying, chanting, or attending services, can provide a foundation from which you can grow and feel nourished in your spirituality. External spiritual support can also come from individuals, either from a spiritual context (clergy or other spiritual counselors) or from people around you everyday (friends or family).

There is a traditional Irish custom of having a "soul friend" when engaging in a personal spiritual pursuit. A soul friend is a person you can turn to during the process of your spiritual development, someone who respects your journey, listens to your challenges and joys, and provides advice.[65] A soul friend is a safe source of spiritual support and is as likely to be your neighbor as a monk or a nun. In my life, the support of friends and family has been invaluable. My mother in particular has played the role of a soul friend. Of course, she will always be my mother first and foremost, but she has the flexibility and perspective to honor who I am as an adult and support me on many different levels as I travel my spiritual path.

In some aspects, organized religion is a beautiful system. A functional safety net has been set up so that there is someone dedicated and available to hear you when you need to be heard. However, since all of us contain the divine within, you don't need to limit your support to people who have made spirituality the focus of their professions. You may be fortunate enough to have someone in your life who will allow you the freedom to be who you are, someone to act as a sounding board and support for you when you need them, regardless of what your beliefs are. That person may be trained in counseling, or may have a natural ability for providing this type of support. Tap whatever resource is available that feels comfortable.

Service

Service to others is a significant aspect of many of the great religions. Jesus taught his followers to care for others in need, regardless of their station in life, as they would care for him directly. Buddhists extol peaceful coexistence and serve their communities through non-violence and respect for all creatures. Shamans traditionally work for the greater good by stepping out of their personal needs and working on behalf of the planet and all its creatures. In her teachings, Sandra Ingerman places great emphasis on working with the helping spirits to "be of service." For example, instead of asking for something you think would be helpful, ask the spirits, "What can I do to be of service now?" That intention allows cooperation with the spirits, who often have a greater understanding of the highest good than we do.

It is important to be in service to other people on some level, to be an active part of a community whether it is a physical community, or the energetic community of humans, animals, and other beings on this planet. Many modern spiritual philosophers, including Ken Wilbur and Ram Dass, believe that to genuinely reach a state of enlightenment, we must have compassion and a willingness to serve others.[66] Giving of oneself sets up a healthy dynamic on many levels. It gives you an opportunity to come out of yourself. Any chance you have to step away from your ego, even for a brief time, can yield remarkable results. Volunteering, or working for someone else purely for their benefit, can actually serve you, by helping you put aside your worries and persona temporarily. The power behind any action you take in your life lies in your intention. Serve for its own sake, rather than for spiritual extra credit. Service doesn't work like chips at a poker table. You are the only one playing this game. Don't worry about the potential winnings, just immerse yourself in the game.

Is it possible to serve God as you are serving yourself? I believe that if God has an intention for us, it is for us to fulfill our purpose, to be passionate about our lives, and to be happy. I'm not talking about perfection, having everything you think you want. I'm talking about a sense of peacefulness and happiness that comes from feeling in alignment with your true nature. Even the Dalai Lama says, "The purpose of our lives is to be happy." In many ways serving yourself can be very much in alignment with serving God. Not selfishness, indulging yourself at the expense of others, but connecting with your true wishes and who you really are, and then doing the best you can to express that uniqueness.

You may find that one of your deepest ways of expressing your spirituality is in taking care of children, for example. When you are in the act of caring for children, there are obviously mental and physical components; it engages your mind and your body as you communicate on their level and take care of their physical needs. However, there may be something about the relationship you have with children, a natural ability to perceive their needs, or create a safe haven for them, which transcends what you are doing physically, and takes you to a new place spiritually. It may feed you in the same way that going to church can. It may plug you in to the creative force of the universe and your own inner divinity in the same way that praying can. Be open to finding unique ways to serve that light you up. Those things may become part of your spiritual practice.

To make your greatest contribution, be in contact with your inner divinity. Allow your sacred intelligence to guide you and help with your decision-making. That is how you can be of service to God and your fellow beings. At the same time, it provides a sense of purpose and serenity in your life. When I put out the intention that my will and the will of God are the same, I am stating that I wish for what God wishes for me, that I will accept what is most in harmony with my higher purpose or what Spirit intends for me. In that willingness to cooperate, I find peace.

Everything has balance on some level in the universe. The interplay between giving and receiving is no exception. We must learn to do both. Many of us wish and pray for things: material things, emotional states, and situations. By giving, you can set up the dynamic to receive as well. Remember that you are as worthy of receiving as those you are willing to serve. You must honor and care for yourself, and that includes knowing you are deserving of happiness and joy in this lifetime. Open yourself to an abundance of kindness and care as you share those things with others. Allow the natural flow of the universe to bless you with its abundance and let it flow out from you with grace and generosity.

Creativity

You may find that one of the most fulfilling ways of expressing your spirituality is in singing, writing, dancing, or painting. Creative activity is one of the most enjoyable ways to tap into the power of the universe. When you are engaged in creating, you can lose the layers of yourself that don't serve you and connect more directly with your inner divinity. You may already have a creative outlet in your life that serves this function, or you may enjoy experimenting and finding new methods to generate spiritual energy. Don't worry about producing anything, but revel in the process. Expand your definition of creativity. Focus on "creating." It can be your life or your relationships that take most of your creative energy. You can create a garden or a mood. Creativity doesn't need to be expressed only through the arts.

Your spiritual support is what feeds you. When you sing, if your body, mind, and spirit go to another level and you expand and feel joy, exultation, and a unity with all beings, then singing might be a central element of your spiritual support.

Michael Harner, the president of the Foundation for Shamanic Studies, relates the story of Aua, an Eskimo-Iglulik shaman, who stepped into his true calling after a revelatory experience involving song. Aua had waited a long time to feel his power rise up. One day he felt that power. He said, "I felt a great and inexplicable joy, a joy so powerful that I could not restrain it, but had to break into song, a mighty song, with only room for the one word: joy, joy!" [67]

Artists have historically made the connection between divine energy and creative pursuits. Visual artist Piet Mondrian said, "The position of the artist is humble. He is essentially a channel." Painter Jackson Pollock said that his paintings had a life of their own and he was simply trying to let them come through. There is often a sense that artists are allowing some vital force to work through them. I've felt this sensation at times with my own art, the awareness that I'm opening myself as a conduit for color and shape to form on canvas, or for clay to take shape in space. From early in my life I felt most drawn to visual art. In retrospect, I believe it was a spiritual outlet for me. At times it became unsatisfying when I was creating to please a teacher, working with materials that didn't speak to me, or comparing myself to others. But when I engaged it as a prayer or meditation, I traveled deeply both inside and outside of myself. Now I work intentionally to infuse my art with healing energy. I feel I'm serving both myself as I paint and others who may experience the energy emanating from the paintings.

Nature

Perhaps you feel most connected to your inner divinity in nature. If Spirit is indeed all around us, if God has created the world we live in, then isn't it good and valid to honor God through God's creations, to honor Spirit through the amazing generative and curative power of the natural world that it created? By making relationships with the elements of nature and with the spirit world in its natural form, you create a network for yourself that can support you in all aspects of your life. It's like a network with human beings. Lawyers network with other lawyers. They send each other clients, or consult on cases. Physicians have other doctors they trust, and to whom they send patients. It is the same for just about any profession or avocation; if you network in your community, you will connect with people who will recommend you, or do you a favor. This type of community is a nexus for relating to others. It works in the spirit realm too. As in the physical world, it's up to you to create that network and nurture the relationships. Then you can reap the benefits of those relationships.

In shamanic cultures throughout the ages, people forged relationships with, and accepted support from, the natural world. In *Section 3: Your Environment* we talked about the living essence of everything around you. In shamanic cultures, developing relationships with specific spirits of nature, the trees on your land, the wind, or the sun, was very important. The nature of those relationships, whether they were maintained and cared for or ignored, was believed to set the tone for whether or not the natural environment supported the community. The Koyukon people of Alaska believe that the forest, and the other elements of nature, have eyes and monitor human activity closely.[68]

Some of these relationships come from interaction with specific spirits of nature and the subsequent cultivation of those relationships. Others are a more spontaneous, free-form union with nature. The natural world is one of my greatest sources of spiritual solace. I've had sublime experiences just taking a walk. Some years ago I took the following notes after a woods walk.

> I've just returned from a walk on the yellow trail at Capon Springs. We've had several rainy days in the midst of a rainy season. The woods are dripping. The moss is emerald and the beings on the rocks (maybe lichen?) grow larger and meatier than I've ever seen them. The birdsongs overlay each other in trilling harmonies. The brooks are so full that waterfalls have formed all through the woods, as water flows lushly through established and rarely used beds. The sound of falling water is everywhere, cleansing my soul.

I often sense the unity of all life most exquisitely through forays into nature. I begin to feel more comfortable with myself as I feel the nurturing energy of the natural world around me. Here is another passage of mine from a walk many years ago.

> Insects hummed circles around my head, flirting with my eyes and biting my throat. Cicadas vibrated in the tall maples of the thick, buzzing forest, their winged symphony slowly drowning out the smooth gurgling of the Capon Brook, as the forest closed around me. The path was narrow and rocky. Loose shale made for tenuous footing and sharp rocks pressed uncomfortably under my feet, bending my soles to their geologic geometry. Midday sunlight, thickened by haze, coated the leafy canopy and drizzled to the forest floor pooling—illuminating fallen leaves the colors of native skins, bright orange fungus on dead branches, spirals of green lichen on mottled rocks, and glistening spiders' webs.

Watching my boots alternating in their awkward movements I seemed out of place—my pace too urgent and purposeful to blend in the forest's graceful ease. My body, stiff from stress and disuse, sought an illusive union with the earth to bring me into her balance. Continuing along the path, smearing black bug bodies on my sweaty calves and waving my arms frantically in front of my face to ward off the insects, I felt the forest watching. I was a blundering, strangely colored creature, but she watched without analysis or scorn.

I paused for a rustling, assumed it to be a deer, lovely, but common, and almost kept to my tuneless march. But the movement seemed too quick and scattered to be a deer, so I squatted still on a rock at the edge of the trail. Three fox kits trotted through the crackling leaves, golden rust and gray. They blended perfectly with the forest floor. Only their buoyant play exposed their separateness. Mosquitoes feasted on my blood as I watched them flow together and apart, pouncing and cleaning themselves, engaged in their environment, and without fear as only the very young can be. I lost sight of them in the distance and returned to the trail. A loud, sharp barking stopped me cold and I walked quickly in the other direction. Turning back I saw the mother fox's silhouette, close through the underbrush as she repeated her warning. I stayed a moment listening to her deep raspy call, then stepped surely back on course, my soles now molding comfortably to the relief of the earth beneath my feet.

What struck me about this piece when I came across it after so many years was that I was still seeking spiritual union with the earth. I hadn't been introduced to shamanism, or even learned to develop my intuition formally, but I craved that union and felt it in my body. I was stiff and awkward at the start of the walk and practically merged with the forest by the end. For me, this is an example of how we hold this ancient connection within us always. We know how to commune with nature on all levels. We need to remember it, unearthing it from the deepest levels of our psyches, rather than learning it afresh.

You may come across places in nature that feel different to you somehow. You may become more peaceful when you enter, or maybe more alert. There are places on the earth where the membrane between the spirit worlds and physical worlds is thin. Treat these places with reverence. Ask permission and use your intuition to ascertain if it is appropriate for you to stay and/or to return. If you feel confident that you are not trespassing, you may wish to revisit these spots as a source of spiritual energy.

It is not always possible to be out in idyllic natural settings. For whatever reason, you may find a meditation helpful, instead of, or in addition to, a walk. One way to glean spiritual support from the world around you is to use your imagination to create a garden for yourself. This personal Eden is a place of peace, power, and happiness for you, and can take any form you can imagine. Create yourself a natural sanctuary. Start with a series of meditations or journeys and develop it over time. The place may evolve and change. You may simply feel it, an energetic place that doesn't have a visual counterpart for you. You may perceive it visually or tactilely, learning the crevices of the rock wall, the curving shape of the flowers, or the slippery feel of the silk sheets draped over the chaise lounge. Who said it can't be a decadent garden? Feather this nest with whatever instills a sense of comfort, serenity, and safety in you. Create for yourself a strong imaginal Eden, a haven for your deepest self, a cradle for your inner divinity. This is a place where you can go to be absolutely safe and comfortable in your own skin. You can create this place through a meditation or through your imagination. See the exercise at the end of the section for a guided visualization to connect to this place.

Whatever practices work for you, make them part of your life. Everything you do is a spiritual practice of sorts. Every moment you are working or playing or having a conversation, you have an opportunity to act from your spiritual core and express your inner divinity. I'm not talking about proselytizing or talking overtly about spirituality. I'm talking about being the light, being the person you wish to be. Don't relegate your spiritual engagement to a specific time or place. Unleash your spiritual awareness and expression in your everyday life and give it free rein. See how this incorporation of your spiritual life with your everyday life will feel natural and right. The distinction is an illusion anyway.

PRAYER

"He who prays searches not only his own heart but plunges deep into the heart of the whole world." Thomas Merton

Prayer is perhaps the most ubiquitous way of connecting to the divine and seeking spiritual support. All faiths include some aspect of prayer, communication with God, or the creative life forces embodied in nature. For example, early aboriginal cultures prayed to the gods of weather to bring favorable conditions for their crops and hunting expeditions, Jews pray to God to bring the Messiah to the earth, Catholics ask the Virgin Mary to pray for their souls in this life and at the time of their death, the Baha'is, among others, pray for peace. Dr. Ron Roth, a former Catholic priest, teacher, healer, and mystic, asserts that "authentic" prayer has three fundamental elements. The first is what he terms the "Spirit of Wholeness," the voice within us that comes from our inner divine being. While praying, we must listen to our inner voices at least as much as we talk. The second aspect is faith. For Roth, faith is acknowledging that the divine resides within us, rather than having faith in a particular church or dogma. The third component is the original definition of prayer. In Sanskrit and Aramaic the word "prayer" is non-existent. The closest we can come to it is *pal al*, a Sanskrit word meaning "seeing yourself as wondrously made."[69] In all three of Roth's requirements for genuine prayer, he comes back to the underlying principles of inner divinity. To pray effectively, recognize that you embody the Holy Spirit, listen to the voice of that spirit as you pray, and know that you are of God, not separate from God.

Many types of prayer are practiced around the world. Petition is probably the most prevalent form. Prayers of petition involve asking for something you do not have. You make a request from a place of want, essentially saying, "God, please give me X," or "Please allow X to happen." When we ask for safe travels for our loved ones, or for a speedy recovery for a sick friend, or for a new car, we are petitioning. Prayers of petition often come from our most basic place of yearning. We perceive that there is something we lack, and ask God to give us what we want. This style of prayer has been used for millennia. In ancient times, when religious groups sacrificed animals they were often bartering with the spirits. "I'll give this to you, if in return you give me something, or protect me from something." When shamans journey, they are often pleading with the spirits to provide healing and assistance for their patients. When Christians ask God in the Lord's Prayer to "forgive us our trespasses," they are petitioning the Lord. However, petitioning potentially distances you from your experience of the divine. In contrast, there is another way to manifest your dreams from a place of gratitude and partnership with the divine.

Decree is another method of praying that puts the present time in a more favorable light, giving you more power in each moment. Praying through decree is essentially connecting with your inner divinity and calling forth the power of your creative fire to bring something into existence. In the Book of Job there is the statement, "Thou shalt decree a thing and it shall come to pass."[70] For prayer to be truly powerful, let your feelings well up and open yourself to the spark of the divine within you. Let yourself experience what you are decreeing with all of your being and all your senses. Prayer through decree is about offering your gratitude and praying from the standpoint that something has already happened. Instead of saying, "Oh God, please give me your support." you might phrase it, "Thank you, God, I know you are supporting me always in your light and love." Then let yourself feel that light and love with every cell. We've discussed the power of language and the way words affect your reality. By speaking with the divine from a state of abundance and gratitude rather than lack and despair, you are more likely to experience your life as abundant. When you are in a state of grace, filled with divine energy, and you state something, you are evoking it as truth. You are calling it into being by stating it as fact, rather than fantasy.

Intercessory prayer is when you're praying on behalf of someone else who is sick, dying, grieving, or in need. For example, "Oh Lord, please take care of Jane, allow her to get well." Or, in the style of decree, "Oh Lord, thank you for taking care of Jane and holding her safe in your arms." Many forms of energetic healing today have intercessory prayer at their root.

Prayer can be an individual activity or it can be performed in groups, amplifying the message. You can design your own prayers, having a conversation or sending an energetic message to God. You can also use specific texts. In the Navajo Blessing Way over three hundred ceremonial prayers are memorized and sung.[71] There are many very specific Christian prayers, for example The Lord's Prayer and the Hail Mary. The prayers are used for atonement, during mass, and in the sacraments. Many prayers and blessings are passed from generation to generation, tying us to our ancestors. There can be comfort in everyone knowing the same words and having the same intention.

Prayer has been the subject of numerous studies in recent years. Some of them have concluded that there is a connection between religious involvement (including prayer) and improved immune and endocrine function, lower mortality from cancer, and decreased blood pressure.[72] Prayer and other religious activities have even been shown to increase longevity. Duke University investigators conducted a study that tracked the effects of private religious activities like prayer and Bible study on survival. The investigators factored in demographics and health status (including depression and stressful life events), and determined that persons with no disability and little or no private religious activity in 1986 were 63% more likely to die during the follow-up period of 6.3 years than those who prayed.[73]

As with any ritual, the power of intention is vital. While praying, stay engaged and present on all levels. Focus your energy, your emotions, indeed your whole being, on your prayers. You may find power in the rhythm of repetition, transcending the words themselves and delving into higher realms. You may find repetition numbing and need to find a more spontaneous way of conveying prayers. Experiment with what works for you, knowing that when you pray you have the power of the universe behind you.

MEDITATION

"The mind's babble goes on forever. The secret is to learn to meditate."
Dr. Judith Orloff

As ubiquitous as prayer, meditation has formed the backbone of many spiritual practices throughout the ages. Across continents and cultures, the benefits of meditation have long been felt by spiritual practitioners, and in modern times have been documented by scientists and medical researchers. Meditation is an effective method of developing spiritual support. Meditation methods involve a variety of intentions, from clearing your mind and expanding your consciousness, to regulating your physical systems of breathing and musculature to help foster a state of relaxation. Meditation can be a purely physical practice for stress reduction, or it can have a spiritual dynamic. The effects on the mind and body are well documented. Even when there is no overt spiritual component to meditation, it trains you to be more aware of your surroundings, more focused in your interactions with other people, and more present in your body. Meditation lowers anxiety and helps practitioners manage stress. It even has significant health effects, including the reduction of colds, headaches, and hypertension.[74]

The following is a brief sampling of the meditative practices of different faiths. I encourage you to experiment with them and with others of your own discovery, or to design your own meditative practice using your sacred intelligence and intuition.

Buddhists seek the ultimate goal of enlightenment, literally "to become light," to transcend the limitations of the physical body and move into a purely spiritual state of being. Mindfulness meditation, when you clear your mind and observe your thoughts from a neutral perspective, is a helpful tool. Most of us find it difficult to get distance from our own thoughts. We get caught in the rip tide of our internal dialogues and struggle to find our way back to peaceful shores. During mindfulness meditation, seek a peaceful state of mind, but do not force an empty state of mind. When thoughts come up, as they inevitably do, you acknowledge the thought, take note and let it go.

While meditating, the ancient Essenes focused on three aspects of their life: thoughts, body, and feelings. They would concentrate on the phrase, "Peace to my thoughts, peace to my body, peace to my feelings." Their meditation was akin to prayer, as they were decreeing peace to come to their whole being.[75]

Often a mantra is used during meditation. A mantra is a spiritual word or phrase which is repeated during meditation to retain focus. Practitioners of Transcendental Meditation are given a personal mantra to repeat throughout their meditation practice. A mantra can be a vehicle to connect with divine energy. Kabbalists repeat the words of specific prayers until they feel they have transcended the word itself and connected with the vibration or spiritual energy behind the word's meaning, thereby transporting themselves to another level of spiritual evolution. This process of intense focus is called *kavannah*.[76]

One school of Hindu religious practice is Bhakti. In this school, the preferred method of meditation is to focus on an aspect of the divine, especially through chanting. Vishnu, as the ultimate deity, has many aspects, including Rama and Krishna. Devotees choose any divine being, or *ishta*, to keep at the forefront of their minds as they meditate.[77] Eastern Orthodox Christians recite the Jesus Prayer, or "Hesychasm," in much the same way, simply evoking the name of Christ without distraction.[78]

Meditation can be a foundation on which to build a spiritual practice of your own. There are many reference books and classes available to help you discover the personal benefits of meditation. Experiment with some different methods that appeal to you. What is most important with meditation, as with prayer, is that the practice holds meaning for you. The practice is simply a vehicle for you to connect with the divine energy within you and all around you. Rote meditation is as ineffective as rote prayer. Enter into your meditations with an open heart and allow the spirit of creation to flow through you and from you.

CREATING YOUR RELIGION

"A person has no religion who has not slowly and painfully gathered one together, adding to it, shaping it, and one's religion is never complete and final, it seems, but must always be undergoing modification." D.H. Lawrence

Existing and Designed Anew

Many of us are born into a particular religion. There is great value in an ancestral lineage and the handing down of spiritual practice from generation to generation; however, many of us want something other than the structures of the major religions of the world today. Give yourself permission to follow your own spiritual path. It is not an either/or choice. Your choice is not only to accept what you were raised with or turn away from spiritual practice. Let yourself explore the faiths and spiritual practices that feel most at home for you.

Unfortunately, some religious organizations of the world today have lost sight of the intention of their creators. Acts are committed in the name of Jesus Christ and Allah that are antithetical to their teachings. As human beings we may not have the capacity to take information from direct revelation, the prophets, or from other spiritual beings, translate them into a language we can understand, and then set up a structure to manage that religion, without changing or warping the original message. Remember Pema Chödrön's thoughts about the Tao being ineffable at its core? She asserted that we would be remiss in thinking that we had fully comprehended its message. Organized religion historically has had a tremendous amount of power over people. Once a spiritual message becomes tainted with the human egoic desire of wielding power, the message can't help but become twisted. During the Crusades, the Christian leaders of the time used their spiritual influence over their people to convince them that political wars were holy and sanctioned by God. History has shown that, in addition to religious goals, those wars were also fought for power, land, and economic gain. Jesus specifically warned his followers against allowing power and money to hold a higher standing than the loving worship of God and kindness to one another. As religious practices have evolved through the centuries, we need to reevaluate whether we have been good stewards of the original spiritual messages and responsible about how they are presented and disseminated to the world today.

Be judicious about what you accept or reject. You may have a birth faith that works partially for you. It doesn't mean you have to wholly deny or embrace that faith. My maternal bloodline is a prime example. My mother is a Catholic and also practices shamanism. My grandmother's spiritual practice was Judaism and she studied shamanism as well. Even monotheistic religions have an aspect of choice in their practice. Although Catholicism clearly views Jesus as the Son of God, there are many saints to connect with and to form more personal relationships with through prayer. You may feel an affinity for Mary or St. Francis of Assisi, and accept spiritual support more comfortably from them. We can consider the Biblical directive of "no gods before me" as referring to the "primacy, not exclusivity" of God as the source of spiritual support.[79]

Most of the major religions of the world today have esoteric and ancient origins. By exploring the roots of your birth religion, you may find that the initial messages of the religion's founders and practices of its followers move you more deeply than the structures of those religions today. Daniel Goleman states, "All too often, religious institutions and theologies outlive the transmission of the original transcendental state that generated them. Without these living experiences, the institutions of religion become pointless, and their theologies appear empty. In my view, the modern crisis of established religions is caused by the scarcity of the personal experience of these transcendental states—the living spirit at the common core of all religions."[80]

That direct connection to the divine through personal experience has been important in my spiritual development. I find that observing and connecting with the natural world is a fundamental part of my being. I'm fed spiritually by the simplest moments in nature, such as watching birds, or fish, or clouds. Connecting with nature is an aspect of my spiritual support. I was raised Catholic, and many parts of the basic tenets of Christianity still speak to me. For example, I do try to follow the basic guidelines for living that Jesus taught to his disciples. I love that Catholics honor the divine feminine through Saint Mary. However, I'm disappointed that women are not allowed to attain the highest levels of spiritual leadership in the Catholic Church. I also find intense spiritual support from my personal relationships, especially in being a mother and feeling transcendent love for my child. One of my most consistent practices is taking time each day to express gratitude for my life, and shamanism is a fundamental part of my spiritual support and practice.

I work with an amalgam of spiritual philosophies and methods. There are arguments for and against approaching spiritual discipline this way. There is potentially great value in working within a structure of spiritual practice that has existed for thousands of years. Is it possible that if you start to pick and choose what aspects of faith are appealing to you, you may be limiting how far you can take your spiritual development? There may be elements of a faith or a religious practice that you don't feel comfortable with, but that are necessary for your evolution. But if you find the tenets and rules of an existing religion confining, sexist, or unacceptable for some other reason, feel comfortable creating a system that works for you. You might find that doing some research and some personal exploration yields a more fruitful crop for your spiritual nourishment than accepting or rejecting a particular faith in its current form. Do what works for you; however, don't shy away from the hard questions. Don't choose your spiritual practice because it seems easy or uncontroversial.

The rituals, sacraments, and ceremonies of faiths around the world may contain great power as they've been passed down, or they may have become rote in practice. Likewise, the rituals, sacraments, and ceremonies of your own spiritual practice, something you've created, can hold tremendous power or become mechanical. Be open to stepping into some existing practices and experiencing them with fresh eyes. Experience the power that originally existed at the creation of those ceremonies. Also consider creating your own rituals, your own ceremony, remembering to keep those practices meaningful. You may find that going outside in nature, reveling in the beauty that Spirit has provided, offering your gratitude, and praying for the healing of the world, has power for you. You may volunteer in a neo-natal care unit, sitting peacefully with the tiny premature babies and beaming them love. You may offer God a dance of celebration each morning. The power is in the intention you hold while engaging in those practices. Experiment and find something that fuels your inner light.

Discipline and Flexibility

For me, the practice of developing intuition and opening to intuitive guidance came before my exposure to the discipline of journeying in a shamanic way. "Core shamanism," as I was taught the practice, does involve a basic set of rules. For a long time, I followed those rules and kept my journeying practice quite separate from my intuitive practice. I was meticulous in trying to follow the rules of journeying. Over many years, in my studies and practice, I realized those artificial separations weren't serving a purpose any more. I mostly received information as a sense of knowing, rather than through a more specific structure. As I prepared to start a journey the answer to the questions I was journeying for had already popped into my head. I fought it for a long time, and stuck with the guidelines for journeying I'd been taught, only to receive the same information. Other people I knew were having similar experiences.

I've become less rigid about following certain rules for accessing the spirit world. I've allowed the different ways I get information, or that information is sent through me, to combine in a more fluid and flexible approach. It feels like a reunion, condensation, or even an expansion, of methods. I strongly encourage you to have discipline. I needed discipline to practice the basics of core shamanism and to work with people intuitively. Over time I branched off and experimented in different ways with confidence that I knew how to navigate non-ordinary reality. I wasn't going off rashly into the other world without knowing where I was or what I was doing. That would have been potentially unsafe for me and my clients. But once I became proficient in the discipline I was able to build a new structure from a strong foundation. With any field, art, or vocation, there is great benefit in mastering the basics and learning from teachers with remarkable experience. Once you have those basics mastered, you take your work to a new level if you allow your inner compass to guide you.

Spiritual Planning

Contemplate your spiritual beliefs and consider creating a framework for your spiritual struggles before you actually enter into a crisis. It is quite common for people to "find" religion when they are hurting, grieving, or afraid. That's fine, but when you're under stress or in pain, it can change the nature of your relationships, including that with your spiritual support. I suggest you explore and design your spiritual life at a time of your own choosing, rather than under pressure.

When people are in crisis, they often wish they had a spiritual guide to provide answers. The work comes before that. The work comes in developing that relationship so you can understand what your guidance is trying to tell you or show you. When you're in a heightened emotional state, it is quite difficult to have the discipline and the focus to develop a practice, and the clarity and discernment to sort out profound spiritual guidance from simple emotional desires.

Having spiritual support can also guide you through the logistical aspects of crises, like illness and loss. The rituals and routines that go along with spiritual structures can be helpful. In the Jewish faith, there are very specific rules for how and when to bury the dead, and what happens during the grieving process. Sitting *shiva* is the time for gathering as a community to remember and mourn the dead and to share food and comfort. There is solace in knowing what is traditionally done at certain times. Congregating and knowing what the rituals are going to be gives you a guidebook of a sort to know what to do. At times when emotion can be overwhelming, many of us need that support. A preexisting structure can allow you to focus on your deeper feelings and needs without having to make decisions about religious practice and ordinary practicalities.

Even happy life events can cause stress. They provide a great opportunity for shared celebration and also a reminder of support from the community. Shortly after my daughter was born, in addition to being baptized in a lovely ceremony led by a dear friend, she was honored with a shamanic ceremony. I will never forget how clear and wide her eyes were as a group of about seventy-five shamanic practitioners rattled in a circle for her, singing and welcoming her into the community. As a new parent I appreciated that the ritual also signified that I had support in raising her, as other adults were available to guide and mentor her through life.

Scientists are now recognizing that participating in spiritual or religious communities and activities can have dramatic effects on your life. Researchers report that religious people are statistically better able to handle the stresses of illness, grief, and divorce and are less likely to be depressed, anxious, or suicidal than non-religious people.[81] Scientists have more difficulty in sorting out whether the psychological benefits come from the religious activities themselves or the sense of community and connection that is often a part of spiritual practice. I've participated in group-oriented practices and those that are deeply personal. I suspect we need some form of both to reap the greatest rewards from our spiritual investments. Shamanism combines these two aspects. Journeying can be an individual experience or a group activity, as in a drumming circle or a community ceremony. I'll discuss shamanism in depth, as it is the practice I'm most comfortable with.

SHAMANISM

"Shamanic journeying is a joyful path to regaining the knowledge of how to bring our lives back to a place of harmony and balance." Sandra Ingerman

Shamanism is the oldest spiritual practice on the planet. It has been part of society on six continents for tens of thousands of years. Definitions of shamanism vary; however, shamanism is consistently viewed as a series of methods for enlisting the help of the spirit world, and honoring the spiritual aspect of everything found in nature. The term "shaman" comes from the Tungus people of Siberia, "săman" (pronounced SHAH-mahn).[82] Traditionally, shamans play many roles in their communities, including priest, healer, magician, leader, psychic, psychopomp, hunter, herbalist, mystic, ambassador, and warrior. Shamanic practitioners today may be called upon in similar capacities.

Michael Harner asserts, "The enlightenment of shamanism is the ability to light up what others perceive as darkness."[83] Shamanic practice allows a tremendous amount of flexibility in connecting to the spirit world. Whether through dancing into an ecstatic state, or lying perfectly still and calling on a spirit, different methods work equally well. There is no human with the authority to dismiss or accept your interaction with the spirit world. There are guidelines more than rules. In shamanism, you seek information directly from spiritual helpers. You don't need another human being as an intermediary to engage the divine forces of the world.

One of the things I appreciate about shamanism is the lack of dogma. There are so few things one needs to accept on faith or on someone else's word. A "shamanic" faith comes mostly from one's personal experience. In some ways, this absence of a man-made structure with an organization of systems and rules has allowed shamanism to sidestep the traps some major religions have fallen prey to in the process of being managed by human beings.

In shamanism you learn to alter your state of consciousness, to shift your mental processes, to perceive things differently. You learn to shift focus from your physical body and create an opening to see and feel the spiritual world around you. When you seek out the help of your spirit guides, more often than not, they will answer you and offer help. The language of the spirits can be mysterious and beautiful, symbolic and confusing. Developing expertise in interpreting the messages of your spirit teachers can be more challenging than finding them in the first place.

A shaman straddles two worlds, the spiritual world and ordinary, everyday reality. While in ordinary reality, or the "ordinary state of consciousness," the shaman obeys the rules of the consensual reality of her group. In modern western cultures, for example, those rules include gravity and the linear progression of time. In non-ordinary reality, or the "shamanic state of consciousness," however, those rules are quite different. While journeying to the spirit worlds, the shaman or shamanic practitioner moves outside the construct of linear time and is able to access the past, as well as the future. The concept of the shaman's flight defies many contemporary beliefs about the laws of nature. The shaman "flies" through the air, self-propelled or on the back of a beast. The shaman travels through the dense earth to reach the lower worlds. These activities are commonplace and perfectly normal while in an altered state, but absurd while in what is considered a "normal" state of consciousness.[84] The shaman is experienced and skilled in the operating systems of both worlds and acts as an intermediary between them. After entering the spirit world, she engages her spirit allies to obtain benefit for an individual or the community, by asking for healing or retrieving information.

Levels of Commitment to Shamanic Practice

There are essentially three levels of commitment to shamanic practice: community member, shamanic practitioner, and shaman. People who use the beneficial techniques of shamanism in their personal lives, mostly for themselves, can be called community members. Many shamanic techniques of spiritual exploration are available to any sincere and disciplined person. One does not need to be a shaman to engage in shamanic practices for personal guidance and spiritual fulfillment. All of us have the potential for amazing results from using shamanic techniques. This section is meant to give you a sense of what shamanism is as a spiritual practice, with the hope that you will explore it more deeply if it calls to you. One of the exercises at the end of this section is a shamanic journey, the cornerstone of shamanic practice. Experiment with some shamanic methods and attitudes towards engaging the world and see if they feel right to you. If they do, practice more and see where that path takes you, knowing you are using techniques that your ancestors of all cultures and continents have used before you.

At the next level of commitment are shamanic practitioners, who have often made the decision to offer shamanic healing to others. Shamanic practitioners have worked with shamanic techniques of divination and healing, developed a sound relationship with their spirit helpers over time, and feel called to use their connection to the spirit world to help others. They may offer specific kinds of services, such as journeying for information or providing soul retrievals, or they may act in a broader capacity within the community, by leading groups in ceremony, teaching others to journey, and providing a wide range of healing sessions. Practitioners usually devote significant time to continued learning and personal growth, through interaction with their spirit helpers and ordinary reality teachers and peers.

Shamans are in service to others at a level of commitment that is profound. The title of shaman is typically an honorary title, given to someone who, through lineage, initiation, or the possession of extraordinary gifts, lives a life devoted to being a "spiritual activist," a consistent and dedicated presence in the community for healing, peacemaking, and wise counsel. While shamanic practitioners may offer help to others as they are inclined, a shaman may be called upon regularly as an important figure in the support system of a community.

There is a clear distinction between the shaman and the average person using shamanic techniques to connect to the spirit world. Shamanism is akin to other spiritual practices where followers share the space and methods of worship within their community. Catholics pray with their priests during mass; however, their weekly attendance and prayer cannot be compared to the commitment the priest has made to devote his life to Jesus and the Catholic faith. Likewise, the shaman and the people of shamanic cultures may take part in similar spiritual activities; however, the shaman has felt a particular calling or commitment to practice her faith with more intense devotion and discipline. You may choose to practice shamanism or make a commitment to become a shamanic practitioner. Shamans, however, are typically called, not created. They are distinguished by the miraculous results of their work.

Core Shamanism

I practice "core shamanism." In the 1950s and 1960s, Michael Harner, an anthropologist and scholar of shamanism, was working with the Conibo and Jívaro tribes in the Amazon area. He gleaned as much information as he could about the tribes' shamanic practices as an outsider, until he earned the tribes' respect and was initiated into their shamanic traditions. With these groups he began to learn about shamanic techniques firsthand. After profound spiritual experiences in the Amazon, he studied other shamanic groups and discovered that different cultures with diverse worldviews utilized surprisingly similar techniques to achieve results in healing and divination.[85] As founder and president of the Foundation for Shamanic Studies, he coined the term "core shamanism," defined as the "universal, or near-universal, methods of shamanism not bound to any specific cultural group or perspective."[86]

Harner defines a shaman as a "type of medicine man or woman especially distinguished by the use of journeys to hidden worlds otherwise mainly known through myth, dreams, and near-death experiences."[87] To take that "journey," shamans alter their state of consciousness at will. From those "hidden worlds" the shaman utilizes a body of ancient techniques to facilitate healing and balance for themselves and others in their communities. Harner makes the distinction that shamanism is a methodology, not a religion. Shamanism is a spiritual practice available to just about anyone. The techniques are valuable for personal use, as well as for helping others.

Shamanic Revival

Although certainly not as widespread as it once was, shamanism is garnering much contemporary interest, what Harner terms a "shamanic renaissance." There is a resurgence of interest in shamanic practices and beliefs in the West. In many places where shamanic practices were abandoned or prohibited, attempts are under way to revive and honor age-old cultural traditions. Whether for renewed cultural appreciation or for personal and professional use, many people in modern societies are studying and practicing shamanism.

Teachers like Michael Harner, Sandra Ingerman, and other faculty at the Foundation for Shamanic Studies present the concepts of core shamanism as a set of ancient and universal practices readily adaptable to the challenges and circumstances of modern life. By distilling shamanic customs to their basic principles and methods, it is possible to avoid the rote mimicry of performing rituals outside the cultural context in which they were developed. Although the teachings of core shamanism lack the culturally specific nuances of traditional shamanism, they help make these techniques accessible to a wider audience. The availability of this type of teaching has increased overall interest in things shamanic.

The concept of living in balance and harmony with nature, so vital in shamanic traditions worldwide, is echoed in the environmental movement that began in the 1970s. Increased environmental concerns and heightened awareness of the delicate and complex relationships and interdependencies in our natural ecosystems have also influenced the resurgence of shamanism and other more nature-based spiritual practices in the West. Shamanism is "spiritual ecology." It celebrates the profound beauty of the natural world, teaches communication with other beings, and expounds thoughtfully on the role of the human being within the universe.[88] This merging of spiritual and ecological concerns aligns well with shamanic philosophies. Shamanism can also be melded with other religions to form a personal practice that engages the spiritual world and the natural world more holistically.

The Shaman's Journey

The use of the journey is the fundamental element of shamanic practice. The term refers to a shift in consciousness, whereby the shamanic practitioner's soul is believed to depart the body and travel into the spirit realm. Shamans induce this altered state through singing, drumming, dancing, and/or ingesting hallucinogens. While journeying, the shaman travels to a dimension outside of time and space. It is from within this spirit realm of god, goddess, and universal life force that the shaman's true work is accomplished. Essentially, as a practitioner, you learn to access the divinity surrounding you. You shift your focus to your inner divinity, your spiritual essence, and engage the world from that perspective.

Monotonous percussion sound, called "sonic driving," is the most common method for entering this altered state. The beat used is fairly consistent across cultures and is typically about 220 beats per minute. Scientists have observed that this rhythm alters brain waves and blood chemistry. In a study among the Salish of the Northwest Coast of North America, shamanic drumming created a shift to the theta wave EEG frequency (4–7 cycles/second), which is closely associated with dreams, hypnosis, and deeply meditative states.[89]

The drum is the most important tool used by the shaman and shamanic practitioners. Shamans have been observed using drums across the globe. The drum is referred to as the shaman's "horse" or "canoe," as it is the vehicle that brings the shaman to the spiritual worlds.[90] Drum design varies across cultures, but they are typically hand-held, round, and made of animal skin. Today you can purchase drums made of hide or synthetic materials that function well for shamanic work. You can decorate your drum or leave the face of the drum unadorned.

Rattles are often used instead of, or in addition to, the drum. It's very simple to create your own rattle. Even ordinary objects like a bottle of aspirin, or a pack of Tic-Tacs, make an excellent sound for journeying on your own. Experiment to see what percussion sounds work best for you. CDs of drumming, rattling, singing, and even didgeridoos can be purchased from the Foundation for Shamanic Studies.

Regardless of the mode employed, shamans enter an altered state. The shaman's perception shifts from the sights and sounds surrounding the physical body to the landscape of the spirit world. To fully immerse themselves in their perception of the celestial realms, shamans block out input from their five senses and the physical world around them. Disturbances are minimized, a covering is often worn over the eyes, and great care is taken not to disturb someone who is journeying.

In core shamanism and in many other systems, the spiritual worlds are divided into three levels. The distinction between the levels is mostly semantics, as the cosmology of the spiritual worlds is more aptly described as a hologram, where each level can be accessed from another; however, the traditional shamanic worldview describes three distinct layers. The *upper world* is reached by traveling skyward, past a cloudy layer or membrane. The *lower world* is reached via a tunnel descending into the earth. The *middle world* overlays the physical world with which we're most familiar. Shamanic practitioners can meet spirit teachers in any of these worlds; however, the upper and lower worlds are the most common places to connect with helpers who have reached a level of spiritual evolution beyond our own. Knowing which world you are in is an important part of journeying safely. It's helpful to have a teacher when first learning to journey. See the *Resources* section to locate qualified teachers in your area.

Helping Spirits

One of the fundamental underlying principles of shamanism is the existence of spirits. Depending on the culture, the emphasis is on relationships with nature spirits, ancestral spirits, power animals, or spirits in human form. Usually, a combination of different types of spirits is engaged and honored. Shamanic cultures are animistic and believe that all natural objects, from plants to animals and rocks to thunder, possess a spirit. In previous sections, we've discussed the concept of a vital energy surrounding or infusing all things. As you go through your day, you are affecting and are affected by the energetic components of the people you encounter, the information you hear, the home you live in, and the land you live on. Shamanism takes that concept a step further and suggests that you can develop personal relationships with the spirit beings with whom you coexist. Just about anyone, not only traditional shamans, can acquire a helping spirit and make a connection with the spirit realm to boost their personal power.

These are compassionate and healing spirits. They sympathize with humans and the struggles of life on earth. They are willing to help when contacted. Many helping spirits once lived on this earth. Their souls passed on, and at the time of death either went to the lower or upper world. Some very benevolent spirits choose to stay in the middle world to assist more directly in matters of the earth and the human race. These spirits have a larger perspective, but they are not all powerful. They need our help to bridge between the worlds. I've found that the support from my helping spirits has sustained me through many difficult times. I've found solace in the loving embrace of my power animal, and comfort from the supportive words of my spirit teachers.

Once a shaman has connected with a spirit who is willing to work with her, that spirit is available and able to assist the shaman in many ways. The shaman likewise has made a commitment to help the spirit. The spirit can take the form of an animal (called power animal) or a human (spirit teacher or tutelary spirit). A relationship is built with these spirits over time and with repeated journeying. These helping spirits, or allies, protect the shaman physically and provide emotional support, wisdom, and vital energy. When journeying, the shaman or shamanic practitioner often relies on the power animal or teacher to serve as a guide in the lower, middle, or upper worlds. By shape-shifting, or merging, with a helping spirit, the shaman is able to embody the power and skills of that spirit for a period of time.

Most people with an interest and willingness to learn the techniques can successfully meet a power animal or spirit teacher. Power animals are typically sought out in the lower world and tutelary spirits in the upper world. This is not a fixed rule, however, as spirits are not confined by space or time. Some people believe a power animal is a spirit being that stays with you because it cares for you and enjoys being able to experience life in a physical body. Others think a power animal is a symbol for one's subconscious wisdom. Almost everyone has a power animal, and some have several. Perhaps you had an invisible animal friend as a child or have always been fascinated with a particular kind of animal. This animal may be your power animal; however, you don't choose a power animal—the animal chooses you. There is no hierarchy of power animals. A mouse can be as strong a spiritual guide as a lion. To maintain a connection with your power animal, take the time to learn about it, learn to feel its presence, communicate with it, and honor it by doing things that it enjoys, or things that it asks of you.

Talking about helping animal spirits is a wonderful way to introduce shamanism to children. Children often have a natural affinity for animals and they provide a good entry point to discuss the spiritual philosophy of shamanism. At four, my daughter was having trouble sleeping at night because she was afraid of the dark. I suggested she focus on an animal spirit, which could help her. Earlier I tuned in to see if I perceived an animal spirit around her and I saw a beautiful white wolf. I told her that this wolf could help her if she was scared. She said that felt good. We didn't talk about it after that. A month or so later we were taking a walk with her grandparents. Grandpa had been reading her Little Red Riding Hood and joked, "Stay on the path, don't talk to strangers, don't talk to wolves." I spoke up, "We like wolves." Fairy tales are historically cruel to certain animals and instill haunting fears and negative impressions about animals and witches. I try to correct these misconceptions for my daughter. She added, "Yes, I have a wolf spirit who helps me if I'm scared." Grandma asked, "Do you call her?" She said, "No, I don't call her out loud because Mommy would think I needed her. I just call her in my mind." I was happy to hear it was part of her thinking and she was aware of having that spirit with her.

The shaman's relationship with helping spirits is developed over time. For the Jívaro of the Amazon, "the guardian spirit is often a power animal, a spiritual being that not only protects and serves the shaman, but becomes another identity or alter ego for him."[91] This animal spirit is akin to the *nagual* of Central America and Mexico.[92] Great care is taken to honor the spirits, as they are key to the success of any shamanic ritual or treatment. By following established rules and rituals of engaging the spirits, the shaman appeals to them to bestow their good favor and protection. By appeasing these spirits the shaman helps maintain balance and harmony with nature, for an individual and for the community as a whole. You can create this balance for yourself by connecting to the helping spirits around you and then making them a part of your life, through whatever methods feel comfortable to you. The Navajo describe this balance with nature as *hozhogo*, which means harmony, beauty, cooperation, and loving relationship.

Divination and Healing

The shaman typically journeys to helping spirits to obtain information or facilitate healing. Because the shaman's journey is believed to be outside the construct of time and space, the shaman can obtain information about distant past or future events, or from remote locations. Traditionally, the shaman's help was enlisted to find lost objects, locate herds of deer to hunt, and predict the outcome of events. You can utilize this technique to ask advice and guidance.

The divination journey can provide one form of spiritual support. Its most effective application is not necessarily as a predictive tool, but as a source for wisdom and advice. I'm certified in Harner Method Shamanic Counseling, which is a method of learning to use shamanic journeying to gain personal insight and counsel. Formulate concise simple questions to ask your helping spirits. Avoid two part questions and ones that might invade someone else's privacy. Remember that spirits exist outside of time and space and may have different definitions for "soon" or "good for you." Always incorporate other methods of decision-making, like intuition, instincts, logic, and research before making vital decisions. Often the language of the spirits is metaphorical. You must practice your interpreting skills and put them to the test over time to be sure you are understanding what the spirits are trying to convey to you.

Healing is the other main reason that shamans and shamanic practitioners enter the spirit world on a journey. This will be discussed in more detail in *Section 6: Your Health*. Even without advanced training, which shamanic healing requires, you can simply journey and ask your spirit allies for help, or to do what is needed for the highest good. The healing journey is analogous to intercessory prayer.

Shamanism: Ancient Practices and Modern Applications

Shamanism reunifies practitioners with spiritual power. This occurs through their relationship with and assistance from spirits, and equates to an increase in personal power. You may evoke that personal power through your biological heritage or through your spiritual heritage. Some people know their biological ancestry, either through journeying or through ordinary reality knowledge, and some people don't. Some of us come from a culture with a rich, documented shamanic tradition to draw on and some of us don't. Knowing your biological ancestry and the shamanic traditions and techniques of that ancestry is not a prerequisite to looking at the world with shaman's eyes and walking on the world with shaman's feet. Although traditions handed down from generation to generation are extremely valuable, shamanism is an individual practice at its heart. Shamanism is primarily about direct revelation. Even if you know nothing about your ancestry, you are not missing out from the shamanic perspective. Core shamanism has made the rich world of shamanic practice available to Westerners and others who do not have a cultural support system for shamanic work. For that, our society is indebted to Michael Harner and the other faculty members of the Foundation for Shamanic Studies. They have done much to disseminate shamanic knowledge, to preserve shamanic traditions in their native lands, and to reintroduce shamanic practices to traditional cultures who have lost their shamanic knowledge.

Work directly with the spirits, work directly with your own intuition, connect to your inner divinity and you connect to the divine knowledge of all the traditions of shamanism throughout the ages. Remember the hologram. You don't necessarily need to know from what country your ancestors came. From your place in time and space right now you can access the vast experience of the ancestors of all times and places past, and the descendents of all times and places to come.

Shamanic drumming circles can be a good place to find human companionship and support while exploring journeying. Circles meet with different frequencies, sometimes weekly or monthly. The structure of circles varies, but typically they will include time to "call in" and honor the helping spirits, drumming to start shifting your state of consciousness, and time for journeying and sharing. They are a supportive arena where it is often appropriate to share the joys and challenges of your practice. Our circle meets twice a month. After the initial rituals of smudging, rattling, and drumming, we typically do one group journey and one personal journey. We always make time to send healing to people who have requested help and sometimes will devote time to hands on healing for one or more people in the circle. Over time we have developed a deep sense of trust and safety in our circle. We take turns leading and teaching, and support each other in times of crisis. Each circle is different, so contact the leader to know what to expect. The Foundation for Shamanic Studies keeps a list of ongoing circles.

People seek the direct connection to "spirit" that shamanism offers. As in the arena of health care, people are looking for new ways to fulfill their spiritual need for healing and balance. In record numbers, people are turning to alternative religions or a self-made compilation of spiritual practices. Duane Elgin describes this trend as a "personalized, customized form of faith, which minimizes rules and absolutes ..."[93] In an article for the *Utne Reader*, Jeremiah Creedon wonders if this "pastiche spirituality" is signaling the formation of a universal belief system, "gleaned from all the others."[94] According to a USA Today/Gallop Poll conducted in 2002, one third of Americans consider themselves spiritual, but not religious. For many people, this spiritual shift is not a new construction, but a revival of traditional practices. Its fundamental focus is on the experience of the individual within the context of a "spiritual" world; a world with a spiritual dimension of equal or greater relevance to the human condition than the physical dimension modern society values so highly. There has been a loss of confidence in many hierarchical institutions, both governments and organized religions. Shamanism offers one possible alternative, a way of interacting with each other and with the divine that, for some, seems more accessible and satisfying. Harner talks about this concept as an overarching "shift to spiritual democracy."[95]

From healing to divination, personal spiritual practice to creating harmony with nature, our ancestors believed strongly in the interconnection of all beings. The centuries old trend towards a human-centered, scientifically explained reality might be shifting back to more ecologically sound and spiritually expansive ways of living. Shamanism always adapts to the culture and time in which it is practiced. This adaptive quality may be key to shamanism's role in our rapidly changing culture. Do shamans understand the fundamental nature of reality at a more profound level than most of us today? That is clearly a controversial question. By looking closely at the beliefs and practices of shamanic cultures across the globe, and perhaps even experiencing a shamanic journey for ourselves, we can broaden our understanding of reality versus fantasy, truth versus mythology, and matter versus spirit. Modern society has drawn the lines between those concepts definitively, and perhaps erroneously. From the blurring of those lines, or at least the open-minded explorations of their boundaries, the ancient wisdom of the shamans can play a part in the creation of a healthier, more sustainable future for us as individuals, and as a planet.

CLOSING

"If the Mind dwells upon the spiritual things, then it follows that it becomes what it has dwelt upon, what it has lived upon, what it has made itself a portion of."
Edgar Cayce

Since the dawning days of human history, we practiced some form of religion. We've worshipped heaven and earth, the sun and the moon, gods and goddesses. Some spiritual practices have turned to nature as their source of awe and inspiration, others to an omnipotent God. Regardless of the form our devotion takes, as a species we have embraced the spiritual world with vigor and conviction. That conviction combined with cultural hubris has sometimes led to bloodshed in the name of the gods. Historically, tolerance and open-mindedness regarding spiritual issues is not among our greatest attributes. The United States of America was founded on the basis of freedom of religious expression. We're still fighting to preserve that right today. Despite the challenges of our relationship with God, and with each other in the name of God, we crave a connection to the divine at a profound level.

Our societal and individual searches for meaning and solace repeatedly turn inward to a spiritual practice that feels like home. Some of us have found our spiritual home. Some of us have moved several times in the quest for one. Some of us are still searching to uncover the feeling of support and comfort that faith can provide. Some of us view faith itself as a self-delusional folly. Others are simply disinterested. Whether we recognize it or not, we are spiritual beings. On some level we long to be at peace with that aspect of ourselves and everything around us.

That peace can be found in part through creating a spiritual support system that includes people, spirits, and methods of devotion. Through community interaction or private prayer, you can build a base upon which to create a fulfilling life. By standing in awe of the miracle of the natural world or by losing yourself in creative vision, you can touch the divine energy that is within you and all around you, often unseen but ever present.

In centuries past, and in many cultures today, religious options were limited. You were whatever religion you were born into. We have myriad choices in our society today. You can choose to accept your birth religion, convert to another, or create your own. However you decide to craft a spiritual practice for yourself, keep in mind that the web of life encompasses all beings and all religions. There is not one true way. All paths that incorporate love, compassion, and kindness can lead you to the heart of Spirit. I've shared some of my search with you. If what I've explored moves you as well, try it. If not, know that it is one path, but not "the" path. Let your search be one of exploration and joy, rather than a quest for some ultimate level of knowledge. Let yourself be changed by the wondrous surprises and synchronicities that happen when you open yourself to divine energy. And above all, know that you do not need to *find* a way to be a spiritual being. People often tell me they know they are spiritual on some level, but they are searching for some outside way to *feel* spiritual. You are a spiritual being *now*, and always will be, regardless of how or whether you choose to practice. Remember that God's kingdom is inside you. Your sacred intelligence is all you need to navigate the unique course of your spiritual expression. Your inner divinity is your guiding light to peace, power, and happiness.

EXERCISES FOR SECTION 5: YOUR SPIRITUAL SUPPORT

Refer to the *How To Use This Book* section in the *Introduction* if you have questions. Relax your body and clear your mind before you begin, be open to the information you receive, and write down your experiences when you are finished.

What is God?

* Contemplate your definition of God or Spirit.

Sources of Spiritual Support

* Make a list of your existing spiritual support structures.

* Toning Meditation
Sit quietly and allow your body to relax as you concentrate on your breathing. Breathe fully and deeply. Once your body is relaxed, begin to "tone," allowing a resonant sound or word to fill your body. You may repeat one word, or let the sound be free flowing and changing. Continue to tone until you generate an inner power, a power that transcends your thoughts and personal issues of the moment. Let yourself be transported on the vibration of your own voice. When you are ready to stop, focus on your breath for a few moments and open your eyes.

* Higher Self Meditation
Sit quietly and allow your body to relax as you concentrate on your breathing. Breathe fully and deeply. Once your body is relaxed, imagine a comfortable space with two chairs facing each other (you can substitute couches, mats, or whatever else you wish to sit on). Picture yourself sitting on one of the chairs. Create a peaceful and welcoming space. Invite your higher self to join you, appearing across from you. Your higher self may appear to you in any number of ways, so don't let your expectations prevent you from perceiving it. Spend some time there communing with your higher self, maybe having a conversation or just enjoying each other's company. Before you end the meditation, ask if there is a word or phrase you can use to help you remember the feeling of unity with your higher self. When you are ready to leave, thank your higher self, become aware of your body and your breathing, and open your eyes.

* Make a list of the ways you are serving yourself, others, and God.

* Volunteer in your community.

✳ Receiving Meditation
Sit quietly and allow your body to relax as you concentrate on your breathing. Breathe fully and deeply. Once your body is relaxed, imagine you're soaking in a warm bubbly bath. (You can substitute lying on a warm sandy beach, or bathing under the stream of a beautiful waterfall, if you wish). Your only intention is to allow yourself to receive, to soak up the warmth. The water is a cleansing, healing gift. Enjoy it and allow yourself to be pampered by it. When you're ready to stop, bring yourself gently back to an awareness of your body and open your eyes.

✳ Express your spirituality through a creative pursuit. Try painting, singing, dancing, gardening, writing, or any other creative endeavor that calls to you. Open yourself to what wishes to emerge from you. Pay attention to the process, not a product or outcome.

✳ Personal Eden Meditation
Sit peacefully and relax into your body and breathing. Picture yourself walking along a path for a moment, until you find yourself at a large gate. Open the gate and step into your garden. Explore the garden, noticing as much about it as possible. Create anything you want in the garden to feel comfortable and content. Enjoy your time in the garden and return whenever you wish to feel the loving support of nature around you. When you're ready to leave, exit though the gate, walk a few steps along the path, return to an awareness of your body, and open your eyes.

Prayer

✳ Create your own prayer of decree
When you use decree, you are calling on your inner divine power and stating something as if it were in existence now. Draft your prayer on paper first to get the wording as you like it. While praying, call it into being, knowing you are fueled with the creative power of the universe. Use all your inner senses to feel your prayer coming to life.

Meditation

✳ Experiment with different types of meditation

○ Mindfulness Meditation
Sit calmly and relax. Simply observe your thoughts. Keep your awareness on holding peace in your mind. Note any thought that floats by, and then let it go.

○ Tension Release

Sit calmly and relax. Breathe deeply and let your awareness rest on your feet for a moment. Consciously relax all the muscles in your feet. When your feet are relaxed, move your attention up to your ankles and relax your ankles. Move all the way up your body, from your calves, to your thighs, to your buttocks, your spine, your arms, your neck, your head and face. Take as long as you need at each part until you can totally relax your muscles.

○ Mantra

Chose or journey for a word or phrase that represents divine energy to you. As you sit peacefully, repeat that word or phrase silently, focusing all your energy on the word itself, and ultimately on the power behind the word.

Creating Your Religion

✱ Consider your use of existing and created rituals or practices. Create a brief ceremony or ritual that has special meaning for you. Be clear on your intent for performing the ritual, and then journey or meditate to be shown the steps of the ritual.

Shamanism

✱ Journey to Meet an Animal Spirit
(*This meditation is included on the* Inner Divinity *companion CD. See the* Resources *section for more information.*)

Ideally, take a shamanic journeying workshop or learn directly from an experienced teacher. Visit www.shamanism.org or www.shamanicteachers.com for information about workshops in journeying. If that is not an option for you, I recommend Sandra Ingerman's book, *Shamanic Journeying: A Beginner's Guide* for a complete set of journeying instructions. Or use the following meditation to meet an animal spirit.

Before starting the meditation, picture a place in nature you have been to in real life, not imagined or in a dream. It should have an opening into the ground, such as a tree with deep roots or a hollowed out trunk, a cave, a lake fed by a natural spring, or an animal's burrow. Hold this place firmly in your mind as we begin. It is your departure place. Also hold the intention that you are going to the lower world to look for an animal spirit.

Close your eyes. Move down into the natural opening of your departure place, traveling into the earth. Use your imagination if you need to. Make yourself small to travel down tree roots or an animal's burrow, or breathe underwater if you're entering through a spring. Move down into the earth through a tunnel or tube-like opening. You may see your surroundings, or you may feel them. Travel through this tunnel until you sense light and emerge at the end.

Once you step out of the tunnel, silently repeat your intention to meet an animal spirit. Explore with all your senses. If an animal is there, introduce yourself and begin to get to know it. If an animal is not present, start to look for one. Take your time and explore. When you're ready to return (in about 10–15 minutes) say thank you and goodbye and retrace your steps all the way back through the tunnel to your departure place.

SECTION 6: YOUR HEALTH
The Universal Spirit of Healing

Your body is an integrated whole. Your physical state affects your emotional and spiritual states and vice versa. Many energy-based and traditional healing models assert that all illness or imbalance, whether physical, emotional, or spiritual, actually originates on the spiritual level. Everything we put into our bodies (food, air, water) alters our energy bodies. Everything we do spiritually (meditation, prayer, visualization) alters our physical bodies. As you seek to live in harmony with the natural and spiritual world around you, you must also learn to live in harmony within your own skin. To reach the ultimate goal of health, find the unity between your body and your spirit, and care for both aspects of yourself simultaneously.

In this section, I'll present a variety of options for taking care of your health. Much of what I discuss comes from the shamanic perspective. I'll describe the healing methods I practice most frequently, including soul retrieval, Reiki, Healing with Spiritual Light, and distance healing. When working with clients, I allow each person's inner divinity to guide the healing process. There is no one technique that is fundamentally better than another when it comes to spiritual healing. The methods are secondary to the healer's compassion and ability to be a clear channel for healing energy, and a client's readiness and openness to receiving that healing energy, and willingness to do their inner work. For some, a combination of techniques proves most effective; for others, one is sufficient. Your job is to sense which methods call to you. There are many healing modalities that address the physical *and* spiritual aspects of the patient: cranio-sacral therapy, naturopathy, reflexology, polarity therapy, La Ho Chi, some forms of chiropractic, Feldenkrais, the Alexander Technique, Jin Shin Jitsu, aromatherapy, sound and light healing,

Rolfing, shiatsu, and the list goes on. The modalities I cover here are not the only options, but some good places to start.

The belief in a life-sustaining, vital energy, such as a universal spirit, has existed in cultures across the world from the beginning of recorded time. Shamanic cultures believed in spirit as the animating force in a human being's life. The Ancient Greeks called it by many names, including *pneuma* and *medicatrix naturae*.[96] Dr. Samuel Hahnemann, the founder of homeopathy, called the universal spirit *dynamis*. [97] In the Vedic tradition, vital spiritual essence is called *prana,* Sanskrit for "life-force." The healing systems of yoga and Ayurveda are based on the cultivation and management of *prana*. Practitioners of traditional Chinese healing systems believe that nurturing the beneficial movement of *ch'i*, or spirit, allows the body to utilize its natural ability to remain healthy. Maintaining the proper flow of *ch'i* in the human body is the goal of such preventative regimens as *T'ai Ch'i* and *Qigong*.

To create health we need to relearn some principles forgotten over the centuries. Some advantages of living in the information age are that we have the tools to compare healing models from the past and present, research the effectiveness of different methods, and consider anecdotal evidence collected from practitioners and their clients. Just as different religions may hold partial answers to the mystery of God's true nature, different healing modalities may hold pieces to the puzzle of ideal health. What strikes me about the beliefs in a universal life force is their fundamental similarity. In exploring the nature of this force, we may need to alter "Western" beliefs about time and space, health and disease, the sacred and the ordinary, the miraculous and the impossible. Perhaps an amalgam of ancient and modern healing methods will give us a more complete picture of health.

You embody the creative power of the universe within you. Your sacred self is whole and complete, and your path to health is unique. You can inspire your body and your spirit to heal naturally. By remembering your own divinity, you encourage your body and spirit to find a state of harmony, where your cells function as they should, where your soul feels at peace.

INTEGRATIVE MEDICINE

"Integrative medicine emphasizes the healing potential of the human body, the doctor/patient relationship, looking at all aspects of lifestyle and emphasizes 'whole-person medicine' meaning you have to look at patients as minds, bodies and spirits and community members, not just physical bodies." Dr. Andrew Weil

Integrative medicine blends elements of complementary and alternative medicine with conventional, mainstream methods of treatment and diagnosis. According to the University of Maryland's School of Medicine, "Integrative medicine aims to enhance current medical practice and, although perceived as a 'new movement,' it in fact re-focuses medicine on its ancient roots and values."[98]

My training and practice utilize some of these energetic or spiritually based modalities, which can be a valuable part of a holistic healing model. Although I'm not going to discuss more conventional medical models here, I believe we should do what works, regardless of the system or philosophy a method supports. Energy medicine can be a wonderful complement to allopathic medicine. Great strides have been made in technology and research that have improved the state of health and quality of life for millions of people. We need to incorporate both these paradigms to provide the most fruitful path to health. In the 20th century, the pendulum swung dramatically to the side of mechanistic medicine. As the 21st century begins, the pendulum is moving somewhat back to a central position, where the mechanics of the spirit are considered as well as the mechanics of the body.

When I have a health problem, I use a variety of methods. I have a physician and I also have an acupuncturist and an assortment of energy healing practitioners I call on. For example, I have a long history of migraine headaches. Many years ago, before I was aware of alternative techniques, I exhausted the allopathic treatment options available at that time. My headaches continued. They stopped suddenly and without an obvious cause around the time I started practicing shamanic healing. They recurred seven years later and I immediately sought out energy-based options as well as medical ones. They were controlled using a combination of medication, herbs, and treatment to balance my energy system, especially acupuncture.

We can do much more to preserve and foster health *before* an illness manifests in our physical bodies. Often conventional medicine is called upon to fix a problem, to treat an illness that already exists. One of the advantages of energetic medicine is that it can help prevent imbalance on all levels. When used in conjunction with living life in a holistically healthy way, energetic medicine can help you to live not just without illness, but with vitality.

It is in comparison to traditional, allopathic models of medical care that we find the greatest differences in approach to healing. In many Western hospitals today, spirituality is not a consideration in the diagnosis and treatment of the patient. The body is viewed as a physical mass made up of discrete organs. The different organs and systems in the body are often treated in isolation from one another. A person goes to a gastroenterologist for stomach problems and to a cardiologist for heart trouble. Contrast this model to the concepts of energy based medicine such as shamanism or intuitive healing, which consider the physical, emotional, mental, and spiritual condition of the patient as a matrix of interwoven layers that cannot be detached from one another for treatment. Times are changing. The holistic model of health care is fast becoming accepted and the connection to our spirituality is being considered more frequently in treatment.

Recent research has shown that patients with a strong religious background who turned to their faith during times of health crisis healed faster and coped with illness "more effectively" than their non-praying counterparts. They also lived longer.[99] Medical schools are beginning to recognize the need to educate doctors in the role of spirituality in healing, both in an intercessory mode and as a component of personal faith. Courses in complementary medicine and the mind-body connection are becoming widespread. Sixty-four schools, including Harvard and Johns Hopkins, currently teach students how to do a "spiritual intake," to understand patients' spiritual needs as they deal with illness.[100]

Natural healing and alternative medicine have experienced huge growth in the United States and other countries. According to a nationwide government survey conducted by the National Center for Complementary and Alternative Medicine (NCCAM) and the Centers for Disease Control and Prevention (CDC), 36 percent of U.S. adults use some form of complementary and alternative medicine (CAM). When prayer is employed specifically for health reasons it is included in the definition of CAM and the number of U.S. adults using some form of CAM in the past year rises to 62 percent.[101] People are seeking alternatives to allopathic, often invasive or drug-based, treatment for illness. Shamanic healing techniques may eventually become a more widely practiced discipline, sharing the near mainstream status of acupuncture and herbal remedies. In Europe, the trend toward physicians using alternative therapies is "overwhelming." Of the 88,000 practicing acupuncturists, 62,000 are medical doctors.[102] In the region of Tuva, just north of Mongolia, a popular clinic offers shamanic treatments in much the same way the hospital across the street offers traditional therapies. Patients make appointments or walk in to see the shaman on duty for that day and receive treatments for a variety of physical and emotional ailments, as well as divinatory services, such as obtaining information about a run-away child. [103]

Pharmaceutical companies can take the lead in using indigenous healers' wealth of knowledge about medicinal plants to benefit a mass market eager for natural remedies. Some, like Shaman Pharmaceuticals, claim to marry the unlikely combination of native wisdom and big business. This corporate validation of the extent and value of indigenous knowledge can also increase awareness of the relevance of traditional healing to modern society. Hopefully, in their zeal to patent and market "shamanic" products, they will remember to show respect for the shamans and their communities by repaying them in equitable and appropriate ways. Thomas Carlson, M.D., director of ethnobiomedical field research for Shaman Pharmaceuticals, seems to have insight into the importance of respecting this ancient knowledge. He explains, "Our ability to survive as a species might depend on how well we integrate the wisdom of traditional forest cultures. It's not just that shamans know plant medicines. Shamanistic cultures have evolved harmonious systems of living with their biological environments."[104]

Given the rise in interest in alternative healing modalities, and the success of allopathic medicine in areas like surgery and vaccinations, it seems only logical to try to distill the most effective elements of alternative and allopathic treatments into a new form of medicine. This effort to unite the two schools, integrative medicine, is a clear signal that the paradigm of health care is shifting.

Choosing a Practitioner

The attitude of your health care practitioners can also profoundly impact your healing. Be aware of the way you feel energetically in the presence of your health care providers. Are you sensing their compassion? Do they listen and communicate in a kind way? You need to be sensitive to your doctor's regimen of seeing patients under tight time constraints, and understand that their attention must be shared with many patients; however, you should feel comfortable with your practitioner's level of attention and care for you. Whether you're seeing a medical doctor, a therapist, or an alternative practitioner, you should feel safe and respected. Remember that the treatment itself is only part of the healing process. Your practitioner's words and attitudes affect you as well.

When I was pregnant, I was seeing a group of obstetricians at a well-known teaching hospital. I'm sure they were excellent technicians and I would have had a fine delivery; however, after meeting several of them, I wasn't comfortable. I was approaching birth as a natural process. I wanted medical interventions available if necessary, but wanted to use as few of them as possible. It's hard to imagine a more vulnerable time than when you are giving birth. I wanted someone there who shared, or at least respected, my approach. I mistakenly thought this was the only hospital that my health insurance covered, and, as my due date approached, I felt increasingly anxious about my relationship with the doctors. Then one day I had a check up with a doctor whom I found patronizing, bossy, and disrespectful of my wishes. With the help of my doula (birthing assistant) I found another hospital covered by my insurance. My new hospital allowed me to use a midwife, which was my original preference. At the last minute, I switched and had a wonderful experience with the practitioners and the new hospital. When I took a stand for my own care, and my baby's, I had help to find the right way for us.

When medical doctors limit your options by disregarding natural and alternative techniques, or essentially give up on finding a cure for difficult problems when allopathic methods don't work, they can instill a sense of hopelessness. As a client, you must remember that there are many paths to health. Dr. Andrew Weil explains that although he hears of many "incurable" conditions being cured around the world, he is surprised at the inability of many medical doctors to have faith in the body's ability to repair itself. Especially during a time of crisis, when patients are vulnerable, this belief can be passed easily to a patient. "In my experience, shamans who serve as healers do much better. Regardless of what methods they use … they are master psychotherapists. They're especially good at taking the belief and power that people project onto them and reflecting it back in the service of healing."[105] Believe in the possibility of miracles, while you do everything practical you can to heal yourself.

As I mentioned, when I work with clients I typically combine modalities. When designing a plan of treatment, I take into account the issues my clients are currently facing, their goals, and the intuitive and spiritual guidance I receive. I do an assessment journey to consult with my helping spirits. Plans are based on a person's individual needs and vary accordingly. Two sample plans follow to illustrate possible combinations of healing techniques.

A young woman is seeking emotional healing. She is having difficulty finding balance after a series of personal and professional disappointments. She finds herself dwelling on traumatic events from the past and is unable to feel the energy and enthusiasm for life that she once had. I might suggest the following sessions for her: an extraction to clear energies that are connected to her inappropriately; a soul retrieval to reconnect her with parts of her essential self that separated during crises in her life; several energetic healing sessions to infuse her spiritual body with healing and rejuvenating energy; and a custom designed ceremony to celebrate and manifest her intention to live her life joyously and powerfully.

A middle-aged man is seeking to connect to sources of spiritual guidance and gain clarity about his life path. He is taking a fresh look at his life and feeling confused, particularly about his career options. An appropriate program might include the following: an intuitive reading to gain insight into the causes of his situation and the most desirable options for the future; Harner Method Shamanic Counseling (a method of teaching journeying skills) to access his own spiritual teachers; and a guided visualization designed for him to connect with a deeper level of his subconscious for insight and problem solving.

By working with different modalities, I can help facilitate healing on different levels. Some of the techniques are purely energetic and there is little talking involved. When I do intuitive consultations, I'm acting more as a counselor, providing advice and helping clients see themselves and their choices more clearly in order to create the lives they want. Obviously, practitioners have different styles of working. When you're seeking a holistic healing practitioner, I recommend that you pay attention not only to the types of work they do, but especially to how you feel in their presence.

Spiritual healing is deeply personal. There is a level of intimacy involved that requires trust and comfort for both the client and the practitioner. Use your instincts to decide if you feel comfortable entrusting yourself to a practitioner. Personal referrals are always reassuring, but remember that the right practitioner for your friend may not be the right one for you. There are many gifted people working in this field. You may feel relaxed and open with one and nervous with another. It is not necessarily a reflection on the practitioner's technical or personal skills, but simply a good or poor energetic match.

There are some practical ways to find qualified healing practitioners. Often professional organizations can refer you to someone in your area. For example, Sandra Ingerman maintains a Web site (www.shamanicteachers.com) listing people she has trained who have demonstrated success with clients. The Foundation for Shamanic Studies maintains a list of people certified in Harner Method Shamanic Counseling. Where a person trained is not necessarily a stamp of approval for their work, but it can help you start your search. Some of the best shamanic practitioners may have been taught directly from the spirits without formal training through an individual teacher or organization. Before meeting with a practitioner you can ask how they got started in the field, how they've learned their practice, and what methods they use. In addition to providing you with some concrete information, it will give you a chance to see how you feel intuitively about them before committing to a session.

The practitioner creates a healing environment, engages you physically and psychologically to help you receive healing energy, and implements technical skills; however, the practitioner is not "healing" you. You and the universal life force around you ultimately bring about the healing. Don't abdicate your power to a practitioner, but work together as partners to bring harmony to your systems. Use your sacred intelligence to sense what works for you and have confidence in those instincts.

SHAMANIC HEALING

"Everything that's ever been known, everything that can be known, is available to the shaman in Dreamtime." Michael Harner

The existence of Spirit or spirits is a fundamental premise of shamanism. Spirit permeates everything: the bodies, as well as the souls, of human beings and animals, plants, rocks, the earth, air, and the universe itself. It is the animating force behind all living things. It is the energy that exists within everything, living or inert. Spirit is the basic power of the universe, a vast energetic web that sustains and interconnects all creation. Spirits are ancestors, power animals, teachers, healing allies, and natural forces such as wind or rain. According to shamanic cultures, your relationship to spirit dramatically affects your quality of life. Your job is to live responsibly in your community, to respect yourself and your neighbor, and to follow any practices necessary for you to create harmony with the world around you. If you get into trouble, the shaman can intervene and attempt to restore your health and balance through her skill at negotiating the spirit world. According to shamanic scholar Åke Hultkrantz, "medicine and religion are two sides of the same coin" for the Native North Americans.[106] This premise holds for other shamanic cultures as well. The distinction between "ordinary life" and the supernatural is less pronounced than in Western cultures. Health is considered a natural state. Maintaining a harmonious relationship with the spiritual world is necessary for sustaining that healthy state. It would serve us to consider this holistic view of health more closely. If you are a being created of matter and spirit, why artificially separate those aspects of yourself for treatment? Why not consider the requirements of a healthy body and a healthy spirit to be two parts of a whole?

From the shamanic perspective, all illness, misfortune, or imbalance, whether physical, emotional, or mental, has a spiritual origin. The shaman addresses the spiritual nature of illness by diagnosing the condition and working with the spirit energies within and surrounding the patient. Their goal is often to affect the physical; however, they believe the physical world is a manifestation or reflection of the spiritual world. The shaman seeks to establish spiritual health and balance, which frequently correspond to a physical state of health. The helping spirits are the true healers. In any shamanic healing practice, the shaman is acting as a conduit, a bridge between the patient and the spirits, a vehicle through which the spirits can perform miracles.

Shamanic healing is holistic healing. The word "holistic" is derived from the Greek word *holos*. "Holistic medicine" refers to a system of treatment for the totality of mind, body, and spirit, which views each of those aspects as integral and interrelated in healing. Shamanism was one of the first holistic healing systems on the planet. Although the spirits are credited with the primary role in shamanic healing, it is the shaman's task to fully integrate the work of the spirits with the practical realities of the patient's physical, mental, and emotional lives. The shaman takes the totality of the patient into account when determining appropriate treatment, and works with other health practitioners as needed.

One of the basic principles of shamanic healing is that in order to heal, a patient must be reunited with spiritual power. That power is equivalent to the concept of inner divinity. It is a reawakening to the sacred vitality we hold within ourselves at all times. Shamanically, power loss can have several causes, including the loss of life essence, or soul, due to trauma or illness, the invasion of the body by spirits or spiritual intrusions, or separation from a protective spirit guide.

As in allopathic medicine, diagnosis is the first step in seeking a cure. For shamans, this step usually involves talking with clients about their symptoms and the relevant circumstances of their lives. However, more important than the patient's description of the ailment is the shaman's perception of the spiritual basis of the illness as viewed in an altered state of consciousness. When I work with clients shamanically I do an assessment journey. I'll journey to my helping spirits and ask for advice about which kinds of treatment are called for, and in what order. Typically, I work in concert with my intuition and my spirit guides to develop a plan for treatment. I also ask some other important questions, such as, "Is it appropriate for me to work with this person?" There are times when the client/practitioner match is not a good fit. If I'm guided not to work with someone for whatever reason, I'll try to recommend other practitioners or avenues for treatment.

Soul Retrieval

The concept that pieces of a person's psyche can detach is ancient and widespread. In modern psychology it is termed "dissociation." In shamanism it is called "soul loss." Soul loss results from trauma or crisis. It may be a physical trauma, such as an accident, illness, surgery, abuse, or near death experience, or it may be psychological trauma, such as the loss of a loved one or emotional abuse. Soul loss can happen over time in the case of a chronic problem, or dramatically during an acute episode.

Soul loss is a self-protective response to a threatening event, used to shield the psyche from the full impact of trauma. By partially vacating your body during a time of distress, you are numbed to the full effect of the ensuing pain. In extreme cases, people report watching their bodies, as if from a distance. One of my clients was in a terrible car accident. Seconds before the crash, she found herself watching the accident from above. She was injured in the crash, but she did not feel the pain of impact. After the crash was over, she returned to her usual vantage point inside her body. If you are facing extreme pain, it is an instinctual reaction to avoid it however possible. You escape the pain by escaping your body. According to shamanic scholar Mircea Eliade, sickness is considered a "flight of the soul." The technique used to heal the effects of soul loss is soul retrieval.

In many instances people can recover fully from traumatic events, even if a part of their spirit or essence left their bodies temporarily. A soul part can return to a person naturally and reintegrate with the larger psyche after the crisis is over. Soul loss becomes problematic when the person's spirit is unable to reconnect with the separated parts after the crisis is over. In this case, symptoms of soul loss begin to surface. Symptoms vary, and can include depression, addictions, chronic fatigue, memory lapses, and immune deficiency disorders.[107]

In many cases clients express a perception of the experience of soul loss. There are some classic statements that indicate soul loss has occurred. For example, when a patient says they "have never felt the same" since a particular event, or they don't feel "fully present in their body," or they feel like "a part of them is missing." Typically a practitioner will do an assessment or diagnostic journey to determine if soul retrieval is recommended.

During a soul retrieval, the shamanic practitioner journeys with the intent of finding any of the patient's lost soul parts that are ready to return home. Soul retrieval techniques vary and are evolving over time. Typically, after identifying a spirit as a fragment of the person's soul, the practitioner communicates with it to determine the situation that caused its flight and the gift it brings back. Then she journeys back to ordinary reality, retracing her steps and holding the lost soul-part. Once back from the journey, she performs a ritual of reunification. It involves blowing the soul-part into the patient through the top of the head, and then into the area around the heart. Ingerman emphasizes that what is returning to clients is simply part of their essence, a neutral energy that is part of their larger spiritual body.

Soul retrieval is one of the techniques I employ most frequently with clients. The following is an excerpt from a newspaper article written about my work, which details a soul retrieval I did with one of my clients. It is always important to remember that the spirits are the true healers. As I took that journey, I was able to bring back parts of Helen's fragmented soul, because my helping spirits guided me.

> Helen Beckham grew up shy and sheltered, which made it easier for her later to bury the things she wanted to forget. She had gotten married, gotten on with her life. But four years ago, while on her way to visit her parents in Greensboro, a car accident brought it all back: a hospitalization for an illness that required humiliating, invasive treatments when she was a fourth-grader; and, at the age of 14, the rape by a family friend on the cold bathroom floor of her church.

> "It just seemed like my whole life was just shot down in that moment," Helen recalled of the wreck, which damaged her lower back. "I really felt alone in the universe, that the whole thing wasn't fair. Like before, I was doing everything right and, boom, out of nowhere something horrible happened. It really shook me up."

> She tried a mix of traditional and alternative therapies for her injury, and sought counseling for the vivid memories that had resurfaced. All of it helped but none of it made things good enough. She felt as if she had lost pieces of herself along the way, as if she should return to her old church in Greensboro, face her greatest fear and feel whole again.

> Last month, she had a dream that she did just that. After waking up with a yearning to return and somehow make things right again, she set up an appointment with Mara. The two met months earlier at a party, and although Helen was hopeful Mara could help her out, she had no experience with this type of work and showed up for her first shamanic journey feeling apprehensive.

> Any doubts disappeared after it was over. Mara first told Helen that during the journey she had seen a girl about 10 years old sitting at the top of a tree. Helen took that to be herself in the fourth grade, when she

went to the hospital. It made sense to her because she loved climbing trees at that age. She felt safe in the highest limbs.

But more mind boggling for Helen was that Mara also had come across a teen-age girl with long brown hair and bangs sitting on a bathroom floor. "When those words came out of her mouth, I just about fell out of my seat," Helen remembered, still emotional. "I don't know how it works, but she made an instantaneous believer out of me. She was bringing back pieces of my soul."[108]

Another client of mine suffered through rape, physical abuse, depression, and addictions. She describes her experience during and after her soul retrieval session.

Well over a year ago Mara performed a soul retrieval for me. I had always felt something was missing inside of me and that was confirmed by Mara's journey. Several fragments of my soul had separated ... Just identifying these traumatic turning points helped me to find an acceptance of the past and see how deeply I had been affected by those events. I was able to come to terms with those circumstances. I believe those fragments have come back and I have begun on the journey of healing.

Working with Mara enabled me to let go of the limits of my beliefs and enter that magical realm. I felt as if the guides spoke to my heart. I came away feeling connected. Something had been revealed to me that had eluded me, and I was able to really let go of some old wounds. I understood something about myself that enabled me to move on.

Sometimes when I work there is no reference to trauma in the journey, only a remembering of the gifts the reunited parts bring back to a client. I recently did a soul retrieval for Prudence, who had suffered a great deal in her life. I was aware of many traumas that could have presented. Instead, my helping spirits showed me a beautiful female figure dancing. She was made entirely of light. I was mesmerized as she danced gracefully with long flexible limbs. Prudence was brought the gifts of freedom, self-expression, flexibility, and joy. The spirits suggested that she "dance with abandon" to activate the energy that was returning to her. After the journey, Prudence told me that she had always wanted to take dance lessons, but her older sister, who took classes herself, had discouraged her. Even after she finally convinced her mother to take her, her sister threw such a tantrum at the local dance school on the eve of her first lesson that the whole family was "uninvited" from taking classes. As a child, Prudence didn't get to dance. But now, as an adult, she has her dancer back.

Soul retrieval can have profound physical and psychological results and may provide one of the most effective bridges between traditional shamanic healing and contemporary psychology. Although the two modalities originate from different perspectives, there is a common recognition that people who have endured severe crisis respond in a holistic way. Survivors of sexual abuse or people suffering from post traumatic stress disorder are affected physically, psychologically, and spiritually at a level sometimes far deeper than physical wounds indicate. Given the shared shamanic and psychotherapeutic premise that a person's psyche responds to extreme pain by aversion and dissociation, there is common ground for the soul retrieval technique to be used as a complement to Western psychotherapy.

Extraction and Laying On of Hands

As it is possible for someone's energetic or spiritual essence to be lost, it is also possible for a foreign spirit or "intrusion" to be attached to a person inappropriately, causing illness. In fact, soul loss, and the resulting "holes" in a person's spirit body, can precipitate spiritual intrusions. The shamanic technique of extraction removes these trespassing energies. Terms for this kind of healing vary cross culturally; however, the basis of the technique, the removal of a foreign energy from a patient's body, is consistent. Extractions are often used to treat physical symptoms such as infection, tumor, and pain. Typically the shaman begins with a divinatory diagnosis. Using her hands or another tool to scan the body, the shaman senses the energetic vibration of the patient's body, and determines if there is a disturbance in the patient's energy field caused by a spirit intrusion. If an intruding spirit is found, an extraction is performed. In addition to sensing an offending spirit in or around the patient's body, the shaman frequently sees it as an unpleasant substance or creature. As a surgeon removes a tumor or clears a blocked passageway, the shaman removes the spiritual cause of disease or illness.

Shamans work closely with their spirit allies, especially plant spirits, while performing extractions. A shaman may have dozens of allies at her disposal, each to treat a different type of intrusion. In some cases the shaman actually holds these helping spirits in her mouth. This is particularly important during the practice of "sucking" the harmful spirit from a patient. The spirit intrusion is sucked into the shaman's mouth and neutralized by the helping spirits. The shaman is very careful not to swallow and then spits the intrusion out. This very physical process of removal can induce severe reactions in the shaman, including vomiting. Often the spirit of the illness is very similar to the spirit ally that the shaman uses to heal the illness. Possibly this correlates with the homeopathic concept of "like heals like."

I once worked with a woman who had chronic foot problems. She was planning a walking trip to Europe and was concerned that she would have to cut her activities short given the pain in her foot. After a divinatory diagnosis, I saw that she needed an extraction. I merged with my helping spirits and removed the intrusion from her foot. She reported that the problem was better and her trip was successful. Other clients notice physical changes, such as increased healing after surgery, reduced pain from inflammation, or improved mobility. By manipulating the "energy" surrounding the patient and by removing spiritual intrusions, the shaman is often able to relieve physical symptoms.

Power Animal Retrieval

Like soul retrieval, power animal retrieval reunites a lost aspect of the patient, restoring power and vitality. But instead of a portion of the patient's psyche, a power animal retrieval reunites the patient with a spirit ally who can provide protection, support, and guidance. Loss of power can manifest in a variety of ways, from chronic bad luck, to becoming accident prone, to difficulty in accomplishing goals. The concept of a guardian spirit is prevalent in shamanic cultures. In the Puget Sound area, Salish shamans frequently implicate the loss of a guardian spirit or power animal in a patient's misfortune or illness.[109]

To retrieve a power animal, the shaman undertakes a journey to the lower world and seeks an animal spirit who is willing to help the patient. Once identified, the spirit is brought back and blown into the patient through the top of the head and chest, similar to the technique used in soul retrieval. It reconnects patients with their own spiritual resources for guidance and protection. Once reconnected with their guardian spirits or power animals, people are often able to tap into their own intuition and innate healing abilities more easily.

Sometimes I will sense an animal spirit around my clients when we're drumming or rattling, before the journey itself. People are typically excited about reconnecting with a power animal. This relationship seems to bring up a deep sense of connectedness and joy, and often reminds people of the mysterious and fantastic states of mind they experienced in childhood. Frequently there is a renewed sense of playfulness inspired by a power animal. This alone can be healing. One client described the feeling of being with his power animal as "exceptionally jubilant," others have reported a fascination with the animal in their ordinary life and a peaceful sense of support and strength.

A variety of animal spirits have offered to help me. Some are particularly helpful with clients or specific healing techniques and others serve more as personal advisors. One spirit acts as my guide primarily when I'm doing soul retrievals, another for extractions. My primary power animal first came to me in a meditation, before I knew about shamanism. During my first shamanic journey I was delighted to see her again. She has been a consistent companion, providing me with practical advice and unwavering affection. When I feel insecure or afraid, I call on her and am protected and supported. When I need some direct guidance she advises me. And when I need a safe place to rest, she holds me. Some of my most powerful personal healing experiences have been when I invited her to merge with me in ceremony. At these times I'm filled with an immense energy and sense of strength. When the ceremony is over I feel energized and transformed.

Healing Journey

The healing journey is a passive healing technique. It is the basis from which all other shamanic healing techniques are derived. It is simply asking for help from the sacred realm in whatever capacity is needed. The shaman usually journeys and asks for healing of a particular ailment or problem, or simply for the highest good. Shamans take a supporting role to their spirit allies. They make the request and do what they are called on to do in the journey. Although the methodology of this technique is harder to dissect than the others, it can have equally profound results. Sometimes the healing is performed while the shaman is actually merged with a power animal or spirit teacher. In this case, the shaman journeys to meet a spirit, requests to merge with that spirit, and then returns. The shaman then embodies the power of the spirit and is able to transmit that healing power to the patient through a number of vehicles, including song and dance. The healing journey is comparable to prayer. The shaman asks the spirits to show compassion toward the patient, and offers thanks.

One client asked me to journey for her mother, who had a brain tumor and was in hospice. With her mother's permission, I journeyed to my helping spirits and asked them to give her what was needed. My spirits took me to her room and I watched as they helped to calm her fears and reassure her as she prepared to make her transition. They infused her with gentle healing energy and let her know that she was supported. Over of a series of journeys my client noticed a great shift in her mother, from fearful and resistant, to peaceful and ready to let go when the time was right. In any long distance healing work I do there is an element of the healing journey, as I always ask for the spirits to lend their support in whatever way is most helpful.

Lost Souls

Shamans are active in assuring the peaceful existence of a person's body and spirit while they are alive, and are equally concerned with the state of their soul after death. By acting as psychopomp, literally "conductor of souls," the shaman guides recently deceased or confused souls through the landscape of the spirit world safely to the appropriate place. The premise is that a person may become lost or confused after death, unsure of what has happened and unable to negoti-ate the world in the new state in which they find themselves. Shamans, having lived with one foot in ordinary reality and one foot in non-ordinary reality, are familiar with nonphysical states of being. They are able to steer lost spirits in the right direction, allowing them to move into the next phase of existence peace-fully, with as little trauma as possible. Shamans are particularly adept at this role of post mortem escort because they've often faced their own death during initia-tions and the near death experiences that are often the catalyst for a shaman's calling. The ability to travel in the "afterlife realm" is one of the most universal requirements for a shaman. Their excursions deep into the spiritual terrain have brought them to worlds the average person sees only after their physical life is over. Practically all of the shamanic traditions in the world have reference to shamans working in this capacity.

Often psychopomp work is needed when someone has died a sudden or traumatic death. After the tsunami that killed over 170,000 people in Asia in December 2004, survivors reported many sightings of ghosts, the spirits of those killed in the tidal wave, who had not passed on to where they needed to go. One woman watched as rescuers tried desperately to revive an unconscious child, but failed. The next week, she saw the dead boy playing in the hotel lobby, wearing the same clothes he had on when he died. Stories abounded of ghosts stuck near the places of their death, calling for help in the night, or searching in vain for loved ones. Spiritual leaders recognized the importance of performing psychopomp work, for the sake of the living and the dead. "If we don't send them off, the spirits will stay around where they died," says Saengthong Suwanjan, the sixty–year–old keeper of a temple overlooking the sea. "If they can't go anywhere, they will stay here and haunt us. And if they don't know how to get to the next life, they might try to take some of us with them."[110] With many other shamanic practitioners, I've tried to help tsunami victims by acting as psychopomp. The journeying I did was moving and overwhelming at times. The sheer number of confused spirits was astonishing.

One of my clients came in for an intuitive reading. She brought her sister, who was grieving after the death of her son. He died alone when his car crashed into a tree. We started the reading, but it became clear that psychopomp work was needed to help the young man. I felt him close to his mother. He was staying to be near his family, and had a profound sense of guilt for causing the accident. He loved them and hadn't meant to cause them the terrible pain he was now witnessing. He needed his parents' forgiveness. I counseled his mother that she, in particular, needed to let him go. With the help of ancestral spirits who were waiting to help him, we assisted him in making the transition. My client contacted me later and said that the work during that session had a profound healing effect on the family. She said it made a tremendous difference in helping them move on.

When souls are in between stages of existence, dead in body, but wandering this world, they are suffering. They are often confused, angry, and lonely. When they are not assisted to cross over into the appropriate spiritual worlds, they can cause trouble for the living. Without necessarily having malicious intent, they can latch on to living beings. These lost souls are attracted to the light and vitality that the living radiate. In some instances they even enter the body of a living person.

When the soul of a dead person merges with that of a living person, the living can feel a variety of ill effects. Much depends on the disposition of the deceased soul. Some spirits are simply confused, wishing no ill will on their hosts. In such cases, the hosts might feel that their thoughts are not their own, or they are acting compulsively, or the experience of being inside themselves changed dramatically at some point. Other spirits are angry and wish to exert control over their host. This can result in self-destructive or violent behavior, addictions, and suicidal feelings. Some possessing souls are aware of their attachment, and others are not.

One client came to see me reporting that he didn't feel like himself. Jason lacked confidence at times, would obsess about his appearance, and regularly holed up in his house, not emerging for days at a time. Energetic intrusions and possessing spirits exist along a spectrum of levels of consciousness, from very simple energy to human consciousness and beyond. I sensed a possessing spirit, among other issues that needed to be addressed. It was not a human energy, but it was sentient. I worked in a number of ways with this man, through ritual, song, extraction, psychopomp, Reiki, and Healing with Spiritual Light. Our first breakthrough came when I worked with my helping spirits to allow this energy to release its fearful hold on Jason and move upward into a loving place. What it needed most was love and reassurance. Ultimately, the energy cleared and my client felt better and more in control.

Herbal Medicine

Our environment provides a plethora of healing plants. Traditional healers throughout the ages turned to nature as a regular source for preventative and curative medicines. Western medicine has reversed that attitude, often touting pharmaceuticals as a safer alternative to herbal medicine. Dr. Andrew Weil laments this disconnection from nature, "This separation has enormous consequences for our society because, fundamentally, healing is a natural process. If you want to understand healing, you must develop a feeling for the ways of nature."[111]

Indigenous healers' vast knowledge of the healing properties of local flora may be their greatest contribution to "modern" medicine. Since the properties of plants can be observed and tested scientifically, it is an area of traditional healing that doctors and scientists with a contemporary Western perspective can more often accept. Native North Americans used indigenous plants extensively for healing. Mosses and fungi were used to dress wounds, sweetgrass acted as a protective amulet, and calamus root was given for stomachache.[112] Native Americans made great contributions to pharmacology. Western medicine has adopted quinine, used to treat malaria, from the indigenous people of Peru, a bark from an evergreen tree used to treat scurvy was given by the Hurons, and the development of aspirin is directly linked to instruction from the Native North Americans about how to use the bark of the willow tree to reduce pain.[113]

Often the discovery of healing plants was made in a scientific fashion, through close observation and by trial and error. By watching animals' behavior—whether they ingested a plant, avoided it, or sought it out when ill—the shaman deduced a plant's potential medicinal uses. The use of plants in healing usually has a spiritual component, as well as the more easily documented physical one. Although the tangible nature of plants promotes healing in and of itself, the spiritual nature of the plant is of primary interest to shamans. They believe it is the spirit aspect of the plant that prompts a healing response. Often the curative properties of plants were revealed through journeying or communicating with the plants directly. Biologist Lyall Watson studied the shamanic approach to identifying healing plants in Madagascar. He describes the vast number of plant species on the island and how healers must carefully choose the exact species, the specific part of the plant to use, the season in which to pick it, the method of preparation, and the ailment it can treat. He believed they must have been assisted somehow in mining the gems of medicinal information from this enormous pool of choices. "The help it seems comes from the plants themselves. When Watson asked traditional healers how they know an extract from the leaves of a local flowering plant picked in the spring is good for what they call 'milky blood,' he always gets the same answer, 'Oh, it's easy,' they say, 'we ask the plants.'" The effectiveness of this method was demonstrated to Watson when he realized that "milky blood" was leukemia and the Madagascar periwinkle that the natives use to treat it is the same plant from which a major pharmaceutical company derives substances used in their medicines, also to treat leukemia.[114]

The Healing Power of Words and Sounds

From the beginning of recorded time, people have contended that words and sounds have tremendous power to create and heal. The New Testament book of John begins, "In the beginning was the Word, and the Word was with God, and the Word was God."[115] Some traditional Latin American cultures believe the world was actually sung into existence by the non-ordinary realms, created out of nothingness from the vibration of sound. The Mayans believe that the spirits sing us into existence. As their song moves from the spirit world to ordinary reality, the sound takes the shape of humans, animals, and material objects.[116] Vedic chants and shamanic songs have been used throughout the world to invoke healing. In ancient Egypt, some words were never spoken because they were believed to be so powerful that physical change beyond human control would manifest upon their utterance.[117]

This faith in the power of language is expressed across cultures and across philosophies. In fact, according to Robert Gass, a pioneer in the field of healing sounds, one of the definitions of the word healing is "to make sounds."[118] Through singing, storytelling, chanting, toning, speaking, and praying, shamans and practitioners of different healing philosophies around the world help heal their patients. Of the many tools shamans employ, their faculty with words and sound has some of the greatest curative power. Shamans sing to call in their spirit helpers, to describe their journeys, to celebrate and honor the earth, and to convey words of hope to sick and despairing patients. The act of vocalizing also helps shamans separate from their egos and slip more easily into the realm of non-ordinary reality. It can facilitate trance states and other altered states of consciousness. The rhythmic drum and rattle beats used when journeying are hypnotic; shamans are *driven* to the other worlds, riding on the beat of the drum.

The power of words is well understood in many cultures. In indigenous traditions, words and songs are often used in healing. The Sami people of Lapland and Norway talked about "word doctoring," where they used specific phrases to heal conditions such as headaches.[119] Shamans have power songs that bring them strength and medicine songs to heal. Navajo healing rituals typically involve singing over the person to be healed. Hundreds of songs may be included in just one ceremony. The Blessing Way ceremony alone has over three hundred songs. The singers need to be highly skilled, as it is believed that singing the wrong words can actually harm the patient.[120] The medicine songs of the Kung! Bushmen are believed to have a "supernatural potency" called *ntum*. Dancing to rhythmic clapping and chanting was believed to activate the *ntum*, which they feel as a "physical substance in the pit of their stomach."[121]

It is the shaman's job to tell healing stories to patients, to use words to give them hope and help them have faith that healing will occur. Health care practitioners of all traditions must be highly in tune with the way they communicate with their patients. Hopeless words can plunge patients into despair, depriving them of the will they need to heal their illness. Hopeful words, in contrast, empower patients to pursue their healing with an enthusiastic and optimistic outlook. Through her communication, the practitioner who inspires her patients to live fully despite a difficult physical situation gives them an invaluable gift.

I often advise clients to seek a power song, or simply to find a private space where they can tone or sing from their heart. I sing healing songs for my clients and anytime that I'm seeking a sense of harmony and connection to Spirit. The ceremonies when I have invited my spirit teacher to sing through me have been especially powerful. Although I recognize my voice, it takes on an intensity and resonance I don't experience in everyday life. At the conclusion I feel cleansed, strengthened, and infused with a radiant light.

Contemporary and traditional shamans share the viewpoint that, as humans, we hold a tremendous influence over our world. Through the use of our voices and language, we can change that world for better or worse. In a sense, we create our reality by the way we describe it. We bring our health into existence by our belief and expressions about our state of health. Ken Wilber states this concept eloquently. "Language does not merely report the world, represent the world, describe the world. Rather, language creates worlds, and in that creation is power."[122]

Toning and chanting are good methods for stepping out of an egoic state into a more harmonious state, allowing the life force to flow smoothly through you and around you. The repetitive sounds of chanting can cleanse our minds and bodies, helping us align with sacred vibrations, ultimately feeling unity with everything around us. Toning as a group is a remarkable tool for maintaining a state of divine connection. Sanskrit chanting combines the inherent power of sound with the invocation of gods and goddesses. I'll always remember the moment I first heard Krishna Das's music. It stopped me in my tracks and my heart opened. I remember saying, "That is the most beautiful thing I've ever heard." I recommend his music to help connect to the healing energies of sound.

The monotonous percussion sounds used in shamanism are intended to produce a similar awakening. Through drumming and rattling, the shaman and others involved in ceremonial work are guided to a deeper state of consciousness. In that altered state perception shifts to allow a keener awareness of the spiritual dimension. When I drum with clients, they frequently report increased peacefulness and power from the act of drumming. It helps them open energetically to the healing they are about to receive. Drumming and rattling help me connect with my spirit teachers and also heighten my intuition, preparing me to facilitate the healing work.

Experiment with sound. Call a power song to you and sing it with all your heart. Make sounds, allowing different tones to resonate with different parts of your body. Chant a mantra. Inspire your body through the vibration of your own voice, an instrument, or recorded music. Welcome the healing power of sound to flow through you.

ENERGETIC HEALING

"Allow your life experience to be lightly dusted with form." Barbara Brennan

There are many forms of energetic healing in practice today and although the techniques vary, they all work with vital life force to restore health. In this section I'll discuss two methods I use predominantly. Although they are complementary, they approach spiritual energy from somewhat different perspectives. Reiki draws on the *universal* flow of healing energy to rebalance a patient's energy system. Healing with Spiritual Light focuses on creating space where the perfection held *within* each individual's divine potential for health can manifest.

Reiki

Reiki originated in Japan in the end of the 19th century. The word "Reiki" means "Universal Life Energy." Universal life energy refers to essentially the same substance as the other healing systems and philosophies we have examined so far. In fact, the second part of the word "Reiki," "*ki*," relates etymologically to the Chinese word "*ch'i*," the vital force animating all beings. "*Rei*" signifies the universality of this energy, what shamanic cultures often call spirit. It signifies the spiritual aspect of living beings, the life force that flows through everything in the universe, your divine energy.

There are a variety of Reiki systems used today. I practice the Usui System of Natural Healing, or "Usui Shiki Ryoho," named for Dr. Mikao Usui, the founder of the system as we know it. Dr. Usui sought out the wisdom of the spiritual and healing traditions of his time. He learned Chinese and Sanskrit, he read the Indian sutras, and he studied the great spiritual healers. He supposed that if Buddha and Jesus embodied healing powers, then somehow the knowledge of how to develop those abilities must be available in the present day. Through his studies, rigorous personal practice, and a profound encounter with spirit, Dr. Usui brought a powerful healing technique to his community. The techniques he was shown involved specific hand positions, the use of esoteric symbols to start the flow and quality of the healing energy, and a method for training practitioners that involves initiations called "attunements," designed to open a student as a channel for the Reiki energy.

Reiki is a remarkably simple practice. When acting as a conduit for Reiki, a practitioner maintains a positive intention focused on the client. The practitioner concentrates on specific areas of the body in need of healing and harmonizes all the systems of the body. Practitioners place their hands on or above the patient, shifting the hand positions to cover all the major organs and glands in the body in the course of a session. Reiki energy flows where it is needed and helps restore balance by inspiring a person's systems to regulate themselves. Reiki can enhance the body's natural ability to heal itself, foster mental and spiritual equilibrium, clear blocked energies, cleanse toxins from the body, and invoke a deep sense of relaxation, among other benefits. It can also be sent from a distance.

Reiki energy works to harmonize the flow of energy through a person's chakra system. As we've discussed, the chakras are a network of energy centers in the body. There are seven major centers located along the spine from the coccyx to the crown of the head. When the vital energy is flowing in a balanced way, with no blockages, people enjoy physical and emotional health. When the flow of energy through the body is obstructed in some way, or if there is a dramatic difference in the rate of flow from one chakra to the next, illness or discomfort may result. Reiki helps to regulate and balance the flow of energy through the chakras.

Reiki works on physical problems as well as emotional or psychological ones. It can help with acute injuries or chronic illness. I've used it successfully on burns and bruises. When my daughter was a toddler she fell face first out of a stroller onto a hard floor. I expected a huge swelling, but I did Reiki on her for a while and she walked away without a mark. I recently burned myself while cooking with hot oil. The oil splashed onto my hand and went up under my fingernails. I could immediately see the marks where blisters were forming. At the time I thought it would be the worst burn I'd experienced as an adult. After a combination of Reiki and ice water, I had no pain or visible marks.

My clients have reported a wide range of benefits from Reiki and combined energetic healing sessions. The most frequent comment I hear immediately after a session is that the client felt profoundly relaxed and peaceful. Simply entering a truly relaxed state can precipitate healing. With the benefit of the Reiki energy, I suspect the body and mind "remember" how to relax and find equilibrium naturally. The most consistent feedback from clients over time is an increase in energy, calmness, and centeredness; a decrease in pain, anger, and stress; improved sleep; and a heightened awareness that manifests in increased intuition or a sense of connectedness to nature and others. One client said "After one Reiki session, I slept like a log, for the first time in months after chronic sleeping problems."

One client who suffers from thyroid issues described the results of her healing sessions: correction of slow metabolism and constipation, improved circulation, improvement of slow mental processing and confusion, and slowed heart rate. "My heart doesn't feel like it is working so hard. I could also feel the spirits working on my thyroid ... and clearing out the 'cotton' in my head." After one session another client taking thyroid medication visited her doctor and discovered she could reduce her medication significantly. Of course, I always tell clients to seek medical guidance when it comes to medications and allopathic treatments. It's never advisable to change prescription medications without consulting a physician.

I've seen Reiki help immediately with feelings of depression and despair. One client came to me with depression and sleep difficulties. She was experiencing frequent and persistent bouts of crying and writer's block. The later was especially problematic, as she was an author with an impending deadline. After the first session she said, "I'm feeling tremendous benefit. I came home and practically melted into bed last night and slept better than I have in a long while. The next day, I didn't feel like crying for the first time in a long time." She described her experience after a few Reiki sessions, "I'm writing again after being blocked for a long time. I'm feeling better overall. My depression has lifted. Other people have noticed the big change in me. Cumulatively, I am feeling so much better."

In one scientific study, the long-term effects of Reiki on symptoms of psychological depression and stress were evaluated. Forty–six participants were randomly assigned to one of three groups: hands-on Reiki, distance Reiki, or distance Reiki placebo. The subjects were not aware of which group they were in. Upon completion of treatment, there was a significant reduction in symptoms of psychological distress in treatment groups as compared with controls, and these differences continued to be present one year later.[123]

I often combine Reiki with Healing with Spiritual Light and shamanic techniques. It is harder to tease out which technique is affecting what, but easier to see a difference in my clients. Consistently my clients report that energy healing sessions bring them a sense of connectedness, confidence, well-being, increased energy levels, peacefulness, and stress reduction. Since I'm always asking for help from the spirits when I work, I particularly enjoy when clients perceive the helpers in the room too. Often they will sense a presence during a session. For instance, sometimes they feel someone working at their feet, while I'm working near their heads. One client described a vision of a woman with long dark hair he saw during a session. His description matched the spirit I was working with at the time.

Reiki is relatively simple to learn. It's a wonderful system for self-healing. Once you learn the basic techniques, you can apply them to yourself as often as you like. It is an effective preventative method for maintaining your health on all levels. By using Reiki as a spiritual practice, not only a response to crisis, you can often avoid problems before they manifest. Using Reiki on yourself is like stoking up your divine energy, connecting with your inner divinity and allowing it to soak into every cell, permeating your body with vitality and well-being.

Healing with Spiritual Light

Healing with Spiritual Light, one of the methods I work with the most, originated from experiments with polluted water. Sandra Ingerman explored how inner states affect the world around us. She documented the effect that cleansing personal toxins and embodying divine energy had on polluted water placed nearby. In her book, *Medicine for the Earth: How to Transform Personal and Environmental*

Toxins, Sandra explains how she began to work with water, the foundation of all life. She sought to determine if toxins could be transformed or cleaned by using purely spiritual techniques. She helped participants reach a state of pure consciousness where they embodied their inner divinity; they were instructed to let go of anything separating them from their essential spiritual identity, such as thoughts, emotions, and physical sensations.

Her inspiration was the concept of alchemy. She is clear in explaining that the effects on the water are purely a reflection of the personal work of the participants. Although Ingerman was interested in recording the effect on the water, the premise of the study was to see how the ancient premise of "as above so below" would manifest when participants focused on their inherent divine natures. Ingerman wondered if by transmuting personal toxins the water would be inspired to heal as well, returning to its natural state of perfection.

In order to glean quantitative data from her work, she designed an experiment to test the level of toxicity of a sample of water before and after she led a group in healing ceremonies. She started with deionized water and then contaminated it with ammonium hydroxide. Ammonium hydroxide is a common pollutant that comes from decaying vegetable matter or as a by-product of human or animal waste. When ammonium hydroxide is added, water becomes very alkaline. Plain, uncontaminated water has a pH of 5.5. After the ammonium hydroxide was added the pH level jumped to 12. The water was poisonous to drink in that state.

Her group had worked for days, journeying and preparing for the ceremony. Participants were instructed to think of the water as being in a divine state, and not to *try* to change it. They were simply to transfigure into a state of pure divinity. During the ritual, they used drumming, rattling, chanting, and singing. The water was tested again after the ceremony and the pH level had gone down to a 9. Water with a pH level of 9 is safe, although unpleasant, to drink. The results were remarkable, especially considering that the change in the water was a by-product of the transformation of the *people* during the ceremony.

Experiments conducted at McGill University investigated the use of water "charged" by a healer. In this case the healer held bottles of water for a certain period of time each day. Plants watered from those bottles grew significantly better than those watered from the "uncharged" bottles.[124] The human body is mostly water. If energetic methods of healing can produce such exciting results in restoring water to health, it's not much of a leap to assert that they can do the same for a human being. And that's exactly what began to happen.

In working with humans, what she calls Healing with Spiritual Light, Sandra is bringing the concept of transfiguration into her personal healing practice and teaching others to do the same. The technique is remarkably simple and based on ancient ideas about healing. The premise is that our fundamental state is of unity with the creative forces of the universe. We are divine. We possess the innate ability to heal ourselves, not through force of will, but through the vital life force that flows through us. The greatest healers in history have recognized their own divinity. The profoundly spiritual light they cast shone on all those around, sparking the light within the people they touched. There was no manipulation or treatment needed for people to heal; their bodies were inspired by the divine healing light of these masters to find a balanced state for themselves.

There are many tales of the healing powers of these great spiritual masters. Sai Baba has been said to heal people in need of immediate operations, to cure cancer, and to provide all sorts of miracles simply with his presence. Jesus gave sight to a blind man, allowed a paraplegic to walk, and healed a leper, essentially by saying, "it is done." Sandra Ingerman describes filling with divine light and embodying our true natures to bring about healing. She is essentially referring us back to the master healers of the ages. Their awareness of their inner divinity was a key factor in their ability to heal others.

Sandra also emphasizes the importance of being responsible with your personal energetic toxins. Since everything is made of energy, your emotions affect the physical and spiritual worlds around you. We've discussed this in other sections, but it is pertinent here because your emotional well-being and the way you deal with troubling emotions have a direct correlation with your level of health. Don't let emotions fester, don't spew them, don't stuff them, manage them. Sandra advises that we utilize methods for "transmuting" the negative energy behind some emotions, in order to neutralize their impact, or even transform them into healing energy. She discusses some methods in *Medicine for the Earth*, and you can meditate or journey to receive some of your own. Experiment with some transmutation methods of your own devising and see which truly make a difference in how you feel.

During Healing with Spiritual Light sessions, a practitioner focuses on creating a sacred space in the room. They embody their inner divinity as fully as possible, by transfiguring into divine light and releasing anything that separates them from pure sacred energy. Instead of trying to change the client, the practitioner is seeking to create a harmonious field from which the client's system is supported in finding its own natural state of balance. Clients are seen in a state of perfection.

The practitioner seeks simply to rekindle their client's awareness of that perfection and their inner divinity by creating that state in themselves.

My clients report profound experiences. One client of mine, Alicia, called a day after her session in utter amazement and gratitude. She said, "I felt at one with the world. I have never felt so at peace, so at one with myself and everything around me. It feels incredible." She also related that she had been suffering considerably from grief and the Healing with Spiritual Light session helped her with that issue as well. After receiving her first treatment, another client remarked, "It's amazing how something this simple can be so powerful." One young woman suffering from a variety of ailments got up from the table beaming and asked, "Is this what it feels like to be healthy?" Clients consistently report that Healing with Spiritual Light sessions have helped them find a state of peacefulness that has previously eluded them.

My mother worked in this transfigured state on a woman who was suffering from sciatica. Jamie walked in with pain and walked out without it. She reported, "My sciatica is completely gone! Isn't it amazing! For a few days, the symptoms returned in a very mild form now and then, but nothing like before, and I am now almost totally symptom free—without a single trip to the chiropractor!"

Sandra's technique is about light. This inner light has a sort of profound intelligence that can create a state of equilibrium. By recognizing and respecting this light, you can help bring yourself into a state of physical and emotional health.

DISTANCE HEALING

"Praying is not only following rituals and doing it just right. It's how we feel inside, how our heart connects, and how we live. That's called walking the spirit road."
Bear Heart

Sometimes it is not possible to be in physical proximity to someone who needs help. Given that one of the premises of the energetic healing models we've discussed is the interrelatedness of life and the shared universal spirit that flows through everything, it is not surprising that physical proximity is not as important a factor in healing as intent, concentration, and compassion. Remember the hologram analogy. You can access anything from your point in time and space. Prayer is a form of distance healing. Whether used to affect health from a secular or religious standpoint, distance healing has been shown to help its intended recipients.

Larry Dossey is one of the most noted advocates for the use of prayer in healing. Dossey divides healing modalities into three categories. Era I techniques, such as drugs and surgery, are based on "mechanical, material or physical medicine" and fit with widely accepted ideas of time and space. Era II approaches incorporate mind-body medicine and primarily emphasize the effects of consciousness. Techniques include biofeedback and hypnosis, which cannot be fully explained by "classical physics." Era III is "characterized by nonlocal or transpersonal medicine and cannot be described by classical concepts of space-time or matter-energy." "The hallmark of Era III is what I refer to as nonlocal mind. In Era III, we rediscover the ancient realization that consciousness can free itself from the body and that it has the potential to act not just *locally* on one's own body ... but also *nonlocally* on distant things, events and people, even though they may be unaware that they are being influenced."[125] Prayer, energetic medicine, and shamanic healing are all categorized as Era III approaches. They tap into an unseen energy that transcends time and space, and the barrier between the thoughts and intentions of one human being and the body and mind of another. These techniques do not involve the manipulation of the patient's physical body and typically are utilized without the patient being present with the practitioner. Dossey asserts, "Era III is the breeding ground of miracles. They are usually mediated through some manifestation of non-local mind—through intercessory prayer, for example, or following dreams and visions or a sense of contact with an ineffable 'other.'"[126]

Dr. Elizabeth Targ's study on the effects of distance, energetic healing on AIDS patients included healers from eight healing traditions, including Christians, Jews, Buddhists, Native Americans, shamans, and graduates of bioenergetic and meditative healing schools. The healers had an average of seventeen years experience in their field. They were instructed to treat a different person each week on a rotating basis. Targ asked the healers to focus their mental energies on a patient's health and well-being for an hour a day, six days a week, for ten weeks. The results of the experiment were significant. Patients who received distant healing intentions had significantly fewer new AIDS-related illnesses, had less severe illnesses, were hospitalized less frequently, required fewer days of hospitalization, had fewer doctor visits, and also reported significantly improved moods.[127]

Prayer is founded on the idea that we are greater than our bodies; that our intention and our consciously focused efforts can affect the material world, without being limited by space, place, or time. A *Journal of Scientific Exploration* article exploring collective consciousness asserts that even inanimate objects can "resonate" with and respond to human consciousness.[128] The idea of physical objects acting as a conduit to deliver healing power is ancient. Shamans have used tools in healing for ages: crystals, medicine bags, wands, and drums. These objects were infused with power that could be transferred to a patient upon contact to facilitate their own healing. Traditional healers have blessed talismans and charms of various sorts before giving them to the sick person, in the belief that they are able to mediate the healer's wishes.[129] Reiki healing cloths printed with a form of the symbols used in Reiki sessions are also believed to aid in healing.

Intermediary objects are used in prayer healing as well. In *Reinventing Medicine*, Larry Dossey describes the experience of a girl who was in an auto accident that fractured her neck and injured her spinal cord. She was not expected to live through the night. The parishioners in Lisa's family's church created a prayer cloth for her. Each person held the cloth and prayed for healing for Lisa. Lisa had the cloth attached to her body the whole time she was in the hospital. Each day Lisa got a little better. With only a thread of spinal cord attached, a girl who wasn't expected to live through the night, and probably shouldn't have survived the ambulance ride, survived.[130]

The three methods of spiritual healing that I practice regularly are shamanic healing, Healing with Spiritual Light, and Reiki. They all work from a distance. I used a combination of modalities to work long distance with David. David had suffered years of depression, was struggling with his marriage, and felt physically out of control. I started distance healing at the beginning of April. In the first week of May, he reported that he'd had the best month in a very long time. He was mystified, because nothing has really changed in his life circumstances, he just felt different.

Another client of mine was suffering from depression and had a variety of environmental sensitivities and a sense of desperation with her life circumstances. She described that, with each distance healing session, she felt a sense of calm flowing through her, which allowed her to better cope with her situation. She had more energy and an increased sense of well-being, which gave her the hope and determination to work to improve her life.

I worked with Steven, a three–year–old boy who was having episodes of acting out. His father was concerned over a recent custody battle and the ensuing transition of living arrangements. He was also worried about the effect Steven's mentally ill mother might have had on Steven's emotional state. After two sessions, his father reported that he was "doing better, with fewer 'episodes,' most of the ones that have still occurred have been easier/quicker to terminate. I've thought things were getting better before, only to see them 'flare up' again, but it feels different this time, so I'm hopeful that this is a more fundamental shift." Steven was also able to start talking about his mother, which he seemed unable to do before. His father reported that he was doing significantly better after a few more sessions.

Spiritual healing work is based less on employing a particular technique or philosophy than on drawing on the love, compassion, and intent of the healer and the helping spirits. In most cases, this work is about people calling on a higher power—spirit, God, or the patient's higher self—to help one another. These results clearly indicate that somehow the spirit or focus of one person can affect the physiology of another. They indicate that spirit can indeed affect matter, as shamans for thousands of years have professed. When you tap into the power of your inner divinity to inspire positive change, you are accessing the universal spirit that embraces us all, actively creating a healthier world for yourself and those around you.

OTHER FACTORS IN HEALING

"The power of love to change bodies is legendary, built into folklore, common sense, and everyday experience. Love moves the flesh, it pushes matter around.… Throughout history, 'tender loving care' has uniformly been recognized as a valuable element in healing." Larry Dossey

The Vital Role of Love and Compassion

Love and compassion are fundamental elements of spiritual healing work, and should be one of the foundations you look for in a practitioner. Practitioners must be compassionate to act as conduits, allowing healing power from the spirit world to be transferred to the tangible one. They should be motivated by genuine respect and love for their healing partnership with the spirits to remain strong.

For the shamanic practitioner, part of creating a space where healing can take place is venturing outside herself—to step outside her ego. The shaman's experience as a human enables her to relate to the pain and suffering experienced in this world. However, her challenge is to wed that genuine personal understanding to power, which comes only from moving entirely outside of herself. This philosophy also applies to other spiritual healing modalities. Whether using Reiki, Healing with Spiritual Light, or shamanic techniques, I recognize the assistance from the spirit world and my duty to work cooperatively with that world. I open my heart to the spirit world in order to help my clients open themselves to the healing energy available to them. Ingerman describes her personal experience with entering a profound state while doing shamanic healing work: "... my energy feels so expansive I can't imagine any building that could contain it, and I am in a state of egoless divine love. Some shamans burst into tears as they sing because of the love that is coursing through their heart."[131]

This principle of loving interaction is ubiquitous in spiritual healing work. Prayer of all denominations is based on the power of selfless, compassionate intention. Dr. Ron Roth refers to Jesus' non-judgmental attitude towards healing his people: "(T)his quality of unconditional love is the most important attribute we can bring with us to our healing work—whether for ourselves or for others ..."[132]

Without love, the shaman, or any other spiritual healer, is simply practicing a technique. Techniques are not enough to inspire deep change. Love is the fundamental substance of spirit. Love is at the heart of your inner divinity. Love is the fuel by which humans transport themselves into a state of harmony and compassion, a state where we can heal ourselves and our fellow inhabitants of the earth, indeed the earth itself.

Attitude

Your attitude impacts your health. Some of these effects are common sense, although frequently ignored. If you abuse your body, mind, or spirit, you are likely to develop an imbalance or illness of some sort. If you abdicate your responsibility for your own health, the odds are good that your health will ultimately deteriorate. If you ignore signs that your system is off balance and needs treatment, you will ultimately get caught in a tangle of health related problems. Take responsibility for the *preservation* of your health, and you will need to do less to restore it. Listen to what your instincts and your body tell you about what needs attention.

Simply having a positive attitude can help the healing process. Studies of blood flow to the brain during times of sadness and happiness indicate that positive emotion puts the brain temporarily at rest, which is exactly the desirable state for healing.[133] Opening yourself to the process itself can also be beneficial. This is akin to the intention, "Let my will and God's will be the same." With this intention you are accepting rather than fighting, you are aligning yourself with the universal flow, creating harmony in your healing process. When you fight against something, it typically pushes back. A more effective attitude is to put your energy behind your own healing. Instead of fighting *against* an illness, work *for* your healing.

The processes of health and healing are mysterious. The meaning of your life is mysterious. It is easy to become fixated on knowing as much as possible, on having control and using your intellect to figure things out. Life is too complicated to reduce it to manageable little parts that you can master. Appreciate the vast unknown in your own life. Instead of fearing this misty place, embrace the ephemeral quality of your unfolding life. The future is fluid, complex, and paradoxical. You simply can't know everything in advance; however, you can prepare yourself to make the healthiest and wisest choices in each moment.

Illness evokes fear in most of us, but it can be a tremendous learning experience. Not just in the vein of "What doesn't kill me makes me stronger," but in providing an opportunity to stop and reevaluate. Some of us need a boulder in our path to alert us that we need a course correction. The path to health is different for each of us. Turn to your ultimate source of spiritual support, divine energy, to help open yourself to the healing process, without becoming bogged down in figuring it all out.

Your thoughts, your intentions, your prayers, and your attitude can affect your body and your state of health right now. Healing happens in the present moment. We carry so much energetic baggage from the past that it can settle into our cells, and ultimately cause physical problems. When seeking health, stay focused on the "now." Reliving past traumas or botched decisions will not help you find balance now. Telling and retelling the story of your emotional or physical traumas, either to yourself or to others, does not heal those wounds, it simply directs your energy to them. Don't give attention to what you do not want. Don't feed the negative. Infuse your wishes, your visions, and your body with a positive, loving energy now. Studies have shown that when people suffering from disease surrender and accept their situation, while living to the fullest, they frequently heal more quickly.[134]

Retraining Your Body For Health

Remember to live connected to all aspects of your being. One system can affect another. Your thoughts affect your body and vice versa. I conducted a study that demonstrated people can affect their body temperature by taking a shamanic journey to a helping spirit, and simply asking for a change.[135] I'd like you to try a brief exercise that Karen Webster taught me. Read the next paragraph and then close your eyes and try it.

Take a deep breath and bring the image of your kitchen to mind. Picture yourself walking over to the refrigerator and opening the door. Feel the

cool air hit your face. Reach into the fridge and take out a bright yellow, cold lemon. Feel your hands get chilly holding the lemon until you
put it down on the counter. Take a sharp knife and slice a wedge of the
lemon. See the juice squirt out and drip down your fingers. Smell the
tangy citrus smell. Set the knife down and pick up this fresh wedge of
lemon. As you bring it to your mouth the smell intensifies. Take a bite
of the lemon. Bite down on the cold, sour pulp and chew, releasing all
the lemony juice into your mouth.

How did your body react? Most people report that they start to salivate when they
imagine biting the lemon. If that happened to you, your body reacted to something that was purely imagined. Your visualization created a physical response.
Your mind and your imagination are powerful initiators. They can inspire your
body to act according to their intentions. Think of the potential for healing underlying this simple realization.

You can influence your body's natural state of being. It will probably take some
practice. Many of us have disengaged from our bodies to such a degree that we're
living physically out of balance. We compensate for these imbalances with coping
mechanisms or medications that can compound the problems rather than solve
them. When you listen to your body, you will receive valuable information about
what it needs to be healthy. When you allow your body and mind to relax, you
allow the seeds of health to grow in a hospitable place. When you call on your
divine energy, you fuel your healing naturally.

There are many simple techniques for becoming attuned to your body's state.
The first step is awareness. Practice sitting and simply paying attention to different external areas of your body. See if you can tune in to places that you rarely
pay attention to, maybe the back of your neck, or your ankles. Take a thorough
sensory inventory of your body. Note how each part feels. Jot down some notes
about the different sensations you experience. Next, turn your attention to different systems, such as your circulatory or respiratory system. Feel your intake of
breath and the corresponding expansion of your body. Note the way your breath
leaves your body. See if you can become aware of your pulse, of the coursing of
blood back and forth from your heart. Just watch and become familiar with how
these processes feel for you. As you become more sensitized, focus your attention
on different organs and see what insights come to you about their state of health
and their harmonious functioning with the other systems of your body.

Take a tour of your insides. Imagine food moving down your esophagus, into your stomach and intestines. Visualize the flow of air down your trachea and into your lungs. Picture it, sense it. Conjure the insides of your bones and see what they feel like and look like. This method is related to shamanic divinatory diagnosis. You are heightening your awareness of your body by shifting your consciousness to receive information. It is a very intuitive process. Listen to what your body has to convey. You may see images that symbolize the state of your systems. Of course, if you are having a medical problem, see a health care practitioner, but these exercises can help you develop the ability to assess your baseline state of health and potentially sense when something is off balance before a problem materializes.

Experiment with affecting your body through your intention and imagination. Focus on warming your hands, or slowing your heart rate. Feel your hands getting warmer, as you picture rubbing them together over a campfire. Feel your heart relax as you visualize settling into a comfy couch for a rest. Gently and firmly state that it is happening and then imagine it with all your senses. You probably salivated at the thought of biting a lemon. Might you be able to increase your immune system's response to a virus with the same power of your thoughts?

Call on an aspect of the divine to help you affect your health. Summon your inner divinity to align your physical body with its highest potential for healing. The potential is vast. Your sacred intelligence applies not only to the spiritual aspects of your life, but to the physical as well. Use your instincts about what your body needs. Intuit the most appropriate treatments and practitioners for you. Focus on preserving and creating your health in the present moment, and you will have less work correcting imbalances after they manifest as disease.

CLOSING

"Healing is not a quest to solve your mysteries, but to learn how to live within them."
Caroline Myss

The search for effective health care inevitably leads to a system that treats the totality of a person's body, mind, and spirit. Even modern medicine has proven that we're not machines made of flesh that happen to house a consciousness. If imagining a tangy spurt of lemon juice squirting into your mouth can elicit a response from the salivary glands, then it is only logical that our ability to perceive and process the non-physical can and does affect our physical bodies. We are a web of complex interactions woven from our thoughts, our emotions, our bodies, and the vital energy that flows through us.

Dr. Jean Achterberg describes the shamanic view of health as "maintaining communication with the animals and plants and minerals and stars. It is knowing death and life and seeing no difference. It is blending and melding, seeking solitude and seeking companionship to understand one's many selves."[136] If we're indeed connected to one another and all the creatures and components of the universe by an invisible web, then it makes perfect sense for insight into healing to lie in the analysis and engagement of the intangible substance we all have in common, the universal spirit. Your acknowledgement of your inner divinity, and the use of your sacred intelligence as a guiding principle for engaging the world, will help you create a more robust, peaceful, and healthy life.

Can spirit affect matter through specific techniques or simply the power of love? Can our thoughts and intentions heal our neighbors? Can the spirits intervene and work healing magic when we ask them to? From a scientific perspective there is enough data to answer "maybe." From the shamanic or spiritual perspective the answer is "of course." We've seen numerous examples of healing through non-physical means: alleviation of pain from a distance; prayer groups improving hospital patients' conditions; and purifying water through ritual and sound. Shamanism is one model, not only of healing, but of *being*, that demonstrates how to incorporate the power of the spirit world into your everyday life.

The critical step is to set aside our mechanistic view of the world and consider that there are invisible forces at work in the universe that can help us in healing. What is there to risk? According to the shamans, the spirits *want* to help us. My sense is that even *considering* the existence of an unseen world that holds incomprehensible energy and power is frightening to many people. It contradicts a worldview that many of us have held on to tenaciously for a long time, a view upon which we've based our decisions, our hopes, and expectations. The possibility of being incorrect in that view is justifiably unnerving; however, perhaps there is a model of reality that is not only more accurate, but more nurturing and supportive for helping us live healthily.

Shamans have traditionally been at the heart of their communities, acting not only as healers, but as leaders, artists, and teachers. In many indigenous cultures they were the scientists. Communities relied upon them for locating food, remembering the creation stories, bringing the rain, healing the sick, and guiding the dead. In many ways the shaman is an excellent model of the holistic healer. Shamans look not only to the body, but to the land, the sky, and the spirits to ascertain where the causes of imbalance and disease lie.

There has been worldwide recognition of the validity of traditional healing techniques. In the Western world we tend to forget that the majority of the world lives very differently than we do. The World Health Organization states that 80–85 percent of the world relied on healing modalities *other than* the allopathic model. They set about encouraging and "training native health auxiliaries, midwives and indigenous healers." They adopted a resolution encouraging governments to assign due importance to the use of traditional systems of medicine.[137] A branch of the National Institutes of Health (NIH), the National Center for Complementary and Alternative Medicine (NCCAM), is actively researching non-allopathic methods of healing, and considering the issues related to integrating these methods with the current medical model. In 2000, NCCAM's director, Dr. Stephen E. Straus, stated their goal concerning the merging of traditional and modern modes of healing. "We want to build the trust of the American people to prove we are open to good ideas and also build trust within all aspects of the medical profession. What we must show are results from diligent research. This is ancient medicine, but a new science."[138]

In healing today there are many mysteries: people heal miraculously, people die inexplicably, new diseases appear, and existing ones mutate. Western culture stands firmly in the scientific end of the spectrum. Ironically, we have in fact placed our *faith* in science. Faith can be a wonderful thing, but it can also be blinding. If we believe absolutely that one model of healing is the "right" one, how can we contemplate the merits of another? We need to take a macrocosmic view and actually implement some of the basic principles of science: gather all the information available, experiment with different methods, consult the experts from different fields and backgrounds, and see what works. Our society has expanded and evolved into a brilliant tangled web. No one philosophy holds the sole answer to healing this planet and ourselves. We need the wisdom, experience, knowledge, and sensitivities of both spiritually and scientifically based healers to unite us in a truly holistic exploration of health. You need to take that path for yourself, finding a balance in your life and in your health care choices to reflect what your sacred intelligence tells you is most suitable and what your divine nature seeks for your highest good.

EXERCISES FOR SECTION 6: YOUR HEALTH

Refer to the *How To Use This Book* section in the *Introduction* if you have questions. Relax your body and clear your mind before you begin, be open to the information you receive, and write down your experiences when you are finished.

Shamanism

* Practice viewing your health as connected to the health of the world around you, and vice versa. Start to develop a sense of kinship with the living beings with whom you share the planet.

* Experiment with the healing power of sound. Call a power song to you and sing it with all your heart. Make sounds, allowing different tones to resonate with different parts of your body, or your chakras. Chant a mantra. Inspire your body through the vibration of your own voice, an instrument, or recorded music. Welcome the healing power of sound to flow through you.

Energetic Healing

* Practice scanning your body intuitively. First sensitize your hands by closing your eyes and holding your hands a few inches away from your body. Move them slowly closer and farther away from your body until you get a sense of where your energy field begins. Then practice moving your hands to different parts of your body and see what your hands perceive.

* Journey or meditate to get a method to transmute and release any troubling emotions you have. See Sandra Ingerman's *Medicine for the Earth* for more detailed discussion of transmuting the energy of emotions.

Distance Healing

* Working with permission, practice intercessory prayer for someone in need. Track the results over time.

Other Factors for Healing

* Practice holding a loving state. Radiate love privately, through meditations and prayers, and as you go out in the world, at work, or in line at the bank.

* Experiment with turning over your pressing questions to a divine being. Release any tension or anxiety you feel and notice if you receive some spontaneous guidance or insights at a later time.

   ✻   Make sure your self-talk is positive and optimistic. Repeat healthy mantras to yourself. Be kind to your body; remember, it hears you.

   ✻   State in meditation that you align your will with the will of God. See how it feels to surrender yourself to the divine.

Retraining Your Body To Be Healthy

   ✻   Take a sensory inventory of your body. Practice sitting and simply paying attention to different areas of your body. See if you can tune in to places that you rarely pay attention to. Note how each place feels and write down what information you pick up.

   ✻   Connect with your different systems, such as your circulatory or respiratory system. Simply become aware of their functioning, paying attention to the way they feel.

   ✻   Try tuning in to your organs. Focus your attention on different organs. See if they communicate with you in any way, or if you can sense their vibration.

   ✻   Take a tour of the inside of your body. Visualize it with shaman's eyes. Watch, listen, and feel.

   ✻   Experiment with affecting your body through your intention and imagination. Think about warming your hands or slowing your heart rate. Feel your hands getting warmer, as you hold them in front of a roaring fire. Feel your heart relax, as you imagine yourself cradled in a gently swaying hammock.

   ✻   Practice balancing your chakras. Hold your hands over each chakra for a few moments, sending balancing energy with your intention. Start with your root chakra and when you intuitively feel it is time to move, place your hands over the next chakra, until you reach your crown.

   ✻   <u>Dialogue with Your Body</u>
(This meditation is included on the Inner Divinity *companion CD. See the* Resources *section for more information.)*

Close your eyes and take several deep cleansing breaths. For the next few moments your attention will be on your physical body. As you breathe in, picture your breath expanding to fill your entire body. As you exhale, release any tension from your body and let go of any thoughts.

Bring your attention to your feet. Wiggle your toes and flex your feet, then relax them completely. Sit for a moment simply paying attention to your feet and listening for any information that comes.

Move to your ankles and your lower legs. Pay attention to those areas and relax your muscles. Take your time. Do your lower legs have anything to say to you? Work your way up to your knees and thighs. Tense and release your muscles to help them remember how to relax. With each inhalation, breathe energy into that part of your body. With each exhalation, release anything that needs to be cleansed away. Concentrate for a moment on your first chakra, at the base of your spine. Gently breathe through it as you imagine the color red. Think about you bones and your legs. Visualize them and see if there is any intuitive information available about them.

Now focus on the lower third of your torso. Breathe into your second chakra as you visualize the color orange. Pay attention to your lower abdomen. Take your time and tune in to your large intestine, bladder, kidneys, sexual organs, hips, and buttocks. Relax these areas and take note if there is anything they wish to tell you.

Move your awareness up to your solar plexus, the area just above your navel. Imagine the color yellow as you breathe deeply into this area around your third chakra. Relax your belly. Feel your stomach and your liver. Ask if there is anything you need to know about those areas of your body. Simply sit with your attention and your breath concentrated on this area.

On your next breath, breathe in a vibrant green. Feel your lungs expand and contract. Feel your heart beating and sense the blood circulating throughout your body. Relax the muscles in your chest, arms, and hands. Release any thoughts as you spend a few quiet moments with this vital area of your body governed by your heart or fourth chakra.

Move your awareness to your throat and neck. Allow the color blue to flood that area of your body with its cleansing energy. Swallow and relax your throat and jaw. Release any tension in your neck and shoulders. This is the area of your fifth chakra. Be present to this part of your body, sensing any information it is conveying to you.

Let the muscles in your face relax. Raise and lower your eyebrows, releasing the tension from your forehead. Pay special attention to your sixth chakra, between and slightly above your eyes. A deep indigo flows with each breath you take. How do your eyes, ears, and nose feel? Relax your mind. Breathe naturally while concentrating on your face.

Imagine a violet light glowing from the crown of your head. Let your attention rise to the very top of your body. As you breathe, imagine the top of your head opening to receive healing energy from above. Draw this healing energy down into your body and let it flow to every part of you, from your fingers to your toes and everywhere in between. Pay attention to your skin. Relax as you soak up this healing energy. Be open to anything your intuition tells you about what your body needs.

You've just reconnected with your entire body. You can go back to focus on any part that needs more attention at any time. When you're ready, take a few more deep breaths and open your eyes.

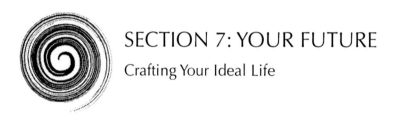

SECTION 7: YOUR FUTURE
Crafting Your Ideal Life

We ask psychics to predict the future, we put money in the bank to prepare for the future, we worry about the future. We spend a vast amount of mental and emotional energy in the future, wishing for some things to happen and worrying that others might happen. The future is a changeable place. There are likelihoods, events that will probably occur, lessons that will be learned one way or another; however, there are also many different possibilities for the future. There is something fundamental we often miss in thinking about the future. You can influence the future right now. The power of your intentions and of your visions can help create the future of your choosing. Your connection to your sacred self helps you envision the state you wish to see realized, the situations that will serve your higher purpose.

The way you approach life now plays a vital role in how your future unfolds. Let's start by looking at ways of being in the present that will reflect on your future; making conscious choices about your attitudes and beliefs now, releasing the past, and letting go of limiting beliefs. There are effective ways to envision a healthy future, to go beyond affirmations to understand how multi-sensory imaging, combined with a strong emotional intention, can shape the future. I'll present different ways of accessing appropriate visions for the future, and of using your creativity and your inner divinity to link to the spiritual field from which the future is born. Finally, you'll learn to pay attention to clues from the universe, like signs and synchronicities, that help you find the path to a future of peace, power, and happiness.

SCULPTING YOUR LIFE

"We must be willing to get rid of the life we've planned, so as to have the life that is waiting for us. The old skin has to be shed before the new one can come."
Joseph Campbell

As you look forward to your future, continually reroute your attention to the present moment. The current moment is your source of power for generating the life you wish to live in the future. What is working well for you now, and what isn't? Which vein of self-talk yields uplifting support and which yields burdensome self-doubt? Which relationships are nourishing and which are draining? In many ways you're creating a mirror of your future with the life you currently lead. A stone sculptor crafts a piece of art one motion at a time. The shape must be roughed out before the details can be finished. The overall form of the sculpture must be balanced and integrated when viewed from different angles. The artist must remain focused on each placement of her chisel or the future of the sculpture is in jeopardy. If the underlying structure of the piece is not sound, no matter how lovely the finishing touches are, the piece will not stay strong over time. Your divine nature is a source for you to sculpt the life you want. By listening to your intuitive sense, you can "rough in" the foundation of your future in present time. The first step in creating your ideal future is to take a look at how you view yourself and your possibilities in the present moment.

Your Perception is Your Reality

Marcus Aurelius said, "The universe is transformation; our life is what our thoughts make it." We form opinions about ourselves at an early age. Our vision of who we are is shaped by what other people have said to us, how we are treated, and what we see happening around us. After a certain point, we accept those opinions as truth. The moment we accept stagnant portrayals of who we are is the moment we sabotage our futures.

Your perception is your reality. What you believe is what you will experience. At a subconscious level, we filter out what does not fit with our view of the world. In *Section 4: Your Intuition* we talked about the importance of recognizing your own filters and biases when working intuitively. That awareness is important when creating your future because the more limiting beliefs you have, the more limited your future will be. One of my clients moved to the South from the Northeast. She moved to be near her family, but she did so with a lot of emotional "baggage." She had deeply ingrained stereotypes about the

South, stemming from slavery and the Civil War. She believed Southern culture was backward and the people were superficial. Nothing compared favorably to her life before moving. She didn't like the South before she even got there. Of course, once she arrived, she saw that the culture was backward and the people were superficial. She experienced that because it was the only version of reality she was allowing through her filters. She entered the landscape inhospitably and was greeted in kind. During our intuitive session, we took an honest look at what opinions she held that were restricting her from experiencing life with the openness and passion to which she was accustomed.

Take stock of the opinions you have formed about yourself. Write them down and take a careful look. Are they accurate? Do they reflect who you are today or are they remnants of the past? Do they take into account the inherent complexity of who you are? Make a list of your beliefs about the world. Review the list and try to determine why you hold those particular beliefs. Did you adopt them based on your own experience or because of something someone said? Now look at each of these lists and, next to each entry, write down the opposite belief. If you said you were an introvert, write "I am an extrovert." If you said you have to earn your way financially in the world, write, "the universe will provide for me even if I don't 'earn' my living." Can these opposite statements also be true? Could those opposing views of the nature of reality co-exist?

I consider myself to be a basically kind and honest person. I like to hold that opinion; it makes me feel good. However, there have been a number of times in my life when I've been less than kind and less than truthful. I'm not absolutely one thing or another. I'm a complex person who has grown and changed over time. You are too. When I was in junior high school, my chorus teacher gave me a lower grade than I thought I earned. I took it as a sign that I couldn't sing. I accepted that definition of myself—bad singer. From that point forward, I was hesitant to sing in front of other people. I lost the joy of it. As an adult I try to defy that image of myself, even if it is uncomfortable. I teach shamanic songs to my workshop participants, I sing healing songs to my clients, and I sing goofy off-key songs to my daughter. I try to fight that negative belief about myself, so I can enjoy singing.

Rigid definitions do not serve you. In the past you may have been told, or made to feel, that you were deficient in some way. Maybe you've absorbed a fearful attitude towards the world. As an impressionable being (which we all are) you likely accepted those opinions, or at least filed them away only to dredge them up later to feed your insecurities. Challenge those assertions now. Create who you are now. Not good at math? Try a different teacher. Think people of other races are fundamentally different from you? Get to know a few. Irresponsible? Get a job and balance your checkbook. Too clumsy for sports? Try yoga or swimming. Too shy? Introduce yourself to two new people this week. You came into this world with an individual genetic makeup, but what you do with that skeleton of an identity is up to you. Don't let your perceptions of yourself and the world hinder your ideal future from evolving.

A client of mine, Jessica, had gone to a psychic and was told that she would never be successful in a romantic relationship. The psychic had essentially condemned Jessica to unhappiness. Jessica gave up her personal power, allowing this person to influence her strongly, and for the negative. She was building her life upon this faulty foundation. When I looked at Jessica, I saw a beautiful light around her, and I told her what I saw. She said several other people had said the same thing to her recently. I kept getting the word "ministry." When I shared that with her, her eyes widened and she said "I've hardly told anyone about that." Jessica had a vision for what she wanted to do. It wasn't fully formed, but it related to theology or a ministry somehow. I saw her with a man whom she may meet through that work who inspired her passion. Jessica left my office feeling more empowered and hopeful about her future. I don't know exactly what will happen in her life, but by seeing a positive vision for her future she was able to start building a strong foundation, and to see a chance to live her dreams. There are many probabilities for your future, but few absolutes. Don't let someone else's words or actions rob you of your will to create the life you want.

Look at how you describe yourself and your life. Pick one incident or episode in your life, an event that has shaped your opinion of yourself and the world. Write it all down, what happened, who was there, how you felt, etc. Then look back at your description and realize that what you have been accepting as fact is simply your opinion. It is one way to tell that story. The story could be told in an entirely different way. By recognizing that the "facts" of the past and the opinions that have shaped your current views are not firm, but pliable, you realize the power you hold to craft your future. If the past is not a static place, you can change the way the past has affected you. Create healthy, vibrant, and hopeful stories for yourself in the present, thereby calling a healthy, vibrant, and hopeful future into being.

Potentials

Quantum physics shows that our typical view of reality is often limited and simplistic. We are used to naming and defining things. Too often we see the world in extremes: black or white, solid or liquid, real or imagined. But when scientists learn that light can be both a wave and a particle, that matter is simultaneously solid and mostly empty space, we need to revisit what we accept as reality. Quantum physics explains that the observer has a distinct effect on the matter observed. Niels Bohr's theory, called the Copenhagen View, states that the observer becomes part of any occurrence or event, simply by observing it. This scientific theory falls neatly in step with the pervasive Native American theory of the web of life, with everything intertwined in relationship, none of us acting in isolation, but moving en masse experiencing and creating life. Science describes light as having the *potential* to appear as either a wave or a particle, depending on how it is observed. There is a moment in time before it manifests as either, a moment when the potential for its existence involves a choice. As individuals and as a collective, we continuously experience those moments of unmanifested and manifested potential, the array of possibilities that lie dormant and the ones that ultimately bloom into being.

Your future is ripe with potential. In each moment the range of possibilities for your future can change. Your decisions alter that range. So do your attitude, your intention, and your beliefs. If you choose a future of limited options, it will indeed be limited, not by an objective "reality," but by your *beliefs* about reality. Quantum physics represents the world as multiple possibilities. Until a choice is made, the world is a curious overlapping of all its alternatives, a phenomenon known to physicists as a "superposition." From the superposition, even seemingly opposing things can occur together simultaneously because they are potential and not concrete. If you can operate from the superposition in your own awareness, you can choose which reality you want.[139] From this perspective, your future is limitless.

Things are rarely as they seem at first glance. When we stop and pay attention, everything we encounter has more depth and complexity than we first recognize. A simple chair, for example, is perhaps comfortable, maybe elegant in design, certainly able to hold a person's weight. When you look at a chair, does it seem to be comprised mostly of air? Of course not, but it is. The amount of solid matter in a chair is tiny compared to the amount of empty space. The most current evolution of string and superstring theories, called M theory, challenges the way we've become accustomed to considering the relationship of matter to time, space and gravity. The fundamental concept behind string theory is still not fully understood, but it asserts the possibility of the existence of multiple realities. Imagine …

living, breathing alternate worlds. Dimensions shift with our point of view; with how we observe, perceive, and engage them.[140] It offers scientific credence to the notion that we can create our own reality. It even aligns with what many spiritual teachers have been talking about for a long time. Myron Eshowsky teaches that parallel universes coexist with us at all times. He believes we experience "bleed-through" from these other dimensions that affects us on a personal and planetary level.[141] Perhaps reality is not as we've grown accustomed to defining it. Consider that what you think is impossible may be attainable. When you look closely, the world may shift mysteriously before your eyes.

Let outdated assumptions and beliefs slough off like an outgrown skin. There is a concept in Buddhism that addresses the potential in each person's life. It is called *alaya*. In Sanskrit, *alaya* means a "personal storehouse of consciousness." Everything that happens in our lives comes from this source. The origins of everything we say, think, and do are held there. "If the causal conditions come together, certain seeds will ripen."[142] You can affect those causal conditions. You can influence which seeds will ripen and bear fruit in your future. Of course, you cannot control all the circumstances in your life. I'm not talking about control; I'm talking about influence. Your *response* to a particular event in your life is more important to your future than the event itself. Reach into that vast storehouse of possibilities. Create your future from a place of infinite potential, where the world is full of mystery and wonder. Let your inner divinity guide you through the wealth of latent futures to the ideal future for you.

Co-Creating: Faith in Action

Philosopher Martin Buber said, "Destiny is not where we wait for God to push us. We take part in creation, meet the Creator, reach out to Him, helpers and companions." Living effectively involves finding a balance between paying attention to what comes to you and being intentional about what you call to you. Many clients come to me and want to know "What's going to happen in my future?" I can't tell them exactly. I can tell them what I see and suspect may happen to them, but the future is not cast in stone. The future is fluid, changeable, and dynamic. There are probabilities, things that you come into this lifetime *likely* to experience, but predicting any one specific outcome is not only difficult, but not particularly helpful. A client of mine recently asked if she would be offered a job in Bangkok. I had a good feeling about it, but a prediction was not what was needed. I told her I was optimistic, but focused on what she needed to do to get the job. I advised her on ways to present herself in the interview that would help her with this job specifically. She got the job, but had I simply predicted that outcome, she might have treated it as a fact, rather than as a potential, thereby neglecting what was necessary to get the offer. Life would be terribly boring if you knew what was going to happen each day. Life's richness would be lost; its mystery and excitement would vanish if you could predict unfalteringly what was going to happen. It would change who you are in ways you cannot imagine.

Set the stage for your desired future to come into existence by working in partnership with the universe. Find the balance between being active, doing everything practical you can do to create what you want, and then stepping back and saying "let's wait for a sign and see what happens." A good example of this comes from a friend of mine. He and his wife were trying to decide where to send their son to kindergarten. They had a number of different choices, and they had been praying and debating about it, worried for a variety of reasons about which was the right choice. They did their research, looked at schools, and talked to other parents. They did all of their due diligence, intellectually, emotionally, and practically, in trying to determine what was the best choice for their son, and they still didn't know what to do. Then one day they were introduced to a woman who turned out to be a teacher at one of the neighborhood schools they were considering. They talked with her and she invited them to come and volunteer at the school. Because of this chance meeting, the child was able to go and spend time in the kindergarten classroom with his mom as she volunteered. They had the opportunity to try a school out before committing to it. It turned out to be a wonderful place for him. They didn't simply sit around saying, "God, tell me what school to choose." They did their part through research and intention, and *then* they said, "God, tell me what school to choose."

People often get confused about this balance. They will mistakenly say, "I have faith I will be taken care of, so I'm just waiting to be shown the way." It doesn't work that way. When you're entirely passive, you're not doing all you can to create the life you want. Periodically, something will fall in your lap, but usually after you've done your part, practically and/or energetically. Be sensitive to coincidences and synchronicities, those gifts of spirit that act as signposts for you, indicating that you're on track or need to move in a different direction. Co-creating involves using your sacred intelligence to escort you through a dance with the universe, sensing when to lead and when to follow.

When my husband and I were considering moving south from Massachusetts, we tried to find this kind of balance. We didn't know where we wanted to move exactly, or even if it was the right thing to do. We had family nearby, good jobs, a house we liked, but we were tired of the New England winters. We played an intentional game. We put out the intention that we were moving somewhere warmer and watched what came our way. We held the intention that we would find the right place for us. We participated energetically. For the next few weeks the Triangle area of North Carolina kept popping up. People talked about it, we saw articles written about it. It wasn't exceedingly dramatic, but the Triangle wasn't a place we were consciously thinking about, and then it was just "there" as soon as we put our feelers out. We jumped on that wave. We looked for jobs and a place to live, again with the same intention: "if it's meant to be it will happen," if not we will stay put. Now we were participating practically. Within a month my husband had a job and we had a place to live. The dance with the universe felt balanced and rhythmic. We've enjoyed living here ever since.

Co-create your future. Have faith, but put your actions behind it. Be sensitive to what people, circumstances, and opportunities show up out of the blue—seemingly without your effort. Also be focused on drawing what you want into your life. Let your instincts tell you when to push forward and when to stop and listen.

FOLLOWING YOUR INNER CALLING

"A nice definition of an awakened person: a person who no longer marches to the drums of society, a person who dances to the tune of the music that springs up from within." Father Anthony de Mello

We come into this world with certain things to learn and experience. Once we get here, our free will plays a large role in determining how we go about experiencing those lessons. Your life is a divine dance. Your core self, your inner divinity, interplays with and overlays the blueprint of your life that the universe has planned for you. Before you came into being in this life, you agreed to certain aspects of your life now. In order to fulfill the agreements you made before incarnating, you need to work in partnership with the internal and external divine forces. There are many ways to do this. Here are the two most important ones: first, listen to your intuition, and second, pay attention to what the universe shows you. By listening to your inner voice when it tells you what makes you happy, or what kind of work you want to do, or who you want as a partner, you make choices aligned with what your higher self needs to fulfill your destiny. By paying attention to what the universe gives you, you allow the loving spirits to help you on your path. Listening to that balance of inner and outer guidance will help you live a life that is truly yours. When you're living a "true" life, one that reflects your personality, your passion, and your gifts, you will find peace. The strength that comes from living in contact with the essence of who you are and what the universe has to offer you is profound. When you're expressing your inner divinity in your life every day, in everything you do, you will find happiness.

The first step in living the life that is rightly yours is to recognize and respect your uniqueness. Look inside yourself. I'm referring to ways of acting, internal patterns of thinking, your vocation, how you spend your free time, everything that makes up your life. I'm not talking only about finding a job you like, although finding fulfillment in your work is part of the equation. You are much more than what you do from nine to five. Role models can be helpful, but for the most part you need to consult your inner guide to determine what is right for you. Once you get a sense of what makes you happy, or even just makes you smile, do it. Do it even if it is unpopular, surprising, or seemingly impossible.

I was walking down the brick path to my house a few months ago, passing the gardens I had planted the previous year. Suddenly, I felt a big grin on my face. I'm not usually a grinner, in fact quite the opposite. But, I realized that seeing the flowers and plants growing made me happy. My intellect dissected that thought a little—why should this simple thing give me so much pleasure? Don't I have other things in my life that should make me smile more? I didn't understand why I found the garden so wonderful. And then I let it go and accepted that cultivating my garden brings me joy, simple as that. Stop questioning it, just do it.

When you stumble upon activities in your life that make you smile, do whatever you can to do them more. This is the classic and wise suggestion to "follow your bliss." Forget about what other people think you should do with your life. Forget about what expectations you've dragged with you from childhood. Forget about the guilt you may feel over doing something purely for your own enjoyment. Do what you are called to do, what makes you feel alive, and what makes you happy. Everything you are called to do might not be pleasurable in the moment. I'm not talking about choosing fleeting entertainment over true meaningful engagement. Throughout this book I have talked about ways of becoming clearer regarding what is right for you. Sometimes we make it more complex than it has to be. Typically, we don't need a bolt of lightning to tell us what we want. Our bodies do a good job if we pay attention. Have you ever accepted a job, and your stomach started to hurt right away? Not just a nervous excitement hurt, but nausea? I have. I took a job once because it seemed at the time like the best option (I needed the money and I was too scared to turn it down because I had no "real" reason not to.)

I cried the night before it started. I didn't know why exactly, I just didn't want to go there. Ultimately, I hated it, and felt sick going to work most days.

You are multifaceted; so is your inner calling. It is an amalgam of how you spend your time and your resources, the personal and professional roles you adopt, and what you create. Your calling may be about having specific experiences or providing a service to others. It may be learning how to heal or learning how to play, learning to receive, or learning to sacrifice. To create the future most in harmony with your divine purpose, follow your dreams. Follow the inner music that quickens your pulse and makes your body move. Explore the path you find most intriguing, that sparks your interest and passion. Pay attention to the subtle and consistent threads in your life that bring you joy. If you haven't found any yet, start exploring!

People frequently come to me with a dream. Some people don't even have the dream yet, they have the precursor to the dream; they know they want to do something that feels exciting with their lives. Some don't know what the specifics are, but have a sense of what gives them joy and what they would pursue if they had no limitations. When you think about your dream, something that really matters to you, it can be scary. If you fully acknowledge your deepest dreams, and then think about *not* achieving them, the level of disappointment can be hard to imagine. It's not so hard to fail at something that doesn't matter to you, but when you care deeply it can be devastating. So devastating that perhaps it's better to live in a state of mediocrity, playing it safe, and not becoming too attached to your life's course? No, it isn't.

Is it better to live disappointed now or take the risks needed to achieve your dreams? Whatever your dream is, accept it. It may be simple, like creating a native herb garden in your backyard, or have a huge scope, like starting a corporation to harvest and market the native herbs of different regions. It may be purely personal, like learning to play the violin at age sixty-five, or you may need to enlist others, to create an orchestra for seniors. The dream may sound ordinary or it may sound crazy, but it is yours. The worst-case scenario is that you tried and it didn't work out. You can handle that. On to the next dream and give that one a shot. Live to the fullest and life will repay you, although not necessarily with what we typically think of as "success." You will be rewarded, possibly with the accomplishment of a deeply held wish, but certainly with satisfaction in knowing that you lived to the best of your ability. Doors will open for you in ways you can't predict purely because you stepped up and took action to create your ideal life.

I have a friend who told me that her dream is to be an international diamond merchant. Who says they want to be an international diamond merchant when they grow up? It sounds a little nutty to some people. It doesn't matter; it just calls to her. She loves the jewels, she lights up with excitement when she talks about handling them. She is figuring out how to do it, but she is hesitant to say it to anyone because it sounds so unconventional. When I first pursued intuition and shamanism there were people in my life who thought it was strange and maybe a little crazy, but it brought me so much joy and satisfaction that I held tight to my dream. Forget about what it sounds like. Forget about other people's reactions.

Remember that your inner calling is different from what you do for your job. Your inner calling is the voice of your soul, the music of your heart. It may guide you to be a peacemaker. If so, whatever careers and relationships you choose, you may be called upon to act as a mediator. The voice may urge you to live in the inner city, or spend time in other countries. Your inner purpose may seem unrelated to your "real" life to the outside observer. Your inner divinity guides your inner purpose. It should be given your utmost attention, as it is the true indicator of whether or not you are living in harmony with your spiritual self.

When seeking your inner purpose, remember that your soul played a role in deciding your "mission" here on earth. On some level you agreed to certain conditions, experiences, and lessons to be learned. Caroline Myss calls that agreement your "sacred contract." To understand this sacred contract, your job is to listen to those whispered voices encouraging you to walk a particular path and heed the fleeting thoughts of what you are called to do or to be. Pay attention to the signs and synchronicities that occur around you. Myss explains that part of that contract is that you discover what you are meant to do. "The Divine, in turn, promises to give you the guidance you need through your intuition, dreams, hunches, coincidences, and other indicators."[143]

A client came to me describing her boredom and dissatisfaction with most aspects of her life, which had recently gone through dramatic change. Beverly had trouble finding a job in her field of business management after she moved to a new state. She had lost her mother a few years prior and now was too far away to spend time with her friends. She didn't know what to do with her time. She was sixty-two, and felt too young to retire. I asked her what gave her joy. She replied, "babies and small children," and her face glowed. That was her first step. She needed to acknowledge what gave her joy and then try to find ways to bring it into her life, both personally and professionally. She had wonderful grandchildren, but needed to find some children to be with more frequently. It didn't matter if she got a job or volunteered, what mattered was the connection she felt with her true spirit when she was with children and the unique and inspiring talent she had with them. She would serve herself, and the children whose lives she touched, by fulfilling her "sacred contract" to cherish the little ones. She is now working as a child advocate in the court system.

Your inner divinity is your birthright and your gift. It is the key to deciphering the code of your inner purpose. Your inner divinity is a blueprint of your spiritual DNA. Your sacred intelligence provides you with the skills to interpret that plan. By strengthening your awareness of your divine nature, you will see a path appearing before you. The path will be illuminated, with each step visible enough for you to walk forward with confidence, and with enough left in the shadowy places of enigma and possibility to keep your journey rich and interesting.

ENVISIONING YOUR IDEAL FUTURE

"The future is not some place we are going to, but one we are creating. The paths are not to be found, but made, and the activity of making them changes both the maker and the destination." John Schaar

Creativity and Imagination

Creativity is a profound link to your spirituality. When you express your creative nature, you are connecting to a higher source of inspiration and tapping the source of your personal consciousness, as well as the universal consciousness. Creativity can take any form. We typically think of classic artistic expression when we use the word "creativity:" painting, dancing, composing, writing. Expand the definition. Redecorating a room can be a wonderfully cleansing and freeing creative activity, as long as you allow your instincts and your aesthetic senses to guide you. If you are *feeling* how to arrange the room, and *sensing* the relationships of colors, shape and texture, rather than *thinking* about them, then it is one good way to loosen up your creative muscles. You create your life much as you do a painting. Think of creativity as any non-intellectual process of free expression.

As I mentioned earlier, when I was young, I was drawn to art more than any of the other subjects I learned in school. I loved it and was also frustrated by it. I often felt something holding me back. I even perceived a translucent membrane, like a dome over me, that separated me from the true creative parts of myself that I longed to connect with. I realized later that when I was frustrated with art, it was often because I wasn't creating my own art, so much as trying to

221

make what I thought was acceptable art. I also realized, once I started exploring my spiritual side, that what I was truly searching for was a connection to that free, formless part of myself that flowed and moved with the universe. Art was as close as I could get at that time. Since then I've put less pressure on my artistic endeavors, because I'm not looking to them to fulfill a spiritual yearning. I also paint or draw or sculpt whatever and however I feel moved. For me, deciding that I'm going to paint a realistic painting of a cactus or a car is stifling. Sitting down with a palette of rich colors and a brush, calling on my helping spirits to work through me, and letting myself go without any clear idea of what the end result will look like, feels liberating.

When using your creativity to tap into Spirit, do what feels good and don't worry what the finished product will look like. You might not even have a finished product. Be in the moment with your work, whatever it is, and let yourself drift with your natural flow of expression. Don't feel limited by what you think art, or music, or dance, should be, just let it be what it is, as it comes out of you. Look inward, realizing you're equipped with all the wonders of the universe. It's all in you, because you're a part of the divine spirit that flows through everything. You contain ample creative power. Don't follow what others have told you is the "right" way to do things, if they don't feel right for you. Allow the ever-changing flow of universal energy to mingle with your own energy and see where you're transported.

When your creativity and imagination flourish unfettered, you develop the ability to create your future. In addition to helping you tap into your instinctual creative nature, your imagination can help you manifest the life of your choosing. You can manifest what you envision. My working definition of "imagination" was offered by my then six–year–old cousin. My family was celebrating Christmas a few weeks early, as it was the only time we could all be together. He was telling my then two–year–old daughter that we were using our imagination to have Christmas on that day instead of on December twenty-fifth. She asked what imagination was. He said imagination was when "you pretend something until it's true." When you pretend something to be true with your whole mind, spirit, and heart you can create it. This is not about wishing something to be true or asking for it to be, it's acting and feeling as if it already is. In the wise words of Elmo from Sesame Street, "It's astonishing what you can do with your imagination."

Visioning

Historically, there have been many ways people try to affect the future, bringing about a desired state or avoiding an unwanted one. Offerings are made to the gods for protection, potions are blended to help people fall in love, wishes are left at holy sites, candles are lit, prayers are said; however, we must take personal responsibility for creating the future. There is help available to us, but we must not rely solely on some higher power to take care of us. As mature members of this planetary community, we must work to craft our futures actively and intentionally.

The myriad possibilities for the future that may or may not come to pass all have one thing in common—this moment. The roads to those imminent times and places all cross at this instant in time. Let's look at some methods for harnessing the latent power of now to affect our future.

Many people have worked with affirmations to activate their will. Affirmations are good to use as a starting point, but they are usually not enough to create the desired effect, in and of themselves. Saying something without feeling it doesn't convince most people, let alone the universe, that it is true. But when you state something and, as the words are flowing from your mouth, you are feeling and sensing and being totally within the vision you've created, then that affirmation or statement has power.

First, of course, you must have a vision to work with. Spend some time dreaming up what you want to be or experience in the future. Proverbs says, "When there is no vision, the people perish."[144] Having an intention for the future is sustaining in and of itself. Like a beacon calling from the distance, it guides you forward in time, as your body moves you forward in space, aligned with your vision of the future, instead of wandering aimlessly.

There are a variety of ancient references to crafting the future through envisioning it in the present, "pretending" that the desired state you are hoping for already exists. By using your imagination to create all the sensations of that future state in the present moment, you are generating the energy of that state. By drawing that energetic blueprint, you summon those circumstances into reality. This "calling" into the present works more readily than if you focus on the future as something distant from you now.

Sandra Ingerman says, "As a culture we have forgotten how to vision, so we have been thrown into the chaos of the universe, manifesting lives based on confusion and troubled thoughts. If we have an opportunity to create a different illusion, let's dream a dream that embraces love, harmony, connection to all, and, most important, joy." In some of her workshops she leads the group in a "visioning party." Each person lets their imagination have free rein in conjuring a healthy and joyful vision for themselves, their communities, and the planet. Ingredients for successful visioning include feeling with your inner and outer senses. What does your desired state look like and sound like? What do you feel inside as you experience it? Envision other people talking with you, congratulating you. Make it real to your body and your mind from the big picture down to the small details. Sandra will often have participants draw or paint an image of their vision afterward.

You may envision inner peace, a more fulfilling career, or a more satisfying relationship with your spouse. Using your imagination to inspire that state may create external changes that bring about your goal, and it may change *you*. You may begin to feel more peaceful, more fulfilled, or more satisfied without anything concrete changing. Either way, you accomplish your goal. Call your vision forth from the heart of your inner divinity, attending to your deepest spiritual needs, and your practical needs will be taken care of as well.

As we discussed earlier, the ancient Essene's philosophy on prayer and manifesting vision included the integration of the intentions of the mind, body, and heart. Our thoughts, feelings, and emotions need to be actively engaged in the process of bringing about the future. The intentional concentration of those energies is what determines which of the many latent possibilities will emerge as reality. With this principle, daily life in many ways becomes one continuous prayer, with each internal and external communication registering on the metaphysical level as an intention for the future.[145]

In many ways we're accustomed to thinking of the future as unknowable. In some respects that is true. We cannot "know" the future absolutely. At its core the future is ineffable. However, we can actively work, as one cell in this vast organism of life consciousness, to create health and balance. Through our thoughts, imaginations, and emotions we continuously emit highly charged signals. Those signals are received by the web of universal consciousness, and ultimately reflected back to us as the future. We are each living visions for the future right now. If those visions are welling up from our sacred selves we are walking the path of beauty and harmony, creating a healthy present and a sustaining future.

Ethics

There are ethical considerations when working to craft your future. Since we live in relationship to others, our futures are intertwined. In *Section 4: Your Intuition* I discussed the ethical boundaries of using intuition and the importance of not invading other people's privacy. Similar issues pertain to manifesting the future.

As we are part of a larger web of existence, our intentions for the future potentially affect others. The goal in creating *your* ideal future is not to manipulate people or situations for your personal advantage, but to affect overall positive change. Be careful that your visions for your personal future do not inadvertently cause harm to others. For instance, it's fine to focus on having a job that is meaningful or to envision a place to live that feels like home. It's not fine to focus on getting a noisy neighbor to move out, or to envision an old boyfriend suffering from a painful disease.

Do not use your powers of imagination and creation to manipulate, control, or manifest things for other people simply because you think it would be good for them. We aren't in a position to determine what is best for others. We do not have the right to try to create a future for them that fits with our personal wishes, however well intended. Work to help others manifest their ideal future only with their express permission and for their intention, not your own.

Keep your focus on creating a good life for yourself, with or without the specific circumstances you intend to manifest. Let your vision express your inner divinity. When envisioning the future for others or the community at large, focus on an overall positive scenario of peace and health and let the details of other people's lives remain under their own influence.

THE POWER OF YOUR FOCUS

"If you think you can do a thing or that you cannot do a thing, in either case you are right." Henry Ford

Intention and Attention

George Bernard Shaw said, "Imagination is the beginning of creation. You imagine what you desire, you will what you imagine and at last you create what you will." Your will is your intention. The power of intention is great. It is especially applicable in creating your future. Concentrating on your intention can be a challenge. Sometimes I have difficulty concentrating. Periodically, I picture myself as

225

a Hindu deity with dozens of arms. During those moments, I'm not feeling like a goddess, I'm feeling that I need more resources, or arms, than I have to do what I want to do in the day. It's a challenge for me to concentrate entirely on writing, when I have laundry to do and errands to run before I pick my daughter up from school. It's also hard for me to pay total attention to my daughter when I'm thinking about the clients I need to get back to or the research I mean to do. I'm better served by concentrating on exactly what I'm doing in the moment, and letting all the rest of it wait its turn. In many ways, I've created the rich and varied nature of my life. Consciously and over time, I envisioned essentially the life that I have right now. I love it, and have no complaints; however, it does not lend itself to long stretches of time to focus and pay attention. I have to discipline myself to keep my intentions clear and my focus honed on the tasks at hand.

Often we start out with a vision, or a simple desire. Initially, we focus on the goal. We are excited and feeding that goal with the power of our intention and emotion. Then, as they inevitably do, obstacles will show up to block our way. Our focus then moves to the obstacles. The obstacles get big and strong on all the good energy we are feeding them. The more we shift our attention to the impediments, the less energy we are sending to our goal, and the goal tends to wither and die. We give up. Keep your intention clearly in mind. Even if you can only grab a few moments each day to attend to your vision of your future, do it.

Our levels of attention naturally fluctuate. Some of us are generally more attentive than others, but the level of attention with which we take in information from the world around us can vary throughout the day. It can also be a learned skill. We've all had the experience of being present with our bodies but not with our attention, listening partly to someone talking to us while we're really focusing on our to-do list, or planning how to exit the conversation. Recently, I was watching television with my husband, and he commented on something we had just seen. Actually, he saw it. I simply took in the images with my eyes, but my attention was so completely elsewhere that I had no idea what he was talking about. Another time he was explaining the merits of various golf clubs he was debating about buying. Although I was happy he was excited about the prospect of his new purchase, I was tired and didn't understand most of what he was saying. I felt my eyes glaze over. My body was with him; my attention was not.

Some professions involve specific training in paying attention. Police officers learn to heighten their level of attention to perceive as many details about a scene as possible, so they can make quick decisions in tense situations. Is the person walking through the doorway a criminal or an innocent bystander? Drivers can learn to heighten their awareness of the details of what is happening around them, which can improve their reflexes and prevent accidents. People who are visually impaired can learn to expand the powers of their other senses, not only to compensate for the lack of sight, but also to perceive in a more subtle and complex way. For example, the sense of smell can detect information often "overlooked" in the typical visually dependent way of perceiving. Our powers of observation serve us in many different capacities and can be developed over time.

Shamans perceive the world at a heightened level, too. Look through your shaman's eyes to comprehend the essence of the matter, to see truth, both literally and symbolically. You do not need to be trained or born into shamanic practice to utilize the keen vision and insight that shamans develop as they seek truth and healing. Start by practicing. Think of your powers of attention like peripheral vision for a moment. Fan out your range of perception. Soak up as many details as you can, both physical and energetic, of the world around you. This peripheral attention can often help you see the under layer of reality that exists all around you, the energetic level of experience.

Once you've practiced this expansion of your attention, try the opposite shift in attention. Filter the extraneous information from your view and bring the relevant information into sharper focus. When you're in particular need of heightened abilities for discerning truth or making sound decisions, look through your shaman's eyes. Pay attention to the patterns that emerge as you hone and experiment with shifting your attention.

The concept of isomorphism provides a helpful analogy for living in ways that bring about balance. The word derives from the Greek *iso*, meaning "equal," and *morphosis*, meaning "to form" or "to shape."[146] Isomorphism demonstrates that there is often a reflection of patterns in nature from the small scale to the large scale. For instance, the structure of a fern is often the same, whether you are looking at the whole leaf, or at just one branch. If you apply this concept to your life, you recognize that, as a creature of nature, the balance of your individual cells is reflected in the health of your body as a whole, and the health of your body is often reflected in the harmoniousness of your life. You can help create balance on the larger scale by initiating balance on the smaller scale. Be aware of the different levels of your life. The way you interact with yourself often mirrors the way you interact with other people and your surroundings. Pay as much attention to the conversation you have with the dry cleaners as you do with a potential employer. If you wish to affect change in your life, start by changing the details. For example, if your life feels chaotic and out of control, start by reorganizing your office. Get rid of the stacks of paper, pay the overdue bills, and create a filing system so you can find what you need easily. This one-day project can "tip" the pattern of your life, and help reduce the chaos. Even initiating change in this one room can help to create a blueprint for the rest of your life to model, a pattern reflected from the small to the large scale.

Create your life now in a way that mirrors what you wish to have happen in the future. Perhaps you currently have a full time job in an office, but your dream is to run a bed and breakfast. Your office job is serving you because you need to build up the capital before you can start your business. Appreciate it as one step in the progression towards your ultimate goal, while at the same time do your research about what it takes to actually run a bed and breakfast. Imagine that it has happened already, not just with your mind, but also with your mind's eye and all of your internal senses. Experience yourself running that bed and breakfast and see what it feels like. If you learn that running a bed and breakfast will take certain routines of organization and attention to detail, start practicing them in your own house. Set up a pattern of expressing gratitude and enjoying the present, while creating a new pattern in your life through your intention.

Simply paying attention, noticing the patterns of your life, is a good step for initiating the change you need to create the future you want. Your inner divinity is the source for a deeper comprehension of those patterns. Look around you with the keen eyes of a shaman, and then look inside you with the same discernment. Draw forth the life you want from the power you already possess.

Signs and Synchronicity

Being in partnership always involves paying attention. In ordinary reality, that means listening carefully when your boss is conversing with you, tuning in to the emotional state of your spouse, or being sensitive to the subtle ways your child may express fear or uneasiness. Similarly, if you wish to collaborate with the universe you will need to pay attention to the many ways that the universe communicates with you.

Sometimes the communication is subtle, and sometimes it is quite obvious. There are usually attempts at reaching you that are gentle before something dramatic happens. Use your shaman's eyes to discern where you need to focus your awareness. Paying attention to signs and synchronicities is one way to "read" the more subtle messages intended for you. You can think of these messages as coming from the universal web of life, your personal helping spirits, or another spiritual source. They are guiding signs or symbols that help you focus your attention where it needs to be. We are often quite clear on what we want the universe to deliver to us, but the best way we can receive the help available is to let go of rigid expectations of how and when we should receive guidance, and start paying attention to what is really transpiring. The Dalai Lama is often quoted as saying, "I am open to the guidance of synchronicity and do not let expectations hinder my path. I find hope in the darkest of days and focus in the brightest. I do not judge the universe."

The universe has a way of putting signs in our path to help us along. Sometimes we call this fate, sometimes coincidence. These events can be life altering. For example, when my mother was a toddler she lived with my grandmother in Staten Island, NY. They took the ferry frequently. One day someone in their group delayed them five minutes to use the ladies' room. The delay, annoying at the time because it caused them to miss the ferry, saved their lives. My mother and grandmother were among the last people to leave the ferry station alive. The Staten Island Ferry fire of 1946 took many lives, but a twist of fate spared theirs. Coincidences can also be trivial: today the dry cleaners lost my husband's shirts. I hate ironing and had decided to have them done for the first time. The delay caused by the search for the missing shirts allowed me a moment of conversation with the man behind the counter. He asked me what I did for work and I told him briefly. The man is a professor with a strong interest in people, psychology, and spirituality. We had lots to talk about. I may have made a lovely new connection in this world. It would not have happened had my shirts been delivered smoothly.

When we travel to see my in-laws in Massachusetts, I will sometimes make a plan with a friend. I have several friends who live in the area. I typically alternate which friends I see, because family time is often short. On this particular visit I'd made a plan with one friend, who unfortunately called at the last minute to cancel. I felt disappointed that I wasn't able to see my other friend during that time, but let it go and agreed to take my daughter to the park. While there, I heard someone call my name. I turned around and the friend I had *not* made plans with, and her family, were at the park! They didn't usually come there on that day and I'd been there only a few times in my life. She said it was "*be'shert*," the Yiddish word that essentially means fate or destiny. Apparently, we were meant to see each other that day.

A spirit came into my life long ago, but in recent years she's changed. There were signs and synchronicities along the way that helped me realize her true nature, but I wasn't tuned into them. For years I worked shamanically with this female spirit. She was lovely, with dark hair and a light blue gown. She often used a healing dust or light metallic cloth for healing work. Years after I started working with her, she

revealed herself to me as Mary. In hindsight, I looked back and saw signs of a connection to Mary that I hadn't recognized.

I found myself saying the Hail Mary prayer during a shamanic initiation. This was
long before Mary as a spirit came into the picture for me personally. At the time, I
thought it was interesting because I was not an active Catholic and didn't say that
prayer customarily, but I didn't give it much thought. At a Health and Healing
Expo at which I was working, I had an intuitive reading with a friend of mine.
She said she felt Mary's presence very strongly around me. She didn't know of my
connection, and at the time, I didn't either. During the reading she handed me a
beautiful photograph of Mary with flowers and candles. She said she loved this
photo and didn't know why she was guided to bring it to the Expo that day. She
was told to give it to me.

Sometime after that, I told my mother about the transformation of my spirit teacher
and the synchronicities involving Mary. She looked at me wide eyed. My mother
and I have been working with female spirit teachers for years. Their names were different, although they possessed a similar loving and serene energy. We've journeyed
to them hundreds of times, created rituals in their honor, and invited them to work
with us for healing and communication. She said, in astonishment, that the female
spirit she had been working with had also revealed herself as Mary around the same
time. Neither of us had shared this information with anyone. We both pay close
attention to the Mary connection now. I've become increasingly interested in and
devoted to Mary. She is frequently present when I'm doing healing work.

The natural world is a rich source of information to help us in our lives. Shamans
and native peoples of all cultures turn to nature to help interpret and predict life.
The appearance of a particular animal may represent a message from the spirit
world, especially if the animal is rare or acting uncharacteristically. The formation
of a tree trunk may contain information when it is viewed from a particular perspective and time. The timing of a gust of wind may be an indication to be quiet,
or to prepare for upheaval. As I'm writing these words a gentle rain bursts forth
from brilliantly sunny skies, each drop glittering radiantly as it falls to the ground.
I take it as a small gift and go outside to say thank you.

Signs don't have to be extraordinary to be meaningful. We often make the mistake
of waiting for a miracle or a catastrophe to start asking, "Was that a sign?" You'd
pay attention if your child complained of getting bullied on the playground. You
wouldn't wait until there was bodily harm before acting. If your boss said you needed
to improve your performance, you'd take action and not wait until she threatened

to fire you. Nature is ordinary and miraculous at the same time. Don't wait for a tornado to strike to pay attention to the forces of nature all around you.

A friend relates her interpretation of a sign she saw in nature during an extremely difficult period for her family.

> My daughter and I had a very bad episode this morning with screaming and crying, and I ran out of the house to get some space and perspective on the situation. I was sitting with my head in my hands. I picked up my head and out in the middle of the street there was a small vortex of very light street dust rising higher in a perfect tunnel (not funnel, which made it even more unusual). The dust vortex just floated gently around tracing small circles on the road and then collapsed. I have seen leaves in autumn swirl around on the street in a vortex shape, but never light dust. This was totally unusual and cool. I took it to be symbolic or a kind of message that yes, our lives were in turmoil at the moment, but "the dust will settle."

What I love about this description is the way she interpreted the sign. She made the metaphorical connection between an unusual event in nature and the immediate situation in her life. She gleaned wisdom and comfort from this mysterious occurrence. Often signs are symbolic and it's important to think flexibly to interpret them fruitfully.

My five-year-old daughter and I were outside, enjoying picnicking, looking at the sky while lying on a bed of moss, playing hide and seek with our pretend fairy friends, and just enjoying being outdoors after a long winter. We found a small speckled feather that my daughter loved. She carried it around for a while, but later set it down to put on her shoes and it blew away. She saw it going and couldn't catch it, but she thought she knew about where it landed. I came and helped look for it. We searched, but could not find the feather. Eventually, we gave up and sat down by the pond. A little while later, at least twelve feet away, behind a rock, a subtle movement caught my eye. It was too soft for a leaf, and I even thought it might be a mole's snout peeking out from behind the slate. Then I recognized it as a feather. We rushed over and picked it up. I can't be sure if it was the same feather or one just like it. My daughter was glad to have her feather back, and I took away a lesson. When we're looking hard for something, we often direct our attention to a small area where we expect to find what we're looking for, our vision limited by our belief. When we sit back, take a breath, and look around with open eyes, what we're looking for often shows itself in an unexpected place.

Another time I lost a favorite sweater. I'd returned to the store where I thought I'd dropped it, talked to customer service, checked the dressing rooms, looked on the floor throughout the store, and even checked on the racks to see if someone had hung it up as merchandise by mistake. I left my name and number and went home discouraged. There was a voice inside my head that was emphatic that the sweater was in the store. I went back the next morning and looked through everything again but couldn't find the sweater. I didn't want to ignore my intuition which said it was there, but I didn't know where else to look. I had essentially given up and was shopping for a replacement when a friend called. I told her where I was and why. She said that she had a spirit helper who was especially good at finding lost objects and asked for her help. After we hung up, I walked to the next aisle and looked down and there was my sweater lying in plain view! I was grateful for the synchronicity of her call, my search, and her spirit helper with a special talent.

Signs and synchronicities can help you navigate everyday living and can also help guide you into a healthy future. I find that some people put too much emphasis on nailing down a specific meaning, a one-on-one correlation with a sign that says, "Do this." Sometimes signs are obvious, but frequently they are mysterious. The important part is to pay attention. As you develop your skills of perception, your skills of interpretation will unfold too.

Pay attention to what crosses your path, listen to the synchronicities, heed the calling of your heart, and find your passion! Do what you love and you will bring excitement and joy into your life. The key to finding what moves you (or acting on it, if you already know) is connecting to that pure spark of divine energy within you.

Paradox

One of the most challenging ideas permeating the concept of spiritual awareness is paradox. Being able to hold opposing concepts in one's mind simultaneously as truth is difficult, irrational even, but it can help. One of the reasons paradox abounds in the field of metaphysics is that, at a fundamental level, we are unable to truly understand the nature of the universe, of God, and of our own divine natures. This is not because we're flawed in some way, but because most of us have not evolved to that level of comprehension. Try explaining to a rock the benefits of a laptop with a really fast processor, or the humor of Woody Allen. The rock is unlikely to be able to relate to you on this level. I've known many people to have wonderful interactions with rocks, myself included. Rocks can teach us a lot, but not directly about certain things that are uniquely human. One day, I believe we will have a better understanding of the nature of reality and universal truths. We've certainly been working on it long enough. Our human-centered approach makes it difficult for us to comprehend the vastness of all that is. To me, two thousand years feels like a long time, but to the universe it is the blink of an eye.

Time can be more fluid and flexible than we think. Some of us have a hard time getting things done and we have the same amount of time as people who accomplish a lot. It's really the way we manage and think about time that matters. Paradoxically, time can be exact; we all can agree on the time of day in a certain time zone; and it can be variable, such as when "time flies" when you're doing something you love, or when each moment is painfully slow, as when you're at the dentist.

Accepting paradox allows us to glimpse the potential nature of reality and therefore our own natures. The paradox of light being both a particle and a wave simultaneously makes little sense to the average person, but it guides us towards a more complete picture of how our present moment relates to the future. Consider these two statements. 1) Whatever is meant to happen in your life will happen, regardless of whether you cooperate. 2) Your active involvement determines what happens in your life. Can these both be true? Accepting the potential for paradox in the way we experience reality opens many doors. "God gives us all we need" and "We are entirely responsible for ourselves." Reconcile those statements. You may not understand how paradox works, but you can start by acknowledging the possibility of the dual nature of reality.

A challenge in understanding the nature of reality, and therefore the creation of the future in both the universal and the personal sense, is that we may not be capable of true understanding at this time. Having the flexibility and open mindedness to let the universe unfold before us, rather than looking through the myopic lens of our own limiting beliefs, better serves us. Allowing for paradox allows you to see more possibilities for your future than accepting a simple linear progression of time and space. You may achieve everything you need in life to be happy, even though it looks very different than you expected.

In our relationship to the spirit world, there is paradox. We separate ordinary reality and non-ordinary reality in our language. We talk about connecting to the spirit worlds; however, the worlds coexist, sharing space and time. There is no bridge needed, other than flexibility of mind and openness of heart. Those qualities allow us to recognize the physical and spiritual nature in everything in the world around us. By paying attention, we understand the interwoven simultaneous existence of spirit and matter. Simply acknowledging the multiple dimensions you live in will help you perceive those dimensions. Remember those prints that were popular in the 1980s that looked like a random spotted field at first glance, but when you focused your eyes in a particular way showed a dramatic 3-D pattern? For some of us, fresh perception can be that kind of "Ah-ha!" experience. For others, seeing the world in a new way, seeing energy flow, feeling spirit in everything is a gradual process of growing awareness. In working with clients I've found that when you are open, attentive, and willing to do your inner work, the veil between the worlds will be lifted in amazing ways. It may not manifest in the way you expect, but in the way that is most appropriate for you at the time. Your inner divinity guides you in an appropriate balance between speaking and listening, acting and waiting, deciding and contemplating. When you work in collaboration with the spirit world, however paradoxical it may seem, your future unfolds more closely to its divine plan.

PEACE, POWER, AND HAPPINESS

"Happiness is not a matter of intensity, but of balance and order and rhythm and harmony." Thomas Merton

We each have individual goals for the future; however, most of them fall under the headings of peace, power, and happiness. Peace, as I use the term here, implies a sense of well-being in the world and in your own skin; the ability to make it through the bumpy places as well as the smooth parts of your life with grace and confidence, and a basic acceptance and respect for who you are. Power refers to personal power, a sense of integrity, strength, courage, and vitality. Happiness is an underlying sense of contentment, joyfulness, and pleasure in living. How we achieve these goals of peace, power, and happiness is highly individualized. We've talked at length about finding the most suitable ways for you to achieve those goals on a practical level. This always involves maintaining a strong connection with your sacred nature, as it is your inner divinity that guides your hand in painting the portrait of your ideal life.

Even if you're genuinely peaceful, it doesn't mean your life is always calm. It means you have achieved a state of inner peace that allows you to maintain your balance regardless of the external circumstances of your life. A letter in *The Sun* magazine described a man who visited a monastery on the Vietnam/Cambodia border during the Vietnam War. The monks were praying, meditating, and doing their work amid the sounds of artillery fire, explosives, and bombs. The Quakers who were working there asked the monks, "'How can you just sit here meditating when there is so much suffering going on and so much work to be done?' By the end of the week, though, the Quakers understood: this was an island of peace, a living example of how life *could* be."[147] Gandhi said, "You must be the change you wish to see in the world." We need to act how we want the world to be. A sense of peace doesn't mean your life lacks extremes of emotion, disruption, or chaos. It means that by finding your inner compass, you have the tools to navigate through life without getting lost. As you wind your way, you're planting seeds of peace as you go—internally, for your own future, and externally, in the world around you.

It takes tremendous personal power to have the focus of those monks, living with a barrage of artillery fire nearby. It's not brute strength and it's not power "over" someone else. Think of the focus you must have to meditate in a war zone, the courage to blow the whistle on a corrupt employer, the strength to be a kind father when you were abused by yours. Those actions call on your reserves of personal power. You develop that power by strengthening your connection to the divine, both from within and by reaching outside of yourself.

Happiness is not always feeling perky, or having everything resolve perfectly in your life. It is something deeper. It is living in a way that feels harmonious, that feels right at a fundamental level. You can be happy and peaceful while knowing that your life is too chaotic. You can accept that a chaotic phase is uncomfortable, but also important for your development. You can accept it and let it be, knowing that when the time is right, you have the power to change that chaos into calm. Likewise, you may desire things in your life that you don't have. It doesn't have to make you unhappy. Perhaps you accept that now is not the time for attaining your material goals, that there is more work to be done, or the circumstances have not formulated to manifest the vision you have. Happiness is not perfection, but it is not served by complacency, or giving up on your ideals.

You can work actively to bring about the happiness that you seek. Happiness is actually becoming a subject of scientific investigation. "Who has it, and how do we get it?" are the fundamental questions, according to an article in *Time Magazine* called "The New Science of Happiness." There is evidence to suggest that our levels of happiness are greatly affected by our genetic make-up. University of Minnesota researcher David Lykken asserts that as much as 50 percent of our level of satisfaction or happiness is based on "genetic programming." Lykken doesn't assert, however, that you are only as happy as your genes dictate. You are not a slave to your biology. "It's clear that we can change our happiness levels widely—up or down." Researchers assert the importance on working on three "components" of happiness: getting more pleasure out of life (this can be about your sensory experience), becoming more engaged in what you do, and finding ways to make your life feel more meaningful. University of California psychologist Sonja Lyubomirsky has found that there are eight fundamental steps that create a more "satisfying life:"

1. Count your blessings.

2. Practice acts of kindness.

3. Savor life's joys.

4. Thank a mentor.

5. Learn to forgive.

6. Invest time and energy in friends and family.

7. Take care of your body.

8. Develop strategies for coping with stress and hardships.[148]

Science is recognizing the importance of understanding how people can lead happier lives on a personal level. Some world leaders are recognizing the importance of happiness for an entire nation. Bhutan's King Jigme Singye Wangchuck coined the term Gross National Happiness, or GNH, when he ascended the throne in 1972. The phrase is a spin on the more commonly used term Gross National Product or GNP. Gross National Product (GNP) measures the total monetary value of a country's production of material goods and services for consumption during a given time. GNH, by contrast, seeks to "define prosperity in more holistic terms and to measure actual well-being rather than consumption."[149] By shifting national focus from the population's level of material consumption to their level of happiness and well-being, Bhutan's king reflects his country's Buddhist spiritual values. He reaffirms the inherent nature of his people by seeking to build an economy that will serve their unique cultural values.

The concept of GNH is attracting attention from other nations. An international conference on Gross National Happiness was hosted by the Bhutan government in 2004. It attracted eighty-two "eminent" participants from twenty countries. "The evolving concept of GNH could well be the most significant advancement in economic theory over the last 150 years," according to Frank Dixon. Dixon is a Harvard Business School graduate who is currently managing director of research at Innovest Strategic Value Advisors. Dixon asserts, "GNH is an endeavor to greatly enhance the sophistication of human systems by emulating the infinitely greater sophistication of nature." He explains that, currently, corporations and even countries are seeking to expand and grow continuously. Dixon notes, "the only parallel for this in the natural world is cancer cells, which by growing exponentially destroy the host body and themselves."[150] Unchecked growth is not a natural phenomenon. Nature works in cycles. For economists to look to the natural world as a model for balanced living is a wonderful shift in ideology. Ranking happiness above material wealth is a radical shift in thinking, which holds the potential to fundamentally change the future for everyone on this planet.

CLOSING

"The future belongs to those who believe in the beauty of their dreams."
Eleanor Roosevelt

The way you live is inextricably linked with the way you perceive yourself. The way you engage life in the moment, through the screen of your self-perceptions, is what gives nourishment to your future. You are feeding your future now with each thought. Sandra Ingerman says we have a "seed of life" within us which contains the light of our divinity. "The seed within also contains the blueprint for our lives on a physical, emotional, and spiritual level."[151] Right now you are tending the garden that will bloom as your future. If you plant seeds full of "I can't succeed," you will harvest failure. If you fertilize the soil with anger and water it with pettiness, the fruits of your future will taste bitter. If you plant seeds of "I am good enough," you will harvest self-respect. If you fertilize the soil with kindness and water it with gratitude, the fruits of your future will taste sweet. Walk conscientiously in the present, sowing healthy, resilient seeds, and you will reap the rewards of a bountiful future.

Craft your present moment with care and precision and you craft a future of exquisite design. Of course, we're not alone in this journey. In more ways than we can imagine, our fate depends on those beings with whom we share place and time, and conversely, their fate depends on us. Your decisions now affect everyone to some degree. It is quite difficult, especially from our individual vantage points, to comprehend whether that influence will be slight or profound. Let's think and behave as if it is profound. Peace, power, and happiness are available to us personally and as a collective. Let's take responsibility for the future manifesting in our individual stories, but also in the stories of our families, communities, and planet. Embody the qualities you feel are important. Treat others as you wish to be treated. Through example, you can touch those around you, sparking their divine light and illuminating their paths more brightly. Your inner divinity is the source for creating the life you are meant to live.

EXERCISES FOR SECTION 7: YOUR FUTURE

Refer to the *How To Use This Book* section in the *Introduction* if you have questions. Relax your body and clear your mind before you begin, be open to the information you receive, and write down your experiences when you are finished.

Sculpting Your Life: Your Perception is Your Reality

* What is working well for you now, and what isn't? Consider relationships, attitudes, job, lifestyle, location, climate, and community.

* List your opinions of yourself and your beliefs about the world. Review the lists, and, next to each entry, write down the opposite. Could these opinions and beliefs also be true? Let go of beliefs that are not serving you.

Sculpting Your Life: Your Life Story

* Write a story of your life. Reread it after some time has passed and notice how what you assumed to be fact can be viewed differently.

Sculpting Your Life: Potentials

* Practice shifting your paradigm of thought. Consider the "pregnant possibility" of each moment of your life, and you can help to create different futures from the rich nugget of potentials.

Sculpting Your Life: Co-Creating: Faith in Action

* Choose something you wish to manifest for your life. Request help from the universe in achieving that goal, and then do everything in your power in ordinary reality to make it happen. Watch how the balance of faith and action produces results.

Following Your Inner Calling

* Write down a list of things you are passionate about. Write down what your ultimate dreams are. Don't hold back; don't aim low so you won't be disappointed. What do you truly want to be, to do, to experience?

* Make a list of things you feel you "should" do or are obligated to do. Be honest in weeding out what is really a duty and what you can let go of to allow more space for your true dreams to manifest in your life.

* Map a route into your future. In a meditative state, breathe deeply and focus your attention inward. Connect to your divine energy. Imagine that energy as a vehicle with no limitations. Visualize yourself being transported

into the future. See where you wind up, knowing that your vision describes one possibility, and not a certainty.

Envisioning Your Ideal Future: Creativity and Imagination

* Express yourself creatively, imagining a possible future. Consider singing it, dancing it, drawing it, or writing about it.

Envisioning Your Ideal Future: Visioning

* Let your imagination have free rein in conjuring a healthy and joyful vision for yourself, your community, and the planet. Feeling with your inner and outer senses, experience what your vision looks like, sounds like, feels like, even tastes and smells like. What do you feel inside as you experience it? Make it real to your body and your mind from the big picture down to the small details, in the present moment.

The Power of Your Focus: Intention and Attention

* Think of your powers of attention like peripheral vision. Fan out your range of perception. As you go through your day, soak up as many details as you can.

* Imagine yourself slipping on a pair of lenses which filter the extraneous information from your view and bring only relevant information into sharper focus.

* Meditation on Love
  (This meditation is included on the Inner Divinity *companion CD. See the* Resources *section for more information.)*

  This meditation represents one of our most fundamental qualities as human beings. The ability to love is innate. The ability to receive love is vital. In this meditation you will explore a variety of different ways of feeling and expressing love. Some may feel effortless to you and others may bring up some unresolved issues or resistance. Simply relax and open your heart.

  Close your eyes. First take a minute in silence and call in spiritual assistance in whatever form feels comfortable for you. Ask for beings of the light to be present with you. Hold the intention that the work you are doing is for the highest good and that you are protected and enveloped in light. Take a moment now to call in Spirit.

  Take several deep breaths. Allow your belly and chest to expand and exhale fully with each breath, releasing any tension in your body. As you let go of any stress in your body, also let go of any worries or preoccupying thoughts. Relax into your breathing.

Picture something that you love absolutely. It can be anything that is easy for you to love, a child, a pet, or a special tree. Hold an image in your mind of that being. Allow yourself to focus on loving that special person or thing as fully as possible. Throughout the meditation, if you have difficulty, return to this image and this feeling. Just sit with this special being for a minute, expressing deep love.

Now pay attention to your heart chakra and feel the sensation of love in your body. Breathe through your heart. Breathing love in and breathing love out. Breathing love in and breathing love out. Pay attention to how love feels as it manifests in your body. Do you feel it in your heart, in your belly, or somewhere else? Sit with this feeling for a moment.

Still holding that feeling of love in your body, focus on loving yourself. Feel love for your mind, for your body, for your spirit, for the qualities you embody, for the things you do. Send yourself love for as many different things about you as possible. Love yourself as you would a newborn child, without expectation, judgment, or criticism. You are a unique and precious being. Spend some time appreciating and feeling love for yourself.

Your body is filled with the sensation of love. Now picture another being whom you love, a person or an animal. And just as you did for yourself, focus on loving them as wholly and purely as possible. Feel it in your body. Hold this being in a loving space. Surround them with gentle nurturing energy.

And now shift to another image, an image of something in nature. Something you admire and love. It can be a tree, a mountain, the night sky, an animal, or a piece of land—anything that exists in the natural world. Hold the beauty of this image in your heart. Focus again on your heart chakra breathing love in and breathing love out. Send your gift of love to this aspect of nature with every exhalation.

Now, shift your consciousness from the aspect of nature to the divine. What aspect of the divine do you love—is it God, a goddess, a nature spirit, an angel, or a spirit teacher? Let your love for this celestial and divine being transport you to a place of peace and serenity. With each breath in, feel your love flow through every part of your body, filling every cell with unconditional, pure love energy for an aspect of the divine.

You're glowing with the energy created by loving. You've expressed your love in many different ways. It's time for you to feel how the ripples you've created by sending out that loving energy come back to you and wash over you.

As you take your next breath, feel the love that is available for you. Feel yourself surrounded by beings of the light, here to nourish, protect, and cherish you. Picture a golden light pouring through the crown of your head. This golden flow of love energy fills your body and expands your heart chakra far outside your body. Soak in the feeling of being loved purely and unconditionally. Relax into the embrace of the divine. Allow yourself to be wrapped in a beautiful luminous cloak that cradles you and infuses you with love and appreciation. Just rest in the warmth of this cloak for a while.

When you're ready, give thanks for the love you've received. And give thanks for your ability to love. As you prepare to come back into the room, you may keep the luminous cloak wrapped around you. The love that you feel in that warm nurturing space is available to you always; you just need to remember that it is there. Take a deep breath and start to come back into an awareness of your body. Feel your heart beating, feel your breath. Remember that every movement you take in your life, every action, every thought can add to the amount of loving energy on this planet. When you're back and ready, open your eyes.

The Power of Your Focus: Signs and Synchronicity

✳ Pay attention to the natural world around you for signs that convey information.

✳ Has an idea, image, or word popped up repeatedly? Keep your senses open to synchronicities and follow them as best you can.

The Power of Your Focus: Paradox

✳ Practice accepting paradox: for example, simultaneously holding the ideas that you are entirely responsible for your future, and that you are held lovingly by Spirit and guided as you need to be.

Peace, Power, and Happiness

✳ Practice the 8 steps to a more satisfying life:

1. Count your blessings.

2. Practice acts of kindness.

3. Savor life's joys.

4.   Thank a mentor.

5.   Learn to forgive.

6.   Invest time and energy in friends and family.

7.   Take care of your body.

8.   Develop strategies for coping with stress and hardships.

 CONCLUSIONS AND BLESSINGS

As we learn to live in harmony within our bodies, minds, and hearts, we also learn to live in harmony with all that exists around us. Health of all kinds depends on a balanced and respectful interaction. Nothing in this world exists in isolation. From the individual cells in your body, which must function cooperatively with the cells surrounding them, to a nation, which must learn to coexist peacefully with its neighbors, relationships hold the key to health and happiness.

The way you experience life is predicated on your relationship with yourself. If your internal dialogue is positive and you carve out the time for silence and introspection, you're tending to your spiritual and emotional needs. You are wise. It is this innate wisdom that guides you to live in the healthiest relationship to yourself. By treating yourself with kindness and respect, you generate positive energy, which radiates from you and is reflected back to you in your experience of life. By unearthing your deeply held motivations, biases, and fears, you can see the world around you more clearly. By acting with integrity and courage, you generate personal power that serves your greater purposes. The awareness of your inner divinity in your daily living allows you to keep true to who you were born to be.

When you have a nurturing and honest relationship with yourself, you can enter relationships with others from a healthy starting point. By recognizing the spark of the divine within you, a natural effect is to see that spark in others. Compassionate and sustaining relationships are based on an understanding of mutual worth. Our worth as humans is reflected in the shining light of our unique spiritual natures. Forgiving each other, and nurturing each other as best we can, serves the greater good.

As you look around you, recognizing the seed of the divine in everything, the world and its inhabitants take on new life. When you view the world through shaman's eyes, the elements of nature pulse with interaction and energy. Places and spaces are animated with their own personalities. Your environment becomes a living, breathing field through which you walk, run, dance, and play. As you are part of nature, the power of nature is part of you. By working cooperatively with your environment, you create a fertile garden from which the seeds of your ideal life can grow and flourish.

Your intuition is useful in every aspect of your life and work. It is an inner gauge, filtering truth from falsehood, sorting dreams from fears, letting you know when you're on the right route and when you've veered off course. When you listen to your intuitive voice you're listening to your sacred self, the wise and balanced voice of your eternal being. Delve into your inner wilderness and you will tap the divine knowledge stored deep within. In each moment, that knowledge can steer you toward a happy and fulfilling life.

Spiritual support is available all around you. Seek it from within you, from your community, from nature, and from helping spirits. Ask for it and open your arms to receive it. Let your spiritual sustenance flow through you and your thirst will be quenched. Visualize yourself as a newborn baby. Cradle this tiny babe in your arms, loving her, soothing her, casting a proud gaze down upon her. She soaks up this loving attention as the trees and flowers soak up the spring rain. Now, let yourself drink from the well of love and support available to you. Listen to the wisdom of the spiritual beings around you and within you. They will support you in establishing the life that most inspires you.

Your physical health overlays your spiritual health. By maintaining health on all strata of your being, you find holism, a level of well-being that moves past the simple functioning of cells to the coordinated and efficient functioning of your entire being. Although there are many modalities and practitioners who can assist you on your journey toward optimal health, you hold the key to your healing. Your faith in your body's innate understanding of what it needs to heal will affect your health. As more people recognize the spiritual component of health, care of the spirit body will become included in mainstream medical treatment. Through your own explorations in healing, you will inspire those around you. Connect with your body (both the physical and the energetic), and engage it in dialogue. From that discussion you will receive what you need to nourish and support your health.

The future is mysterious and fascinating. Our future as a planet is in our collective hands. Your future is in your hands. Craft the future of your dreams *now*, by living as fully in touch with your sacred intelligence as possible. Find something inspiring in each moment and you will create an inspiring future. Envision the life you want and draw it forth from the universe of possibilities. When you awaken to your divine nature, you will be guided into the future by a light radiating from deep within you.

Practically, find a path that suits you. Stay on it until it suits you no longer and then turn as your intuition guides you. Don't put pressure on yourself to perform in a particular way, to be something you are not, or to live up to someone else's ideal. You don't have to do anything to be spiritual, just let yourself *be*. Remember, you are your primary caretaker. Self-care can take many forms. Sometimes we need discipline and sometimes we need rest. Respect your cyclical nature. Take a balanced approach to your inner work. You can only work on deep levels for so long before you need a break to relax and refuel.

The search for spiritual meaning can be challenging at times. When you seek the answers to the mysteries of your soul, you are trying to grasp the ephemeral, to hold onto the sacred smoke that spirals from the fire of your inner being. By exploring the depths of your consciousness, and experimenting with ways of connecting to your divine self, you acquire the peace that you crave.

I wish you joy as you embrace your inner divinity, wisdom as you walk your chosen path, and beauty as you see the world anew through shaman's eyes.

 # RESOURCES

For more information about individual sessions, workshops, artwork, and to order CDs:

Mara Bishop
WholeSpirit
P.O. Box 51553
Durham, NC 27717
Phone: 919-419-1074
www.innerdivinity.com
info@innerdivinity.com

For more information about core shamanism, workshops, articles, drumming circles, and to order journeying CDs:

Foundation for Shamanic Studies
P.O. Box 1939
Mill Valley, CA 94942
Phone: 415-380-8282
www.shamanism.org
info@shamanism.org

For information about shamanism and finding shamanic practitioners and instructors for journeying and shamanic healing:

Sandra Ingerman
www.shamanicteachers.com
www.medicinefortheearth.com
www.shamanicvisions.com/ingerman.html

For workshops, shamanic resources, and to order CloudDancing cards:

Nan Moss and David Corbin
The Shamans Circle: Down to Earth
P.O. Box 330
Port Clyde, ME 04855
Phone: 207-372-8823
www.shamanscircle.com

Companion CD now available.

See the *Resources* section for ordering information.

GUIDED MEDITATIONS
selected from the book

INNER DIVINITY

Crafting Your Life with
Sacred Intelligence

MARA BISHOP

MEDITATIONS

1. Grounding
2. Psychic Boundaries
3. Nature
4. Inner Guide
5. Animal Spirit
6. Dialogue with Your Body
7. Love

WORKS CITED

Achterberg, Dr. Jean. *Imagery in Healing: Shamanism and Modern Medicine.* Boston and New York: Shambhala, 1985.

Alexander, Jane. *The Spirit of the Home: How to Make Your Home a Sanctuary.* New York, NY: Watson-Guptill Publications, 2000.

Arviso Alvord, M.D., Lori. *The Scalpel and the Silver Bear: The First Navajo Surgeon Combines Western Medicine and Traditional Healing.* New York, NY: Bantam Books, 1999.

Austin, Lou. *You Are Greater Than You Know.* Winchester, VA: The Partnership Foundation, 1955.

Bakshi, Rajni. January 25, 2005. "Gross National Happiness." *AlterNet,* http://www.alternet.org/story/21083/.

Barrett, Jennifer. July 1999. "Going the Distance." *Intuition Magazine.*

Bishop, Mara. "Spirit Affecting Matter: Can Shamanism Help Us Heal?" M.S. thesis, Holos University, 2002.

Braden, Gregg. *The Isaiah Effect: Decoding the Lost Science of Prayer and Prophecy.* New York, NY: Three Rivers Press, 2000.

Brennan, Barbara. *Hands of Light: A Guide to Healing Through the Human Energy Field.* New York, NY: Bantam Books, 1987.

Breslin, James E.B. *Mark Rothko: A Biography*. Chicago, IL: University of Chicago Press, 1998.

Brown, David. "Traditional Healing Returns to Tuva: In the Soviets' Wake, a Shamans' Clinic is Thriving in Northeast Asia." *Washington Post, KYZYL, Tuva*. http://www.fotuva.org/misc/shamanism/clinic.html.

Butler, Stuart M., Ph.D.; Harold G. Koenig, M.D.; Christina Puchalski, M.D.; Cynthia Cohen, Ph.D., J.D.; and Richard Sloan, Ph.D. December 22, 2003. "Is Prayer Good for Your Health? A Critique of the Scientific Research" Heritage Lecture #816, *The Heritage Foundation*. http://www.heritage.org/Research/Religion/HL816.cfm.

Campbell, Joseph. *Historical Atlas of World Mythology. Volume I: The Way of the Animal Powers. Part I: Mythologies of the Primitive Hunters and Gatherers*. New York, NY: Harper and Row, 1988.

Chödrön, Pema. January 2005. "No Such Thing As A True Story." *Sun Magazine*.

Choquette, Sonya. *The Psychic Pathway: A Workbook for Reawakening the Voice of Your Soul*. New York, NY: Three Rivers Press, 1994.

Coddington, Mary. *Seekers of the Healing Energy*. Rochester, VT: Healing Arts Press, 1978.

"Complementary and Alternative Medicine at the NIH." *National Institutes of Health, National Center for Complementary and Alternative Medicine Clearinghouse*, Volume VII, Number 2, Spring 2000.

Coolidge, Shelley Donald. June 17, 1999. "You snooze, you win at today's workplace." *The Christian Science Monitor*. http://search.csmonitor.com/durable/1999/06/17/p1s4.htm.

Cortese, Saundra. *The Souls of Our Children*. San Francisco, CA: HarperSanFrancisco, 1997.

Cowan, Tom. *Fire in the Head: Shamanism and the Celtic Spirit*. San Francisco, CA: HarperSanFrancisco, 1993.

Cowan, Tom. *Shamanism as a Spiritual Practice for Daily Life.* Freedom, CA: The Crossing Press, 1996.

Creedon, Jeremiah. July–August 1998. "God with a Million Faces." *Utne Reader.*

Cutter, John. "Spirituality May Help People Live Longer: Discover why some believe that older people who regularly attend religious services appear to have better health." WebMD, Online. http://my.webmd.com/content/article/11/1738_50058.htm.

deFur, Peter L. December 1999. "A Scientist Caught in the Web of Life." *The Networker.* Volume 4 (6), http://www.sehn.org/Volume_4–6.html#a3.

"Dorothy Maclean: A Spirit in the Smokies Interview," May 25, 1999. *Spirit in the Smokies: Magazine of New Paradigm Living.* http://spiritinthesmokies.com/interviews/dorothym.html.

Dossey M.D., Larry. *Healing Beyond the Body: Medicine and the Infinite Reach of the Mind.* Boston and London: Shambhala, 2001.

Dossey M.D., Larry. *Reinventing Medicine: Beyond Mind–Body to a New Era of Healing.* San Francisco, CA: HarperSanFrancisco, 1999.

Dossey, M.D., Larry. May–June 2001. "What the Leaves Can Tell Us." *Utne Reader.*

Drury, Nevill. *The Elements of Shamanism.* Boston, MA: Elements Books, 1991.

Duke University Center for Spirituality, Theology, and Health. "Intercessory Prayer and Cardiac Outcomes." *Recent Research Findings.* http://www.dukespirituality andhealth.org/research/abstracts/index.html#intercessory.

Edwards, Kathleen. October 2004. Correspondence, *The Sun.*

Elgin, Duane, with Coleen LeDrew. May 1997, "Global Consciousness Change: Indicators of an Emerging Paradigm." http://www.simpleliving.net/awakeningearth/reports.asp#03.

Eliade, Mircea. *Shamanism: Archaic Techniques of Ecstasy.* Princeton, NJ: Princeton University Press, 1964.

Emoto, Masaru. *The Message From Water.* Japan: Sunmark Publications, 2001.

Eshowsky, Myron. "Shamanism and Peacemaking." Foundation for Shamanic Studies. http://shamanism.org/articles/1021409421.htm.

Eshowsky, Myron. Lecture, Reunion of the FSS 4th East Coast 3–Year Program, White Haven PA, October 2004.

Fairclough, Gordon. January 18, 2005. "For Thai survivors, the dead live on in ghost sightings." *The Wall Street Journal.*

Flanigan, Robin. March 28, 1999. "Shamanic journey seeks peace, wholeness: Durham woman taps ancient healing practice." *Herald-Sun.* Durham, NC.

Foundation for Shamanic Studies. www.shamanism.org.

Goleman, Daniel. *The Meditative Mind: The Varieties of Meditative Experience.* New York, NY: G.P. Putnam's Sons, 1988.

Hanh, Thich Nhat. *Living Buddha, Living Christ.* New York, NY: Riverhead Books, 1995.

Hanh, Thich Nhat. *Present Moment Wonderful Moment: Mindfulness Verses for Daily Living.* Berkeley, CA: Parallax Press, 1990.

Harner, Michael. *The Way of the Shaman* Workshop. New York, NY, April 1997.

Harner, Michael. *The Way of the Shaman.* San Francisco, CA: HarperSanFrancisco, 1980.

Hazleton, Lesley. *Mary: A Flesh and Blood Biography of the Virgin Mother.* New York: Bloomsbury, 2004.

Heidorn, Ph.D., Keith C. August 15, 2002. "Weather Almanac. Gods of Thunder Throwers of Lightning." http://www.islandnet.com/~see/weather/almanac/arc2002/alm02aug2.htm.

Helm, H., Hays, J.C., Flint, E., Koenig, H.G., Blazer, DG. 2000. "Effects of private religious activity on mortality of elderly disabled and nondisabled adults." *Journal of Gerontology (Medical Sciences.* 55A, M400–M405. Abstract,

Duke University Center for Spirituality, Theology, and Health. Recent Research Findings, "Prayer and Mortality." http://www.dukespiritualityandhealth.org/research/abstracts/index.html#prayer.

Hendrix, Harville. *Getting the Love You Want: A Guide for Couples.* New York, NY: Henry Holt and Company, LLC, 1988.

His Holiness the Dalai Lama and Howard C. Cutler, M.D. *The Art of Happiness: A Handbook for Living.* New York, NY: Riverhead Books, 1998.

The Holy Bible, King James version

Hultkrantz, Åke. *Shamanic Healing and Ritual Drama.* New York, NY: The Crossroad Publishing Company, 1997.

Ingerman, Sandra. Spring/Summer 1999. "Ethical Considerations in Soul Retrieval." *Shamanism* Vol 12, No. 1

Ingerman, Sandra. *Medicine for the Earth: How To Transform Personal and Environmental Toxins.* New York: Three Rivers Press, 2000.

Ingerman, Sandra. *Soul Retrieval: Mending the Fragmented Self.* San Francisco, CA: HarperSanFrancisco, 1991.

Ingerman, Sandra. *Transmutation News,* July 2003, http://www.shamanicvisions.com/ingerman_folder/ingerman03/july03.html.

Janis, I. P. Defares, and P. Grossman. 1983. *Seyle's Guide to Stress Research.* (H. Seyle, ed.) Vol 3, New York: Scientific and Academic Editions.

Japenga, Ann. "Taking Your Spiritual Pulse" WebMD, Online. http://my.webmd.com/content/article/12/1674_50966.

Kaku, Michio. *Parallel Worlds: A Journey Through Creation, Higher Dimensions, and the Future of the Cosmos.* New York, NY: Doubleday Books, 2005.

Kalweit, Holger. *Dreamtime and Inner Space.* Boston, MA: Shambhala Publications, 1984.

Kavasch, E. Barrie and Karen Baar, *American Indian Healing Arts*. New York: Bantam, 1999.

Kerkut, Prof. Gerald. "Rapidly Dividing Cells." University of Southampton, http://www.geocities.com/gkerkut/index.htm.

King, Serge. *Kahuna Healing*. Wheaton, Ill: The Theosophical Publishing House, 1983.

Klite, Dr. Paul D. May 24, 1999. "TV News and the Culture of Violence." *Rocky Mountain Media Watch*. http://www.bigmedia.org/texts6.html.

Kullander, James. January, 2005. "Sitting in the Fire: Pema Chödrön on Turning Towards Pain." *Sun Magazine*.

"The Last Siberian Shamans." 1996. Novosibirsk Regional Studies Museum Web site, http://nrsm.nsc.ru/.

Leonhardt, David. "Survey: Family, Altruism and Faith Define Happiness." *Sales Success Magazine* On-line, http://salessuccessmagazine.com/articles/700/SURVEY-Family-Altruism-And-Faith-Define-Happiness.html.

Linn, Denise. *Sacred Space*. New York, NY: Ballantine Books, 1995.

Lonsdorf, M.D., Nancy Veronica Butler, M.D., and Melanie Brown, Ph.D., *A Woman's Best Medicine: Health, Happiness, and Long Life Through Maharishi Ayurveda*. New York, NY: G.P. Putnam's Sons, 1993.

Luskin, Ph.D., Frederic. *Forgive for Good*. New York, NY: Harper Collins, 2002.

Mayell, Hillary. January 21, 2003. "Documentary Redraws Humans' Family Tree." *National Geographic News*.

"Michelangelo Buonarroti, The Mid Years (1505–1535)" http://www.michelangelo.com/buon/bio-index2.html.

Misra, Neelesh. January 4, 2005. "Reading Winds, Waves Help Indian Islanders." *The Associated Press*.

"More Than One-Third of US Adults Use Complementary and Alternative Medicine." May 28, 2004, http://www.healthyplace.com/Communities/Anxiety/news/alternative_medicine.asp.

Moss, Nan and David Corbin. Fall/Winter 1999. "Shamanism and the Spirits of Weather." *Shamanism*, Vol. 12, No. 2.

Myss, Caroline. *Sacred Contracts: Awakening Your Divine Potential.* New York, NY: Harmony Books, 2001.

Over, Jill. personal correspondence, October 2004.

Palmer, Martin and Elizabeth Breuilly (trans.). *The Book of Chuang-Tzu.* London, England: Penguin Arkana, 1996.

Parikh, Jagdish, Freidrich Neubauer, and Alden Lank. *Intuition: The New Frontier of Management* (Global Intuition Survey Report) Oxford, England: Blackwell Publishers, 1994.

Paul, Pamela. January 17, 2005. "The Power to Uplift." *Time Magazine.*

Prechtel, Martín, *Secrets of the Talking Jaguar: A Mayan Shaman's Journey to the Heart of the Indigenous Soul.* New York: Tarcher/Putnam, 1998.

Radin, Dean I., Janine M Rebman, and Maikwe P. Cross, 1996. "Anomalous Organization of Random Events by Group Consciousness: Two Exploratory Experiments." *Journal of Scientific Exploration* 10, no. 1.

Rauch, Catherine. "Probing the Power of Prayer: Surprising results follow a study on praying for others." WebMD, Online. http://my.webmd.com/content/article/14/1668_50132.htm.

Reich, John and Ed Diener. Jul/Aug 1994. "The Road to Happiness." *Psychology Today.*

Rheingold, Howard. 1995. "New Medicines from Ancient Bottles: Shaman Pharmaceuticals." On-line, http://www.well.com/user/hlr/tomorrow/shaman.html.

Robb, Vivki. October 7, 2003. "Study shows that forgiveness can be taught." *John Templeton Foundation*, http://www.eurekalert.org/pub_releases/2003-10/cff-ss100703.php.

Robinson, George. *Essential Judaism: A Complete Guide to Beliefs, Customs and Ritual.* New York, NY: Simon and Schuster, 2000.

Rogers, Carl. *A Way of Being.* New York, NY: Houghton Mifflin, 1980.

Roth Ph.D., Ron. *Holy Spirit for Healing.* Carlsbad, CA: Hay House Inc., 2001.

Sands, Helen Raphael. *The Healing Labyrinth: Finding Your Path to Inner Peace.* Hauppauge, NY: Baron's, 2001.

Sarangerel. *Chosen by the Spirits: Following Your Shamanic Calling.* Rochester, VT: Destiny Books, 2001.

Schoemperlen, Diane. *Our Lady of the Lost and Found.* New York, NY: Penguin Books, 2001.

Schultz M.D., Mona Lisa. *Awakening Intuition: Using Your Mind-Body Network For Insight and Healing.* New York, NY: Harmony Books, 1998.

Shore, AG. May–Jun 2004. "Long-term effects of energetic healing on symptoms of psychological depression and self-perceived stress." *Alternative Therapies in Health and Medicine.* 10(3).

"The Structure of Skin." http://www.skin-care.ph/the_skin.htm.

Talbot, Michael. *The Holographic Universe.* New York: Harper Perennial, 1991.

Too, Lillian. *Applied Feng Shui: Pa-Kua and Lo-Shu.* Adelaide, Australia: Oriental Publications, 1993.

University of Maryland Medical School Center for Integrated Medicine. http://www.compmed.umm.edu/FAQs.html.

Villoldo Ph.D., Alberto and Stanley Krippner, Ph.D. *Healing States: A Journey into the World of Spiritual Healing and Shamanism.* New York, NY: Simon and Schuster, Inc., 1986.

Wallace, Claudia. January 17, 2005. "The New Science of Happiness." *Time Magazine.*

Webster, Karen. *Triumvirs.* Volume 1 Issue 3.

Weil M.D., Andrew. January–February 2005. "What Doctors Should Know: Western medicine needs to rediscover the body's mysterious ability to heal." *Utne Magazine.*

Weisstein, Eric W. "Isomorphism." From *MathWorld*—A Wolfram Web Resource. http://mathworld.wolfram.com/Isomorphism.html.

Wilber, Ken. *The Marriage of Sense and Soul: Integrating Science and Religion.* New York, NY: Broadway Books, 1998.

Yant, Monica. 114 April 1998. Interview with Phil Ponce. "Ecological Disaster." *The NewsHour with Jim Lehrer.* PBS, On-line. New York. http://www.pbs.org/newshour/bb/environment/jan–june98/rainforest_4-14.html.

Yudkin Ph.D., Marcia. "Respecting Your Motivational Rhythms." *Twelve Star Publishing, Earthlight Magazine* on-line. http://www.twelvestar.com/Earthlight/Motivational%20Rhythms.ht

ABOUT THE AUTHOR

Mara Bishop is an intuitive consultant, shamanic practitioner, teacher, author, and artist.

Mara has been in private practice since 1995. She holds degrees in Energy Medicine from Greenwich University, Theology from Holos University, and Art and Communications from Clark University. Mara is a graduate of the Foundation for Shamanic Studies Three–Year Program in Advanced Shamanism and Shamanic Healing with Michael Harner and Sandra Ingerman, and Sandra Ingerman's Teacher Training program in Shamanic Journeying and Healing. She is certified in Harner Method Shamanic Counseling.

In her private practice, Mara combines intuitive consultations, shamanic healing, and energetic healing to provide each client with an integrated approach to spiritual healing, personal growth, and emotional well-being. She conducts workshops and is available for speaking engagements.

She lives in Durham, North Carolina with her husband and daughter.

For more information:

Mara Bishop
WholeSpirit
P.O. Box 51553
Durham, NC 27717
Phone: 919-419-1074
www.innerdivinity.com
info@innerdivinity.com

 ENDNOTES

SECTION 1: YOUR SELF

[1]   The Dalai Lama and Howard C. Cutler, M.D., *The Art of Happiness: A Handbook for Living* (New York, NY: Riverhead Books, 1998) 45-46.

[2]   Barbara Brennan, *Hands of Light: A Guide to Healing Through the Human Energy Field* (New York, NY: Bantam Books, 1987) 29.

[3]   Brennan, 45.

[4]   Janis, I. P. Defares, and P. Grossman, *Seyle's Guide to Stress Research* (H. Seyle, ed.) Vol 3, (New York: Scientific and Academic Editions, 1983) 1-42.

[5]   The Dalai Lama and Howard C. Cutler, M.D., 114.

[6]   "Michelangelo Buonarroti, The Mid Years (1505-1535)" http://www.michel-angelo.com/buon/bio-index2.html.

[7]   Martha Washington, "Martha Dandridge Custis Washington" White House web site http://www.whitehouse.gov/history/firstladies/mw1.html.

[8]   Masaru Emoto, *The Message From Water* (Japan: Sunmark Publications, 2001) 8.

[9]   Marcia Yudkin, Ph.D., "Respecting Your Motivational Rhythms" *Twelve Star Publishing, Earthlight Magazine* on-line. http://www.twelvestar.com/Earthlight/Motivational%20Rhythms.html.

[10]   Yudkin

[11]   Shelley Donald Coolidge, "You snooze, you win at today's workplace" *The Christian Science Monitor* On-line. http://search.csmonitor.com/durable/1999/06/17/p1s4.htm (June 17, 1999).

12   "The Structure of Skin" http://www.skin-care.ph/the_skin.htm.

13   Prof. Gerald Kerkut, "Rapidly Dividing Cells" University of Southampton, http://www.geocities.com/gkerkut/index.htm.

14   Thich Nhat Hanh, *Present Moment Wonderful Moment: Mindfulness Verses for Daily Living* (Berkeley, CA: Parallax Press, 1990) 51.

15   Dossey M.D., Larry, *Healing Beyond the Body: Medicine and the Infinite Reach of the Mind* (Boston and London: Shambhala, 2001) 138.

16   Dossey, *Healing Beyond the Body,* 136-137.

17   Dossey, *Healing Beyond the Body*, 133.

18   James Kullander, "Sitting in the Fire: Pema Chödrön on Turning Towards Pain" *Sun Magazine* (January 2005) 7.

SECTION 2: YOUR RELATIONSHIPS

19   Brennan, 75.

20   Thich Nhat Hanh, *Living Buddha, Living Christ* (New York: Riverhead Books, 1995) 100-101.

21   Harville Hendrix, *Getting the Love You Want: A Guide for Couples* (New York, NY: Henry Holt and Company, LLC, 1988) 36.

22   Saundra Cortese, *The Souls of Our Children* (San Francisco, CA: HarperSanFrancisco: 1997) 155.

23   Hillary Mayell, "Documentary Redraws Humans' Family Tree" *National Geographic News* (January 21, 2003).

24   Carl Rogers, *A Way of Being* (New York, NY: Houghton Mifflin, 1980) 116.

25   Vivki Robb, "Study shows that forgiveness can be taught" John Templeton Foundation, (Public release date: October 7,2003) http://www.eurekalert.org/pub_releases/2003-10/cff-ss100703.php.

26   Frederic Luskin, Ph.D., *Forgive for Good* (New York, NY: Harper Collins, 2002) 212.

27   Myron Eshowsky, "Shamanism and Peacemaking" Foundation for Shamanic Studies. http://shamanism.org/articles/1021409421.htm.

28   Thich Nhat Hanh, *Living Buddha, Living Christ,* 100.

SECTION 3: YOUR ENVIRONMENT

29   Dr. Paul D. Klite, "TV News and the Culture of Violence" *Rocky Mountain Media Watch* (May 24) 1999, http://www.bigmedia.org/texts6.html.

30   Lou Austin, *You Are Greater Than You Know* (Capon Springs, WV: The Partnership Foundation, 1955) 52.

31   Jane Alexander, *The Spirit of the Home: How to Make Your Home a Sanctuary* (New York, NY: Watson-Guptill Publications, 2000) 1.

32   Lillian Too, *Applied Feng Shui: Pa-Kua and Lo-Shu* (Adelaide, Australia: Oriental Publications, 1993) 21.

33   George Robinson, *Essential Judaism: A Complete Guide to Beliefs, Customs and Ritual* (New York, NY: Simon and Schuster, 2000) 52.

34   Sandra Ingerman, *Medicine for the Earth: How To Transform Personal and Environmental Toxins* (New York, NY: Three Rivers Press, 2000) 159.

35   "Dorothy Maclean: A Spirit in the Smokies Interview," *Spirit in the Smokies: Magazine of New Paradigm Living* (May 25, 1999) On-line.http://spiritinthes-mokies.com/interviews/dorothym.html.

36   Sarangerel, *Chosen by the Spirits: Following Your Shamanic Calling* (Rochester, VT: Destiny Books, 2001) 47.

37   Neelesh Misra, "Reading Winds, Waves Help Indian Islanders" *The Associated Press* (January 4, 2005).

38   Nan Moss and David Corbin, "Shamanism and the Spirits of Weather" *Shamanism,* (Fall/Winter 1999) Vol. 12, No. 2.

39   Monica Yant, Interview with Phil Ponce. "Ecological Disaster" *The NewsHour with Jim Lehrer.* PBS, On-line. New York (14 April 1998) http://www.pbs.org/newshour/bb/environment/jan-june98/rainforest_4-14.html.

40   Gregg Braden, *The Isaiah Effect: Decoding the Lost Science of Prayer and Prophecy* (New York, NY: Three Rivers Press, 2000) 162-167.

41   Keith C. Heidorn, Ph.D., "Weather Almanac. Gods of Thunder Throwers of Lightning" (August 15, 2002) http://www.islandnet.com/~see/weather/alma-nac/arc2002/alm02aug2.htm.

42 Helen Raphael Sands, *The Healing Labyrinth: Finding Your Path to Inner Peace* (Hauppauge, New York: Baron's. 2001) 30, 36.

43 Jill Over, personal correspondence (October 2004).

44 Lori Arviso Alvord, M.D., *The Scalpel and the Silver Bear: The First Navajo Surgeon Combines Western Medicine and Traditional Healing* (New York, NY: Bantam Books, 1999) 14.

45 Tom Cowan, *Fire in the Head: Shamanism and the Celtic Spirit* (San Francisco, CA: HarperSanFrancisco, 1993) 45.

46 Peter L. deFur, "A Scientist Caught in the Web of Life" *The Networker* Volume 4 (6) (December 1999) http://www.sehn.org/Volume_4-6.html#a3.

47 Dossey, *Healing Beyond the Body*, 204.

48 Martin Palmer and Elizabeth Breuilly (trans.), *The Book of Chuang-Tzu* (London, England: Penguin Arkana, 1996) 162.

49 Nan Moss and David Corbin, "Shamanism and the Spirits of Weather: More Pieces of the Puzzle" on-line http://www.shamanscircle.com/article.asp?ID=93.

50 "Dorothy Maclean: A Spirit in the Smokies Interview," *Spirit in the Smokies: Magazine of New Paradigm Living*, On-line. May 25, 1999, http://spiritinthesmokies.com/interviews/dorothym.html.

SECTION 4: YOUR INTUITION

51 Karen Webster, *Triumvirs* Volume 1 Issue 3.

52 Schultz, 22.

53 Jagdish Parikh, Freidrich Neubauer, and Alden Lank, *Intuition: The New Frontier of Management* (Global Intuition Survey Report) (Oxford, England: Blackwell Publishers, 1994).

54 Schultz, 27.

55 Austin, 54.

56 Denise Linn, *Sacred Space* (New York, NY: Ballantine Books, 1995) 22.

57 Sonya Choquette, *The Psychic Pathway: A Workbook for Reawakening the Voice of Your Soul* (New York, NY: Three Rivers Press, 1994) 14.

58   Schultz, 36.

59   James E.B. Breslin, *Mark Rothko: A Biography* (Chicago, IL: University of Chicago Press, 1998) 135 and 185.

60   Schultz, 42.

61   Schultz, 29.

SECTION 5: YOUR SPIRITUAL SUPPORT

62   Pema Chödrön, "No Such Thing As A True Story" *Sun Magazine* (January 2005) 13.

63   Diane Schoemperlen, *Our Lady of the Lost and Found* (New York, NY: Penguin Books, 2001) 270-271.

64   John Reich, Ed Diener, "The Road to Happiness" *Psychology Today.* David Leonhardt. "Survey: Family, Altruism and Faith Define Happiness." *Sales Success Magazine* On-line, (July/August 1994) http://salessuccessmagazine.com/articles/700/SURVEY-Family-Altruism-And-Faith-Define-Happiness.html.

65   Tom Cowan, *Shamanism as a Spiritual Practice for Daily Life* (Freedom, CA: The Crossing Press, 1996) 18.

66   Roth, 127.

67   Michael Harner, *The Way of the Shaman* (San Francisco, CA: HarperSanFrancisco, 1980) 22.

68   Cowan, *Shamanism as a Spiritual Practice for Daily Life*, 112.

69   Roth, 17.

70   *The Holy Bible*, King James version, Book of Job, 22:28.

71   Hultkrantz, 130-131, Arviso Alvord, 163.

72   Stuart M. Butler, Ph.D.; Harold G. Koenig, M.D.; Christina Puchalski, M.D.; Cynthia Cohen, Ph.D., J.D.; and Richard Sloan, Ph.D., "Is Prayer Good for Your Health? A Critique of the Scientific Research" Heritage Lecture #816, *The Heritage Foundation* (December 22, 2003) http://www.heritage.org/Research/Religion/HL816.cfm.

73   Helm, H., Hays, J.C., Flint, E., Koenig, H.G., Blazer, DG., "Effects of private religious activity on mortality of elderly disabled and nondisabled adults" *Journal of Gerontology (Medical Sciences),* 55A, M400-M405. (2000) Abstract, Duke University Center for Spirituality, Theology, and Health. Recent Research Findings, "Prayer and Mortality." http://www.dukespiritualityand-health.org/research/abstracts/index.html#prayer.

74   Daniel Goleman, *The Meditative Mind: The Varieties of Meditative Experience* (New York, NY: G.P. Putnam's Sons, 1988).

75   Roth, 33.

76   Goleman, 51.

77   Goleman, 41.

78   Goleman, 55.

79   Lesley Hazleton, *Mary: A Flesh and Blood Biography of the Virgin Mother* (New York, NY: Bloomsbury, 2004) 103.

80   Goleman, xxiv.

81   Pamela Paul, "The Power to Uplift" *Time Magazine* (January 17, 2005) A46.

82   Michael Harner, *The Way of the Shaman*, 20.

83   Michael Harner, *The Way of the Shaman*, 139.

84   Harner xix, 46-47.

85   Michael Harner, *The Way of the Shaman*, xvii.

86   Michael Harner, *The Way of the Shaman* Workshop. New York, NY, April 1997.

87   Foundation for Shamanic Studies. www.shamanism.org.

88   Elgin; Harner, xiii.

89   Nevill Drury, *The Elements of Shamanism* (Boston, MA: Elements Books, 1991) 39.

90   Eliade, 173; Harner, 51.

91   Harner, 43.

92   Eliade, 92.

[93]   Elgin.

[94]   Jeremiah Creedon, "God with a Million Faces" *Utne Reader* (July-August 1998) 44.

[95]   Harner, *The Way of the Shaman* Workshop.

SECTION 6: YOUR HEALTH

[96]   Mary Coddington, *Seekers of the Healing Energy* (Rochester, VT: Healing Arts Press, 1978) 43 and 54.

[97]   Coddington, 75.

[98]   University of Maryland Medical School Center for Integrated Medicine, http://www.compmed.umm.edu/FAQs.html.

[99]   Catherine Rauch, "Probing the Power of Prayer: Surprising results follow a study on praying for others" WebMD, Online. http://my.webmd.com/content/article/14/1668_50132.htm, John Cutter, "Spirituality May Help People Live Longer: Discover why some believe that older people who regularly attend religious services appear to have better health." WebMD, Online. http://my.webmd.com/content/article/11/1738_50058.htm.

[100] Ann Japenga, "Taking Your Spiritual Pulse" WebMD, Online. http://my.webmd.com/content/article/12/1674_50966.

[101] "More Than One-Third of US Adults Use Complementary and Alternative Medicine" (May 28, 2004) http://www.healthyplace.com/Communities/Anxiety/news/alternative_medicine.asp.

[102] Duane Elgin, with Coleen LeDrew, "Global Consciousness Change: Indicators of an Emerging Paradigm" (May 1997) http://www.simpleliving.net/awakeningearth/reports.asp#03.

[103] David Brown, "Traditional Healing Returns to Tuva: In the Soviets' Wake, a Shamans' Clinic is Thriving in Northeast Asia" *Washington Post, KYZYL, Tuva.* http://www.fotuva.org/misc/shamanism/clinic.html.

[104] Howard Rheingold, "New Medicines from Ancient Bottles: Shaman Pharmaceuticals" (1995) http://www.well.com/user/hlr/tomorrow/shaman.html.

[105]   Andrew Weil, M.D., "What Doctors Should Know: Western medicine needs to rediscover the body's mysterious ability to heal" *Utne Reader* (January-February 2005) 92.

[106]   Åke Hultkrantz, *Shamanic Healing and Ritual Drama* (New York, NY: The Crossroad Publishing Company, 1997) 1.

[107]   Sandra Ingerman, *Soul Retrieval: Mending the Fragmented Self* (San Francisco, CA: HarperSanFrancisco, 1991) 23.

[108]   Robin Flanigan, "Shamanic journey seeks peace, wholeness: Durham woman taps ancient healing practice" *Herald-Sun* (March 28, 1999).

[109]   Hultkrantz, 66.

[110]   Gordon Fairclough, "For Thai Survivors, The Dead Live On In Ghost Sightings" *The Wall Street Journal* (Tuesday, January 18, 2005).

[111]   Andrew Weil, M.D., "What Doctors Should Know: Western medicine needs to rediscover the body's mysterious ability to heal" 91.

[112]   E. Barrie Kavasch and Karen Baar, *American Indian Healing Arts* (New York: Bantam, 1999) 18-19.

[113]   Arviso Alvord, 112.

[114]   Larry Dossey, M.D., "What the Leaves Can Tell Us" *Utne Reader* (May-June 2001) 66-67.

[115]   *The Holy Bible*, King James version. John 1:1.

[116]   Martín Prechtel, *Secrets of the Talking Jaguar: A Mayan Shaman's Journey to the Heart of the Indigenous Soul* (New York: Tarcher/Putnam. 1998) 7.

[117]   Ingerman, *Medicine for the Earth*, 202-3.

[118]   Ingerman, *Medicine for the Earth*, 201.

[119]   Ingerman, *Medicine for the Earth*. 203.

[120]   Hultkrantz, 130-131, Arviso Alvord, M.D., 163.

[121]   Joseph Campbell, *Historical Atlas of World Mythology. Volume I: The Way of the Animal Powers. Part I: Mythologies of the Primitive Hunters and Gatherers* (New York, NY: Harper and Row, 1988) 94.

[122]   Ken Wilber, *The Marriage of Sense and Soul: Integrating Science and Religion* (New York, NY: Broadway Books, 1998) 128.

123 AG Shore, "Long-term effects of energetic healing on symptoms of psycho-logical depression and self-perceived stress" *Alternative Therapies in Health and Medicine* (May-Jun 2004) 10(3):42-8.

124 Serge King, *Kahuna Healing* (Wheaton, Ill: The Theosophical Publishing House, 1983.) 114-115.

125 Larry Dossey M.D., *Reinventing Medicine: Beyond Mind-Body to a New Era of Healing* (San Francisco, CA: HarperSanFrancisco, 1999) 8.

126 Dossey, *Reinventing Medicine,* 140-141.

127 Jennifer Barrett, "Going the Distance" *Intuition* (July 1999) 28-31.

128 Dean I. Radin, Janine M Rebman, and Maikwe P. Cross, "Anomalous Organization of Random Events by Group Consciousness: Two Exploratory Experiments" *Journal of Scientific Exploration* 10, no. 1 (1996), 143-168.

129 Dossey, *Reinventing Medicine,* 124-125.

130 Dossey, *Reinventing Medicine,* 125-126.

131 Ingerman, *Medicine for the Earth,* 38-39.

132 Ron Roth, Ph.D., *Holy Spirit for Healing* (Carlsbad, CA: Hay House Inc., 2001) 131.

133 Dossey, *Healing Beyond the Body,* 136.

134 Roth, 51.

135 Mara Bishop, "Spirit Affecting Matter: Can Shamanism Help Us Heal?" M.S. thesis, Holos University (2002).

136 Dr. Jean Achterberg, *Imagery in Healing: Shamanism and Modern Medicine* (Boston and New York: Shambhala, 1985) 19.

137 Alberto Villoldo Ph.D., and Stanley Krippner, Ph.D., *Healing States: A Journey into the World of Spiritual Healing and Shamanism* (New York: Simon and Schuster, Inc., 1986) 187-188.

138 "Complementary and Alternative Medicine at the NIH", *National Institutes of Health, National Center for Complementary and Alternative Medicine Clearinghouse,* Volume VII, Number 2, (Spring 2000).

SECTION 7: YOUR FUTURE

139 Nancy Lonsdorf, M.D., Veronica Butler, M.D., and Melanie Brown, Ph.D., *A Woman's Best Medicine: Health, Happiness, and Long Life Through Maharishi Ayurveda* (New York, NY: G.P. Putnam's Sons, 1993) 54.

140 Michio Kaku, *Parallel Worlds: A Journey Through Creation, Higher Dimensions, and the Future of the Cosmos* (New York, NY: Doubleday Books, 2005) 16.

141 Myron Eshowsky, Lecture, Reunion of the FSS 4th East Coast 3-Year Program, White Haven PA (October 2004).

142 Kullander, 8.

143 Caroline Myss, *Sacred Contracts: Awakening Your Divine Potential* (New York, NY: Harmony Books, 2001) 47.

144 *The Holy Bible*, Proverbs 29:18.

145 Braden, 187.

146 Eric W. Weisstein, "Isomorphism" From *MathWorld*—A Wolfram Web Resource. http://mathworld.wolfram.com/Isomorphism.html.

147 Kathleen Edwards, Correspondence, *The Sun*. (October 2004) 2.

148 Claudia Wallace, "The New Science of Happiness" *Time Magazine* (January 17, 2005) A7-A9.

149 Rajni Bakshi, "Gross National Happiness" *AlterNet* January 25, 2005, http://www.alternet.org/story/21083/.

150 Bakshi.

151 Sandra Ingerman, *Transmutation News* (July 2003) http://www.shamanicvisions.com/ingerman_folder/ingerman03/july03.html.

INDEX

O

observation 110, 227
offerings 52, 80, 82
Oprah 117
ordinary reality 116, 154, 185, 188, 234
Over, Jill 92

P

pal al 145
paradox 232-234
patience 47, 50, 65, 112
peace xxvi-xxviii, 2, 11, 64, 70, 77, 103, 138, 148, 234-235
perception 2, 211-218, 227, 232, 234, 239-240
personal energetics 5-9, 33, 37, 42-44, 67
personal power xxvii, 9, 27-30, 36, 65, 71, 103, 159, 161, 213, 234-235
pharmaceuticals 173-174, 187
physics 214
plants 15, 71, 84-89, 173, 187-188, 218
    healing plants 158, 187
play 26-27, 36, 51, 68, 96
pneuma 171
politeness 44-46, 67
Pollack, Jackson 141
portal 108-109, 119
potentials 65, 136-137, 214-215, 239
power animal 159-160, 183-184
    power animal retrieval 183-184
power 4-5, 27-31, 36, 38-39, 46, 49, 65, 71, 80-82, 84, 87, 91, 99, 103, 106, 109, 123-124, 139-141, 145-147, 149, 151, 161, 166-167, 171, 177-178, 183-184, 188-190, 199, 204, 206, 210-211, 213, 222-223, 225-232, 234-235, 240, 242
    giving away power 123
    power songs 189

practitioners, choosing 174-177
prana 5, 171
prayer 80, 90-91, 135, 141, 144-149, 164, 167, 173, 197-198, 204, 206, 224, 230
    decree 145-146, 167
    intercessory 146, 161, 197, 206
    petition 145
prayer cloth 198
praying rain 90
privacy 64, 127, 161, 225
psychic protection 57-59, 68
psychometry 119
psychopomp 185-186

Q

Qigong 171
Quakers xxv, 235
quantum physics 214

R

rattles xxv, 158
razor's edge 30-31
Reiki xxiii, 170, 190-193, 198-199
religion 94, 137-138, 148-152, 164, 168
    creating 148-153
Rogers, Carl 56-57
Rothko, Mark 120

S

sacred contract 220-221
sacred space 9-11, 33, 49, 64, 77-81, 100, 109, 195
Salish 98, 157-158, 183
salivary immunoglobulin 25
sanctuaries 79-81, 100
Sanskrit xxv, 145, 171, 190, 215
Sedona, Arizona 76

978-0-595-40743-9
0-595-40743-9

Printed in the United States
148797LV00003B/6/A

9 780595 407439